PRAISE FOR *TOUGH*

"*Tough* should be essential reading in every class, every grade and for every person that aspires to be better. As a marathoner, Ironman triathlete, road runner, swimmer and 24-year Navy SEAL, this book hits every aspect of mental toughness that I used to accomplish all the hard challenges that I faced over the years. The bullseye is hit with the mental and character traits you need for success and how to navigate and use the traits to make you better, and puts you in a position to make the impossible, possible. Truly a remarkable book!"

—D. McBurnett, Navy SEAL (ret) and author of *Uncommon Grit*

"I spent 20+ years evaluating students during some of the military's toughest selection courses. I know what determination and toughness is. I also know failure. I wish I had this book to reference for those who lost focus and faltered. *Tough* is the most in-depth and comprehensive book on mental toughness I've seen. From the boardroom to the backcountry, *Tough* has something to offer everyone."

—John Barklow, US Navy (ret)

"Powerful self-reflection with an emphasis on integrated personal development. An important read for anyone looking to sharpen their most vital tool... the mind."

—Mark Divine, SEAL Commander (ret), founder of SEALFIT and NYT best selling author of *Unbeatable Mind* and *The Way of the SEAL*

"Greg Everett has written an inspiring and enlightening read for anyone looking to understand what being tough truly means...and why it matters. As a coach, he shares practical tools and incentives that will help to build confidence and create disciplined habits to support your goals."

—Emily Fletcher, Founder of Ziva Meditation and best selling author of *Stress Less, Accomplish More*

"It's interesting timing for the release of *Tough*. We are in the midst of a global pandemic that has changed our lives in ways few of us could have imagined a few years ago, yet the need for physical, emotional and mental resilience (toughness) is an indispensable tool to help us move forward and not just survive, but thrive. Greg Everett's deep insights on this topic, garnered from personal athletic endeavors, coaching and entrepreneurship encompass the message we all need, now and going forward."
—Robb Wolf, bestselling author of The Paleo Solution and Sacred Cow

"*Tough* sets the standard for awareness and recognition of what toughness actually is. The cerebral concepts and explanations of the human reaction to mental and physical challenges coupled with the essentials required to overcome those challenges will enable unbelievable success for every reader."
—Travis Denman MSG (ret), 22-year Special Forces Veteran

"Everett has done a terrific job of taking the intangible attribute of toughness and given us a concrete, actionable, step-by-step process for understanding it and adopting it into our own lives. I am recommending this book to all of my athletes."
—Ben Bergeron, elite CrossFit coach, best selling author of Chasing Excellence

"Life has a way of challenging us when we are most vulnerable. *Tough* is a great litmus test that will help you flush out your weak points. It is a comprehensive guide for all citizens that will help build the mental, physical, and emotional intelligence necessary to thrive...
or you can just hope things work out."
—Tamara Holmes, firefighter, competitive weightlifter, Team USA Baseball player, Women's World Cup of Baseball Offensive Player of the Tournament

"No one is immune to difficult times, hence the importance of toughness. Fortunately, Everett has done an excellent job at detailing an actionable approach to developing this essential attribute that is largely missing in today's world. *Tough* is highly recommended reading."
—Ross Enamait, professional boxing coach

"Leave it to none other than the razor sharp Greg Everett to have us laughing out loud at precisely the same moment we also realize we could stand to be a little tougher. Deconstructing the stereotypical image of what we've come to associate with "toughness," he shows us the true nature of toughness and perhaps more importantly how to get there. This book is likely to make you laugh and nod in unison, and most certainly will light a fire under you."
—Jocelyn Forest Haynes, NCAA D1 and Professional National Champion & MVP softball pitcher, national championship medalist weightlifter

"Toughness is something that is widely misunderstood in our modern culture. We either don't believe we have it, or we overestimate it in ourselves. We often have misguided and negative opinions of it. In spite of all of this, it is necessary for a happy, fulfilling life and it is mandatory for surviving adversity. The question you end up asking is, "what is toughness, and how do I achieve it? In *Tough*, Greg Everett nails the elusive concept of being tough in a way that has not been done before. As someone who knows a thing or two about toughness, I was blown away by his ability to frame the concept of toughness and break it down for anyone to be able to digest and apply in their own lives. As he says, "being tough is less about what we do, than how we do it—and why." If you wonder how you can face adversity, improve your training in sports or self-defense, or just be better equipped to withstand the trials of life, read this book. It just might change your life."
—Varg Freeborn, author of *Violence of Mind*, Violence and Self-Defense Educator and Strength Coach

TOUGH

BUILDING TRUE MENTAL, PHYSICAL & EMOTIONAL
TOUGHNESS FOR SUCCESS & FULFILLMENT

GREG EVERETT

ISBN 978-1-970123-00-5

Publisher's Cataloging-in-Publication Data

Names: Everett, Greg, 1980- , author.
Title: Tough : building true mental, physical & emotional success & fulfillment / Greg Everett.
Description: Terrebonne, OR : Catalyst Athletics, 2021. | Summary: Defines true mental, physical, and emotional toughness, and provides practical tools for thriving through any challenge.
Identifiers: LCCN 2020949388 | ISBN 9781970123005 (hardcover) | ISBN 9781970123012 (Kindle) | ISBN 9781970123029 (ePub)|ISBN 9781970123043 (audiobook)
Subjects: LCSH: Courage. | Mental discipline. | Resilience (Personality trait). | Self-actualization (Psychology). | BISAC: SELF-HELP / Personal Growth / Happiness. | SELF-HELP / Personal Growth / Self-Esteem. | SELF-HELP / Personal Growth / Success.
Classification: LCC BJ1533.D49 E94 2021 | DDC 158.1 E94--dc23
LC record available at https://lccn.loc.gov/2020949388

Also available in digital and audiobook editions

Catalyst Athletics, Inc.
www.catalystathletics.com

becomingtough.com
@becomingtough

For my father, who taught me reason without heartlessness.
For my mother, who taught me compassion without irrationality.
And for both, who taught me there was always more to learn.
Your lessons persist in your absence.

CONTENTS

INTRODUCTION

I seldom read introductions to books after years of finding them too consistently to be turgid, unnecessary decoration, so I won't be terribly offended if you decide to skip this one. The book will stand on its own without it, but if you have a few minutes to spare, let me briefly ease you into what's to come with some background and rationale.

I've been kicking around the idea for this book for several years, and the subjects have been present in my mind in some form for as long as I can remember, albeit absent of any real clarity for most of that time. The structure of the book has changed dramatically from when I first collected some notes for it in 2011 as I cycled through periods of interest, frustration and fleeting feelings of purpose. The final tumbler dropped into place when I realized that what I was trying to communicate extended far beyond the limited scope I'd originally envisioned—that it encompassed not just physical ability or simply the trite notion of resilience, but every facet of our internal experiences, cognitive and emotional processes and mindset, their relation to our external experiences, decisions and behaviors, and the sense of success and fulfillment that results.

I grew up a short, skinny kid—I was naturally athletic and drawn to an array of sports and training itself, but I stumbled through my formative years with nearly crippling insecurity and self-consciousness. The friendships and social interactions I had were far more the product of other peoples' efforts than my own—I was essentially just along for the uneasy ride. I got by and improbably was actually a popular kid in spite of myself by virtue of evidently natural adaptability—I simply became whoever it was most expedient to be as the moment dictated (to be fair, a wildly irresponsible volume of recreational drug use helped as well).

At the same time, I somehow had deep-seated trust in my ability to withstand anything that could come my way. Maybe at that age that particular sense of confidence was derived in part from self-delusion made possible by relatively limited testing, although I had at least my fair share of unwanted tests and arguably more. In any case, the apparent contradictions in my own identity and experiences always stood out to me and made the idea of being tough simultaneously appealing and confusing—appealing because I knew it was necessary, and confusing because the way it was understood by consensus didn't seem quite right.

As an adult, I'm physically on the larger side—six feet tall and 215 pounds (down from my former competitive weight of 231), and if you'll allow me for a moment to be objective without concern for sounding self-congratulatory, comfortably beyond average in accomplishment. I can remember at age nineteen periodically running out of food because the anxiety of having to interact with people would prevent me from going to the store; now I can stand for two straight days in front of a crowd of people giving a seminar. It's taken me many years to rebuild mental habits, move past extant emotional and psychological scarring of various experiences of my younger life, and develop the requisite tools to be capable of being who I now am and doing what I do, a considerable portion of which is available for public scrutiny and criticism.

I've coached the Olympic sport of weightlifting for almost fifteen years up to the world championship level, and was a nationally competitive lifter myself until a blown-out shoulder at the 2015 National Championships effectively retired me. Prior to that I played just about every sport you've heard of, a handful you haven't, and was involved to varying degrees in numerous other athletic and recreational pursuits, from rock climbing to boxing to Brazilian jiu jitsu to tactical shooting competition to solo backpacking through the Sierra Nevada and Cascades. I've worked on an ambulance, I've worked or been friends with many other first responders, law enforcement personnel, and combat veterans from infantry to special forces, and I've been friends or worked professionally with world class, professional and Olympic athletes in multiple sports.

I've had good friends who've both overcome and succumbed to drug addiction, and have wrestled with my own; I've had friends and family who've spent lifetimes battling mental illness, and some who've lost the fight. I've had friendships and many other interactions at all levels with people from the inner city, the trailer, and the ranch, people who've spent time in prison, and people who've been wildly successful in business and other professional pursuits.

As a coach overwhelming of women throughout my career, I've also had unique experience with the way toughness is viewed and embodied by many women, and their dramatically diverse senses of their own limitations and abilities; the varied and often perplexing ways men view toughness with regard to women, and their expectations of what women can and should do; and the differing pressures and constraints on women of various subcultures and the larger societies within which they exist.

In other words, I've accrued an extensive collection of diverse experiences both directly and through relationships with people whose toughness was built, expressed and challenged in markedly different ways, with the range of attitudes and thoughts they had about toughness, and the perspectives others had about their toughness. I've seen the entire spectrum, from people who've accomplished unbelievable physical feats yet fall apart in the face of the slightest emotional challenge or inconvenience, to the physically frail and incapable who've managed to withstand mental and emotional challenges beyond what most of us can even imagine; from the most humble, unassuming war hero and elite athlete to the most arrogant, boastful clown with no real accomplishments to speak of who refuses to shut up about them anyway.

It's been irritatingly obvious to me for a long time that there was something amiss or imprecise about the idea of being tough, even long before

I could clearly understand and articulate what exactly it was, but that this nebulous quality of *being tough* was critical for our individual and collective experience as human beings. I felt compelled and at least adequately qualified to sort it out, and to offer my determinations to anyone interested as I've always been in seeking and developing this quality.

Distilled to its essence, the purpose of this book is to offer a clear and complete concept of toughness—what exactly it means to be truly tough and, more importantly, why it matters—and a straightforward map to allow anyone to achieve it. Each chapter of the book addresses one of the fundamental elements of toughness and the multitude of mental, emotional and physical aspects that it encompasses, and is completed with a set of practical action steps to help you begin and continue to implement the ideas.

To be fair, the provided guidance being clear doesn't mean the process is easy—it will demand difficult reflection and often unflattering self-assessment, and uncomfortable and trying physical, mental and emotional challenges. But I can confidently assure you that despite the difficulty, it's accessible to anyone who decides to pursue it, and that no matter your starting point, your efforts will propel you forward. I sincerely hope you find the process as transformative and empowering as I know it can be.

CHAPTER 1
WHAT IS TOUGHNESS?

Intuitively, we all know being tough is valuable—our natural sense of self-preservation and survival instinct dictate a desire for robustness and fortitude, the ability to weather adversity, to overcome challenges, and to protect ourselves and others. The history of storytelling is replete with the hero archetype—tough men and women who survive harrowing journeys and tests of will, literal or metaphorical, and succeed despite seemingly impossible odds through extraordinary demonstrations of mental and physical strength and resilience. We're all unquestionably drawn to the idea, whether consciously or not, and gravitate toward people we believe embody it, from soldiers to athletes to leaders. We admire and celebrate them, we compare ourselves to them, we strive to emulate them, and we try—however clumsily and often poorly—to teach our children how to live more like them.

But the concept of toughness, with its numerous associations and connotations, becomes murky and even controversial depending on an individual's experiences and the perspective they've shaped. Instead of remaining a pure, simple, essential idea, toughness has been kicked thoughtlessly through the dirt of social constructs and mottled with the debris of misunderstanding and misrepresentation and individually variable emotional baggage. When we talk about toughness, we're often instead talking inadvertently about traits we associate because of our own life experiences with people who represent themselves as being tough, or whom others tell us are tough—not the quality of toughness itself. If our experiences on balance have been negative, we have negative associations with the idea of being tough—violence, aggression, bravado, bullying, even misogyny; if our experiences have been positive, we have positive associations—honor, fortitude, resilience, confidence, and security.

Ask just about anyone in the proper context, and they'll agree being tough is a valuable characteristic. Ask people what kind of person represents toughness, and you'll get a few obvious answers, such as soldiers, first responders or elite athletes. Ask them to define what being tough means, and you'll find people struggle and tend to focus on a single aspect like physical strength or resilience, or a narrow range of abilities you'd expect from a certain type of person or profession, and often fall back on the stereotypes reinforced by popular media. Dig further and ask about the relationship of toughness to gender, masculinity and femininity, emotion, kindness, or social responsibility, and you're liable to get not only a broad range of answers, but even some vitriolic reactions.

This kind of variation in opinion regarding a given descriptor isn't entirely unique to toughness. Even a quality as seemingly innocuous as intelligence may have negative associations for some—someone who grew up as the struggling kid in a classroom full of "smart" kids and a teacher who reinforced with poor instruction and attitude their self-evaluation of being "stupid" likely feels some deep-seated resentment when it comes to the notion of intelligence and education because of the experiences it represents in their mind. But arguably, few if any other concepts of the category within which toughness resides elicit reactions of the same degree of vehemence.

Consider a kid who grows up physically frail, self-conscious and insecure being bullied by another arguably equally if not more insecure kid, who simply happens by nature's whim to be more physically capable. That more physically developed kid is likely to have a reputation as being "tough" because of that physical ability, typically demonstrated through athletic accomplishments, and, importantly, an accompanying act—that is, that kind of kid *acts* tough in a desperate plea for validation and protection from their own fears and insecurity being exposed. This is the perfect formula for someone developing a negative association with the idea of toughness having nothing to do with toughness itself.

If we're going to make any progress, individually and collectively, we need to extricate the fundamental idea of toughness from the tangled mess of experiential, social and media-influenced associations that unjustly encapsulate it. When the wreckage has been cleared away, we can properly examine and evaluate the concept, and fabricate the elements of the structure that support it. This framework is what then allows us to determine the practical steps and incremental objectives necessary to forge our way confidently through the difficult but rewarding process of becoming truly tough.

DEFINING TOUGHNESS

We can't begin to pursue—let alone achieve—toughness if we're not even capable of defining what it is we're trying to become. The process is challenging enough without stepping off haphazardly to stumble around in the dark smashing our toes and cracking our skulls along the way to a destination that doesn't exist. Part of being tough is the capacity to endure and overcome challenges—that doesn't mean we transform every task in our lives into challenges unnecessarily. The classic toughness precept is that if you're going to be dumb, you have to be tough, but fortunately, being tough doesn't require being dumb. There's no reason we can't attack the process intelligently and channel our limited time and energy into the myriad challenges we not only can't avoid, but require for success. Further, it's impossible to undertake the process of becoming tougher without becoming more intelligent, more aware, and more engaged in the world around us.

True toughness is built through the continuing development of four elements:

Character: Who are you?
Capability: What are you able to do?
Capacity: What are you able to withstand?
Commitment: What are you willing to do?

CHARACTER

Who are you? Are you secure in that identity? What are your values? Do those values actually align with the identity you want or believe is you? Do those values in turn align with our vision of being tough?

We can't make sound decisions that guide our lives in the way we want without establishing a clear identity and its corresponding values. Sadly enough, it's more common for business owners and executives to engage in the process of defining an identity and core values for a company, and then enforce decisions that align with those values, than for individuals to do the same on a personal level. Most of us float through life like a fallen stick on a river rather than making clear choices about what we are and where we're going—we spend our lives retroactively describing who we happen to be rather than proactively prescribing who we are.

Even once we've decided—truly—who we want to be, it's not a passive condition in which that identity simply *exists* from that point forward. Our identity is shaped by the entirety of its defining characteristics, from our attitude and outlook, to what we say and how we say it, to how and when we choose to act. We're defining our identity every moment of our life with every choice we make—we don't get to be who we are only on our best days and pretend our poor choices don't count toward the final analysis. We don't get to be one person in one crowd, another elsewhere, then yet another in the mirror—we are the aggregation of all of those personas; and part of that is being someone who has to take on different personas in different circumstances, perhaps to impress or ingratiate or feel safe. In any case, it's *all* our identity.

Do our choices, words and behaviors actually reflect and support the identity we've decided represents us? Does this identity align with what we want and expect to accomplish? It's stunning how much discordance can exist within a given individual. We can imagine our self an elite athlete, yet fail to actually perform the daily tasks demanded for becoming and remaining elite; we can imagine our self capable, but actively avoid any experiences that may invalidate that self-assessment.

It's impossible to be tough without knowing who we are and what we value—we can't stand up for ourselves or what we believe if we're not even aware of what that is. We can't be committed to nebulous ideas—security requires clarity. This doesn't mean, however, that our identity must be immediately established in this process and then remain rigidly unchanging indefinitely. We're continuing to experience life, interact with new people in different ways, gain perspective on not just the world around us, but on ourselves, and being forced to adapt and evolve. Being secure in our identity doesn't mean intransigence—it simply means that we're aware of who and what we are at the present moment, and we're actively working to support that identity with the choices we make every day. In no way does it imply that we're finished with the process of *becoming*—we never will be.

A lack of security in our identities is a primary driver of irrational and meaningless competition, attention-seeking behavior and inappropriate attempts at validation. How can we be tough if we're wasting time and energy trying to convince people around us that we're valuable? That's energy and time we need to be investing into the process of actually becoming or simply *being* who we want to be. Even if the opinions of those around us are consequential, people will ultimately and unavoidably respond to who we *are*, not who we attempt to convince them we are. Our self-delusion about our identities isn't shared by the rest of the world, and our acting is typically painfully transparent.

Character is built by us by choice (or the failure to choose) and revealed to others unavoidably. We make decisions, consciously or not, on how experiences affect our character. It's not a passive process we simply allow to define our character while we sit comfortably awaiting a result. Being tough demands action on every level. We don't have the power to choose all of our experiences, but we always have the ability to choose our behavior in the midst of them and in their wake, and those choices are what define our character.

CAPABILITY

What are you able to do? Self-reliance and independence are predicated on capability—the more we're able to do, the less we're forced to rely on others to do for us. The more we're able to do, the less intimidating and overwhelming unfamiliar experiences are, and the less fear and anxiety they induce. The more we're able to do, the more we're able to help others and contribute to the world around us. And the more we're able to do, the better equipped we'll be to solve any problem that presents itself, and the more prepared we'll be for any possible contingency, from the mundane to the most extreme emergencies.

Continually developing new skills and collecting new experiences doesn't merely give us the ability to perform the specific tasks we've learned how to do—it gives us the tools and confidence to take on new ones successfully. Learning new information and skills is a compounding process. The act of learning develops our ability to learn, creates a growing framework and foundation of information with which we can make future associations in order to assimilate and apply more information, and transforms our perspective on the world and our potential.

Any decent sport coach will encourage young athletes to play as many different sports as possible before eventually specializing later in life in a quest to become elite. The sport of weightlifting is incredibly specific, for example—in competition, the athlete performs three single repetitions of two different lifts, each of which brings a barbell from the floor to overhead. But early development of a weightlifter needs to include an enormous range of physical activity, from running to jumping to carrying to throwing to basic gymnastic movements. These activities develop a physical literacy in addition to actual morphological, physiological and neurological characteristics that underlie future growth and specification.

A common example of this is that children who participate in gymnastics early in life, even briefly, pick up other sports more quickly and easily than their peers. The movements and exercises may have no direct relation to those of the latter sport—what matters is that the child learned how to control their body in a broad variety of ways, and built a body physically capable of performing and tolerating difficult activity. Further, having the experience of learning and even partially mastering athletic movements creates confidence in the ability to learn and master new movements because the process is familiar and no longer intimidating or overwhelming in its novelty.

Similarly, we need to cultivate a lifestyle and mindset that values and seeks new abilities across a broad spectrum, and incorporates this as an unceasing process. Each of us certainly needs to emphasize the areas in which we specialize by profession or choice, but neglecting abilities and experiences outside this narrow bandwidth is a critical error, not just for the previously explained reasons, but also because such different experiences can provide unexpected insights into our specialties—insights that are impossible to predict because of our lack of experience in those peripheral realms. We need to embrace new experiences as opportunities to learn, and continually expand our toolbox.

Much of the resistance to learning and the unfamiliar arises from the fear of humiliation or the exposure of our incapability to our peers. A stunning number of us prefer to live indefinitely hoping we're never actually tested—encouraging others to assume a level of ability and knowledge exceeding the actual—rather than risk a few potential brief moments of embarrassment. This is myopic to say the least, and is an incredibly crippling choice. This of course is related to character, and our security in our identities. Being secure in who we are, we can recognize and accept our present limitations, both because we're willing and able to perform an accurate self-evaluation, and because we refuse to allow those limitations to become permanent. Instead, we actively eliminate limitations through the pursuit of increased capability, and as a part of that often difficult pursuit, we willingly and knowingly accept the possibility of temporary failure and discomfort, whether it be physical, psychological or social.

Character and security allow us to sidestep the elaborate barriers we construct in the way of our own growth—our values dictate priorities, such as learning and becoming more capable over preserving some exaggerated concern over how we're perceived by others, particularly when we're viewing only a single, tightly-cropped snapshot of that perception and failing to consider the sweeping, moving view beyond it.

Continually expanding capability provides us commensurately growing independence and diminishing reliance on others. The encouragement of independence and self-reliance is unfortunately too often misinterpreted as the discouragement of asking for or receiving help, or a push for social isolation. Independence is in no way synonymous with isolation or disdain for social interaction—it's simply the *ability* to take care of ourselves without the need for others' assistance. Each of us chooses what to do with that ability as we define our identities.

CAPACITY

What are you able to withstand? The ability to cope with stress, adversity, danger and the unpredictable is an obvious part of being tough, but how do we develop that ability to its ultimate potential? How much is capacity inherent, how much is a product of circumstance, and how much can be intentionally and systematically built? How are physical and mental capacity related, and how much do we rely on each?

Capacity may be the trait most commonly associated with toughness, and for good reason—this is what we see as the resilience and fortitude to endure extraordinary struggle, especially with more protracted experiences, and to succeed despite stacked odds. We tend to focus on and glorify the most extreme examples—surviving for weeks at sea in a life raft, making it back down a mountain after a fall and loss of equipment in a blizzard, escaping certain death in an attack—and forget that capacity is built and demonstrated at infinite levels of intensity and duration, and through experiences of myriad natures.

Most of us recognize that adversity tends to make us tough, but we often forget that it's by no means a reliable or simple process. We pay attention to individuals who survive adversity and as a result have incredible stories to tell, and neglect to consider the vast number of people who endured the same or similar experiences and were destroyed in one way or another—perishing, quitting, or shattering psychologically, never even recovering to their previous conditions, let alone thriving.

Adversity isn't a magical process that invariably absorbs soft, delicate children and spits out hardened, tough bastards from the other end—it can just as easily break us and turn us into fragile cowards who find every way possible to avoid risk or potential danger in the future. Who we are *before* these trials, and how we consequently experience them, how we choose to view them, and how we manage to use them to a great extent determines how they affect us and influence our lives, character and future choices and success. We must *choose* to harness the power of adversity and put it to work for our benefit, and in order to do that most effectively, we need to be as well-prepared as possible, mentally, physically and emotionally, prior to our most difficult and trying moments.

Much like the development of character is an ongoing process throughout our lives, the building of continuously increasing capacity should be an indefinite project. There are no tricks to instantaneously transform ourselves other than self-delusion—and unfortunately, that's arguably the most dangerous threat to toughness. The procedure of improving capacity follows the same basic structure as capability. We resolve to pursue greater capacity, and to that end, we create and implement methods of achieving it that we actively embed into our lifestyle. This isn't some extracurricular activity we haphazardly tack on every now and then when we happen to think of it the occasional Sunday we have a bit of free time between laundry and lawn care—it's a defining trait of our character and an inextricably vital element of our lives.

Preparation to more successfully and productively handle adversity isn't mindless self-torture—we're not arbitrarily creating discomfort, pain, fear or stress. I can hit myself over the head with a hammer and be pretty miserable, but I struggle to see the potential for any meaningful lesson from the experience, other than that choosing to hit myself with a hammer was a stupid idea.

Steeling ourselves in preparation for adversity, both mental and physical, doesn't mean hurting ourselves unnecessarily or simply repeatedly testing our current abilities unproductively. Preparation is training, not self-destruction; it's systematic and sensible stress inoculation, not pointless misery. This training includes everything from simple daily tasks performed mindfully with clear purpose and habit building, to periodic significant challenges to stretch our boundaries and progressively immunize ourselves against fear, anxiety and intimidation. There must be a well-defined purpose, an effective methodology, and a logical rationale. We're building an electrical circuit to power a machine with an explicit purpose, not clipping a car battery to our eyelids out of senseless curiosity.

A significant piece of this process is the evolution of our mindset—learning to embrace and even seek challenge rather than avoid it, and to consciously determine and control our reactions and attitude in any circumstances. This evolving mindset is in part a direct, independent process, and in part a natural effect of our interdependent work with regard to our character, capability and commitment. We become physically and mentally capable of not simply coping with adversity, but of using it to our advantage and thriving in its wake.

COMMITMENT

What are you willing to do? Knowing who we are, being broadly capable, and possessing the capacity to endure hardship is meaningless if we're unwilling to apply these abilities when it counts to accomplish something worthwhile—anything from saving our own or another's life in an emergency to simply standing up for our identity and values in a social situation. Without the commitment to act, it's all just a private fantasy creating false confidence, which may be more dangerous than not having the abilities at all but being aware of it.

The application of commitment ranges broadly from the repetitive and mundane to the extreme and unpredictable. Are we consistent in the daily routines that reinforce our character, capability and capacity—all those seemingly inconsequential things that in fact not only add up, but compound synergistically and have an enormous influence on the course and quality of our life? Are we also psychologically prepared to cope with severe danger and unpredictability productively by being totally committed to the process and making the necessary decisions?

Some of these things are basic tasks we simply chip away at day to day and use various methods to develop beneficially habitual behaviors and more effective modes of thinking to continuously improve; others are ones we need to contemplate, evaluate and make serious decisions about before we ever find ourselves in a situation that demands that particular type of commitment.

In the midst of extreme danger is not the appropriate moment to step back and consider what exactly we're willing to do in order to get through it. In such cases, the decision about commitment needs to have already been made—the only remaining decisions must be procedural in nature, and ideally largely automated at the point of necessity through prior preparation and training. This doesn't apply exclusively to self-defense type situations, but also to issues of emergency and survival. We need to know, for example, how to start a fire, build shelter and navigate over land before we get stuck in the wilderness so we can simply execute as needed to do what we're already committed to do—survive and thrive.

Much commitment is specific to our chosen profession or lifestyle. If we're athletes, are we actually willing to do what it takes to achieve the goals we've set for ourselves? The hours and hours of often monotonous training, boring recovery protocols, restrictive nutritional practices, missing out on socializing to get in bed at 9:00 every night. If we're in law enforcement, are we committed to consistent, rigorous physical training, frequently drilling our shooting in ways that challenge and expand our skills and automaticity with mechanics while making critical decisions, engaging in authentic force-on-force training to expose and shore up weaknesses and help immunize us against the stress of a fight, gun or otherwise?

Commitment also applies to the most fundamental pieces of life and our character—these are simple and unglamorous daily tasks and mental processes that continuously define who we are and plot the course of our lives. These are the things that are so easy to dismiss as inconsequential and meaningless, yet in truth have enormous impact on outcomes over time. Much of this falls into the arena of discipline, routine and habit building and maintenance—procedures that must be originally developed thoughtfully and with clear purpose, but ultimately transformed into habit in order to preserve as much cognitive space as possible for more complex decisions.

Don't mistake this as implying we need to adopt a monk's lifestyle to be successful. This isn't a call for misery and sacrifice for its own sake. Will there be some sacrifice? Of course. Any worthwhile goal demands it. But in no way are we simply searching for new ways to deprive and torture ourselves as a pretext for calling ourselves tough. We're purposefully establishing a robust structure to support our intentions and ensure we're capable of accomplishing our goals—action, not hope.

CONFIDENCE

Confidence is an inevitable product of the defining elements of toughness. The condition of being confident as a result of achieving reasonable development of character, capability, capacity and commitment underlies the reliable state of peace the truly tough experience.

It's extremely unlikely we'll ever reach the point of perfect confidence, beyond which we never again experience fear, anxiety or doubt, or question our abilities. If we find ourselves at that point, it would be wise to take a step back and look harder—it's more likely self-delusion made possible by having never been tested, not an accurate reflection of our present state. But these feelings will become less frequent and more attenuated over time as we continue to develop, accumulate experience, and find ourselves tested, both intentionally and by chance. Toughness exists on a gradient, and our goal is to continuously push ourselves along the scale.

This state of confidence and serenity is what most of us have always sought, although often unknowingly—we seek ways to relax, to avoid becoming anxious or afraid or embarrassed, to feel safe and secure, and to be pleased with who we are, what we do and what we're capable of. The essential purpose of genuine toughness is to possess the kind of confidence across all circumstances that allows us to be at peace.

MINDSET

It's well established through research and, arguably far more importantly, practical experience, that our minds have enormous power and influence our lives in ways and to degrees it's still impossible to entirely understand and describe. While the actual mechanisms may not always be known, or even seem to be plausible in some cases, the results unequivocally prove the relationship.

The fundamental objective of mindset is to create and maintain in all situations complete control over our outlook and attitude—to never allow external circumstances, other people, emotion or anything but our own rational mind dictate our behavior, influence what we say or how, or alter our perception of objective facts. This is not an intransigent refusal to change the way we think or what we believe based on our experiences, but a refusal to allow change to be the result of anything but our own reasoned thoughts and objective decisions.

Just like we can train our bodies to be more capable of an array of physical activities at progressively greater levels of competence, so too can we train our mind to function increasingly productively and within our control to become a powerful tool for us to exploit to our advantage rather than a seemingly independent entity of whose whims and neuroses we find ourselves victims.

Being truly tough means remaining tranquil and composed amidst chaos, not because we're unaware or indifferent, but because we're in control and making a choice to respond to our environment and circumstances in the way that's most beneficial for us and allows us to function optimally to achieve what we desire or is necessary. Being truly tough means remaining positive regardless of challenges or adversity, not as a product of blanket optimism due to ignorance or naiveté or misguided hope, but because we trust in our toughness and are consequently confident in our ability to endure, overcome and succeed.

EMOTION

One of the most problematic elements of common understandings of being tough is that it requires being unfeeling and never experiencing, and certainly not publicly expressing, emotion. While it's absolutely true that it can wreak utter havoc on us and our lives, emotion also provides the texture to our experiences that makes them worthwhile.

We don't need to eliminate emotion, nor would it be genuinely beneficial—it would simply make us miserable without purpose. Toughness in no way demands emotional sterility. What it demands is the ability, and the conscious action, to control our responses to the people and situations that can elicit powerful emotions to avoid behaving or speaking in ways that may potentially harm us, whether immediately or in the future, and never allowing emotion to prevent sound thinking and critical decision-making in stressful or dangerous situations.

Emotion may be what allows us to actually experience life in a meaningful way, but that doesn't mean it's a reliable guide for our choices. It is, in fact, the worst possible arbiter for our decisions, and yet it's the most seductive and influential. Straightforward reason seems cold and calculating and inhuman to many of us, but that assessment fails to recognize that reason is no less human than emotion—if it's an inherent part of humans' functionality, it must be part of what makes us human. Dismissing it as otherwise is robbing ourselves of arguably the most powerful tool at our disposal. We can even use reason to make decisions that support the experiencing of emotion. Reason doesn't exist to rob us of feelings, but to help us avoid being unduly influenced by them. It's a tool like any other—it works as well as we know how use it.

There's nothing inherently problematic with emotion or emoting—the problems arise from the irrational thinking and poor choices associated with unchecked and unbalanced secondary emotions. Emotion is an inherent part of the human creature, and attempts to eliminate it never produce good results in the long term. Repression leads to a multitude of problems, from amplification to misdirection and even physical symptoms of stress. The goal is to be capable of feeling what we feel without ever becoming victims of those emotions—to allow ourselves to experience these emotions as our bodies intend, to gain what we can from them, and to develop the level of awareness and control that allows us to express what we need to express in productive ways, to channel the energy appropriately, and to avoid the traps we so cleverly set for ourselves. This is why we employ the rational mind, apply our values, and never lose sight of our identities to create the necessary awareness and maintain control over emotion, and to distinguish expressing as communication and connection from complaining as counterproductive self-indulgence or attention seeking.

MASCULINITY & FEMININITY

Toughness is based on attributes that are developed totally independently of sex, yet it's overwhelmingly associated with masculinity. What part of developing broad capabilities, the capacity to withstand challenges, the consistent demonstration of commitment, or security in a clearly defined identity is exclusively attainable by or appropriate for men? Any answer is the product of nonsensical social constructs informing the notion, consciously or not, of gender roles and natures, not a legitimate piece of evidence refuting the previous. It might be argued that being tough is a required element of being masculine because masculinity and femininity are subjective cultural ideas that rational people can disagree on, and that each of us defines in application to ourselves, but the reverse can't be reasonably argued—that being tough means being masculine.

It would be equally nonsensical to pretend there aren't legitimate and significant biological differences between the sexes, and to some extent psychological and emotional ones influenced by that biology, but none of these differences limits anyone's ability to develop toughness. These differences may dictate that we execute certain tasks or develop certain qualities in different manners and to different degrees, but the end result in total is the same: being tough. Further, even pertinent biological differences vary dramatically within a given sex—while we can make plenty of generalizations about them, these aren't entirely accurate across the board.

We know, for example, that men produce far more testosterone than women, and that testosterone supports physical strength through both the development of muscle mass and greater neurological efficiency—the ability to use given muscle mass to produce greater magnitudes of force. In other words, males on average tend to be physically stronger than their female counterparts.

But there are two critical points to keep in mind in this discussion. First, plenty of women are far stronger, leaner, more muscular and more athletically capable than plenty of men, both through nature and training (including an absence thereof on the men's side), endogenous testosterone levels and other natural biological characteristics notwithstanding. Again, we can make reasonable generalizations supported by fact, but we can't presume those generalizations are hard and fast rules—we have overwhelming evidence to contradict them.

Second, an individual of either sex or any gender description who, even with dedicated and intelligent physical training, isn't capable of reaching particularly great levels of strength is not incapable of becoming tougher relative to themselves and even extremely tough in absolute terms. Such an individual may be at a relative disadvantage in that one specific area, but there are far more components to toughness than physical strength, and we all find ways to mitigate the limitations attendant to our weaknesses and exploit our strengths to achieve the ultimate objective.

Unfortunately, toughness has been merged with manhood and masculinity into a single idea in many people's minds, and in the process, corrupted to a remarkable extent culturally and socially. It may be assumed males are always naturally tougher than females, that the condition of being tough is masculine and consequently unbecoming for women, or that being tough means being unkind or violent or aggressive, which traits are then seen as elements of masculinity or inherent qualities of all men.

We need to distinguish toughness from sex and gender and wipe away the odd social coloring it's been painted with—it's a straightforward set of principles defining qualities attainable by anyone through choice and work. Masculinity and femininity, gender roles, definitions and expectations, and other cultural norms can be determined independently—each of us decides what we believe these things to be and that belief, and the behavior, words and acceptance that extend from them, shape the social definitions over time. We'll never reach a global consensus on these ideas, but we can successfully define toughness as an independent concept—and we can use that toughness as individuals to deal with dubious social, cultural and religious pressures on us regarding the others.

PHYSICAL ABILITY

True toughness demands capability and capacity of both the mind and body. Any challenge we face demands mental fortitude, because the mind must always in some way be involved in everything we experience, whether that means controlling emotion and making decisions or simply observing, parsing, interpreting and learning. A challenge may not demand anything directly of the body in the obvious sense—coping with a tragic loss, for example, doesn't require any voluntary muscular effort.

But there are a few simple reasons we need to take the physical elements of toughness just as seriously as the mental. First, of course, is that we're preparing for any contingency, and at least some of those are going to involve physical demands well beyond what we need to be capable of in our typical day-to-day life and therefore what we're presently easily able to manage. The nature and difficulty of these physical challenges cover an enormous array and spectrum, respectively. We can certainly emphasize specific areas with the guidance of probability based on the details of our professional and personal lives. If we never in our life spend time in or around the ocean or other bodies of water, for instance, it's a rational choice to not invest a lot of time and energy into swimming—developing and maintaining a decent baseline ability to swim and stay afloat is arguably enough. If we're sailors by profession or recreation, investing time and energy into being extraordinarily competent and physically capable of swimming and treading water, and consequently comfortable in the water, makes a lot of sense.

Second, ultimately the body is the mind's vehicle—the medium in which it grows and which nurtures or starves it in order for it to thrive or wither—and physical health has a direct and dramatic influence on the health and function of the brain, our mood, our attitude, our ability to manage stress, our focus and our enthusiasm. It's a crippling error to consider the mind as existing in a vacuum and dismiss or trivialize its relationship to the rest of the body and physical health generally.

A final reason, not quite as straightforward but extremely important for our purposes nonetheless, is that physical fitness supports mental capacity, focus and acuity under stress. In other words, without changing anything else, the fitter we are, the more composed, rational, perceptive and decisive we are in situations in which we're afraid, under duress, or dealing with physical strain and fatigue. It's hard to imagine any legitimate argument against this in a discussion of being tough.

Physical training for our purposes here can be broken into two broad categories—capability and capacity. In other words, the ability to perform and the ability to withstand. We need to develop the capability to perform an array of physical tasks at the highest level possible in consideration of our circumstances, and we need to become as robust and resilient as possible to ensure we're able to safely and successfully endure unusual and extreme physical strain and exertion.

The performance side tends to be obvious—we need to be able to push, pull, run, jump, fight and all of the other possible activities that come in handy when we find ourselves in trouble. Physical durability is a bit more difficult to understand, so we can think of it this way: having world class cardiovascular endurance and a knowledge of land navigation has virtually no value in getting us out of the wilderness safely when we break a leg with a little walking over rough terrain thanks to the osteoporosis we allowed to develop with an avoidance of load bearing activity over the years. Fortunately, the kind of physical training that will develop the kind of capability we're looking for will naturally build robustness and resilience.

Understand that this isn't an expectation of training at Olympic levels of time investment and athleticism—like all aspects of toughness, we all start where we are and aim for continual long term improvement rather than a specific universal end point. Some of us will be able to push the physical elements much further than others due to backgrounds in athletic training or simply by virtue of being genetically well-suited for it; and some of us will be working against legitimate physical limitations due to injury history, medical conditions or being dealt a relatively poor genetic hand. That said, all of us are capable of making dramatic improvements in our physical capability and capacity with intelligent and consistent training and supporting lifestyle choices; arguments against physical training are without merit and are at best the result of ignorance regarding training, and at worst just excuses masquerading as reason.

WHO'S THE TOUGHEST?

Toughness isn't a competition. How could it be? How can toughness be measured objectively? Who's tougher: the combat vet who's the lone survivor of a horrible engagement and escapes with life-threatening wounds through enemy territory, or the kid who survives an entire childhood in an unheated trailer with no running water or electricity and two violent drug addict parents who starve and beat her? The two experiences are impossible to compare in any reasonable manner, and how each would fare in direct competition would depend entirely on the circumstances. Are we testing the ability to survive in battle with specific weaponry or the absence thereof, or the ability to survive extended misery and suffering as the result of physical and emotional deprivation and torture? Are we testing only the ability to physically survive a given situation to its natural conclusion, or also the ability to move past it and thrive psychologically and emotionally in the future?

More importantly, why does it matter who's tougher? The truly tough have no desire or need for validation or recognition for what they've done and continue to do—it's simply their life. There's no prize for toughness—at least none the truly tough would find meaningful or worth chasing. The reward is the satisfaction of success and the joy of being at peace in our own lives—being able to simply live and pursue our goals without being saddled with fear and anxiety.

There will always be someone tougher out there, someone who's endured adversity we can't even imagine and is still fighting, and someone who's willing without hesitation to go far beyond what we're even willing to consider.

The toughest person on earth isn't reading books about being tough (or writing them, for that matter)—they're busy fighting with everything they have every day to survive their own life. We need to be content with measuring ourselves against ourselves every day, and when the day comes that we're forced to test our toughness against someone else's, we'll be as prepared as we can be. Not trying to make it a contest with others is part of true toughness—having nothing to prove to anyone but ourselves is the mark of the kind of confidence created by character, capability, capacity and commitment. Continually striving to get tougher than we used to be is the way we get tougher than others anyway.

If you feel compelled to compete, that's why sport exists. By all means, compete—it's generally healthy and beneficial. Just don't make the mistake of conflating athletic prowess with toughness in its truest sense, or capability in real world scenarios. Being a successful boxer doesn't necessarily prepare us for a street fight with someone who has no boundaries or interest in rules or conventions; being a world-class competitive shooter doesn't mean we're capable of successfully handing a real gunfight; being a champion swimmer doesn't mean we'll automatically survive a capsized boat. In sport, we're testing very specific skills in accordance to the equally specific rules of that sport—it's critical to not extrapolate the results into other areas in which there are no rules, no boundaries and no referees.

ACT TOUGH OR BE TOUGH

We can either act tough or be tough—the two are mutually exclusive. Those who are truly tough never boast or seek attention, just like those with true confidence who are secure in their identities don't desperately seek validation. Being tough means accepting without objection or complaint that the rest of the world may never know it. It's more likely than not that we'll never find ourselves in a position in which a public demonstration of our abilities is necessary. This shouldn't be a disappointment—while we might appreciate challenges and find overcoming them gratifying (a mindset necessary to develop toughness in the first place) it makes little sense to wish unnecessary problems upon ourselves; and if those problems are in public view, it's probable that means wishing them on others. The truly tough don't worry about not getting an opportunity to show the world their abilities—they simply prepare themselves well, trust their abilities because of that preparation, and act as needed when needed.

This doesn't mean that if we're truly tough it won't ever be apparent to others—it very likely will through the natural course of our lives. Our behavior, our lifestyle, our attitude, our confidence, and the way we interact with other people all communicate a great deal to those around us without any affectation on our part. Being obvious and being made obvious are two very different things.

One of the defining characteristics of toughness is the absence of desire or compulsion to be recognized for it—this is a reflection of security in our identities and the consequent lack of need to prove ourselves to others. In fact, it can be argued that, much like we tend to point out and criticize the traits in others that we despise in ourselves or fear we posses, acting tough—or, more accurately, in a way that we believe *appears* tough—and drawing attention to our alleged toughness is nearly always an indication of weakness and cowardice. Every bullying story, to use an extreme example, if allowed to play out to its natural conclusion, results in the exposure of the bully as a coward trying to avoid discovery as such.

Just as the greatest athletes on earth never need to open their mouths to remind anyone of their greatness, the toughest individuals in the world will not only never bother telling you how tough they are, but actually conceal it to some extent. In part, this is a natural outgrowth of the humility that attends true toughness, and in part, it's an intentional decision to obscure their true abilities and maintain an advantage in a potential confrontation. In any case, true toughness is a quiet business that doesn't advertise.

AGGRESSION & VIOLENCE

Toughness isn't aggression or violence or loud-mouthed bravado. It isn't a matter of dominating or intimidating others, but of dominating our own emotions, fears, insecurities and irrationality, and establishing control over everything meaningful within our control. Again, this doesn't mean physical or emotional control over the people around us—it means controlling our decisions, our responses to our circumstances, and our mindset in any situation.

Make no mistake—being truly tough undoubtedly demands being physically and mentally prepared for violence. But it demands being prepared to respond appropriately to violence, not to unnecessarily initiate or escalate violence. Picking fights isn't tough—it's the act of a coward who lives in constant terror of their inferiority being recognized publicly and who needs to be continually reassured of their abilities through dubious self-administered tests that unfairly require the participation of otherwise uninvolved parties. Violent reactions to non-violent circumstances are also an egregious violation of one of the primary qualities of toughness, which is complete control of our emotions and reactions through rational thought and decision-making. It's the mark of an immature, mentally weak individual at the mercy of unchecked emotion.

Toughness is being capable of doing what we need to do, and related to that, knowing exactly what that is and executing decisively. It doesn't require action without cause—it requires cause for action. The ability to physically damage someone isn't an imperative to apply it. It's no different from any other ability—a tool in the toolbox to be pulled out and put to work when the situation requires it. And like any craftsman, we should be intimately familiar with our tools—their purpose, their advantages, their drawbacks and limitations, and their optimal application. We don't swing a sledgehammer at every problem we encounter simply because we possess the strength and have one handy. Part of controlling our reactions to everything we experience is the ability to instantly sort through the array of possibilities and select the response best suited for the circumstances. At some point, this may very well mean violence to protect ourselves or others, and it may mean extreme violence in order to respond in kind. True toughness prepares us for this contingency.

We may decide we're unwilling to cause physical harm in any circumstances, we may be willing to do nearly anything short of actually taking a life, or we may be willing to kill in order to save ourselves or those we love or are responsible for. These are our personal decisions to make, but these decisions need to be made thoughtfully and in complete harmony with our values—and critically, they need to be made well in advance of the moment the responses they dictate are demanded. In other words, our preparation with regard to violence is to be capable and willing to do what we believe is right—and to accept the consequences of those actions, whether that means inflicting violence for the sake of protection, or willingly accepting our own or loved ones' harm or death if we refuse to.

EXPERIENCE & PERSPECTIVE

It takes experience to truly appreciate and understand most things in life—we can only get so far with academic theorizing and intellectualizing. This presents a problem when at least some of what we're concerned with are things we can't genuinely practice or even predict reliably, such as certain types of emergencies, threats to our safety, psychological trauma, and other circumstances requiring being tough.

It's possible to model elements of these things to some extent for the sake of training and preparation, but we can never truly replicate the actual experience. No matter how much time we spend at the shooting range, in competition, or even doing force-on-force training with simulated ammunition that causes a reasonable amount of pain with contact, we aren't experiencing the true threat of death and maximally consequential failure of an actual gunfight with an opponent who has no compunction about harming us. No matter how much time we spend hiking or backpacking or mountaineering, even with minimalist gear, we can't genuinely replicate the experience of being lost, alone and injured in the wilderness. No matter how much time we spend wailing away on a heavy bag, we're not experiencing what it's like to do the same with fists or worse coming back our way from someone whose actions are not restricted by the same principles ours are. There are physiological reactions, psychological and emotional states, and interactions of the three that are wholly unique to the actual experience.

This is not to say, of course, that we can't effectively prepare for these things—we absolutely can, although admittedly imperfectly. But we need to always bear in mind that the preparation is not the experience, and we need to recognize its limitations and avoid overestimating our capabilities in a manner that negatively influences our performance when needed. In short, we need confidence as a result of suitable preparation, not hubris arising from a failure to appreciate the true nature and severity of the events for which we're preparing.

As described by the Dunning-Krueger effect, generally the less knowledgeable and competent we are, the less aware we are of it because we lack the ability to evaluate ourselves accurately, and as a result, we're far more confident in our abilities than we should be. Paradoxically, as our competence improves, we actually begin to be more critical and doubtful of our abilities and become less confident than those less competent than us—in other words, we become more aware of what we don't know and can't do, and that increasingly influences our self-evaluation. As we progress further in competence and experience, however, we begin to trust our abilities to a greater extent and regain confidence—but at this stage it's warranted.

We have to be cognizant of this in our pursuit of toughness. It's easy to overestimate how tough we are when we've spent time preparing but have never been truly tested and our experience is limited. If we've spent the last several years religiously watching boxing or MMA and have never been in a fight, it's easy to believe our seemingly extensive familiarity with the sports would translate into competence in a physical encounter with someone. The first time we get punched in the mouth, we're very likely to instantly realize our error. Getting obliterated in a fight for the first time is an extremely effective way to have our perspective and confidence retuned for accuracy.

Our goal in our preparation is to avoid requiring having our teeth knocked out just to learn this lesson—especially considering that such a lesson may bring with it consequences far beyond some unplanned dental work. We do this through the combination of thorough, lifelong, intelligent preparation and continuous, meticulous self-evaluation. And we never ignore the lessons that those with the actual experiences can teach us. In this way, we ensure our confidence accurately reflects our abilities at every stage in the process, and consequently, our decisions and actions are as effective as possible.

TOUGH ENOUGH?

Like nearly all human qualities, toughness exists on a gradient—it isn't tough or not, it's tougher or less tough. We'll very likely never be the toughest person on earth, but it's completely certain that we can be tougher than we are now and continually grow tougher over time with persistent effort, commitment and diligence.

How tough do we need to be? A better question is, How tough do we *want* to be? There's no requirement in life for us to be tough at all—plenty of people are barely clinging to the bottom of the scale, and are only on it at all because it has to be stretched to include everyone. But all of our choices have consequences, and how tough we want to be should be a decision we make based on what consequences we're willing—or unwilling—to accept. Another way to think of it is this: How do we want to live? How do we want to feel, both day to day and when under duress? How confident and secure do we want to feel? How competent and accomplished do we want to be? Our answers to these questions are what determine how tough we need to be—as tough as necessary to meet our self-determined criteria.

In any case, our goal is to always be tougher than *we* were yesterday. We want incremental but consistent improvement across the scale, from seemingly inconsequential daily tasks, to fundamental changes in our character. We need to be tough enough to manage whatever we know our lives will be presenting us—the predictable and mundane first and foremost, and at least eventually working to become progressively more prepared for the unpredictable and extreme. Like everything else worthwhile in life, it's a process, not a final result.

The continuous process of improvement is more difficult than simply *being* tough at a given level, much like losing weight or gaining strength is more difficult than maintaining a present level of either. The process itself is a challenge and can be very demanding and taxing mentally and physically at times. Continuing this process throughout the course of our lives without surrendering to complacency, withstanding setbacks and obstacles, and being willing to fail without giving up, is itself an act of toughness that few can handle, but in return will produce a level and type of toughness that few will attain. Ultimately, the difficulty notwithstanding, it's an invigorating and inspiring process.

WHAT'S THE POINT?

Finally, but no less importantly, what's the point of all of this? Why is all of this hard work and potentially discouraging self-examination worthwhile? If part of being tough is being largely unable to gain recognition for our abilities and credit for our work, what's in it for us? If we're not competing to determine who's better and the best, what's the reward at the end of the road?

The first point to remember is that the road doesn't end. This isn't a quick project we work on during our free weekends for the next six months before moving on to the next one. This is a process of personal growth we chip away at all day, every day until we give up or run out of days. Don't let the idea of an unending process be discouraging—being tough isn't a distant endpoint with nothing between it and our present condition. Every single little step we take along the way is making us tougher, and consequently every forward step is achieving the objective on some scale.

This process of becoming tough isn't some miserable existence of sacrifice and deprivation in which nothing but this goal of growing tougher exists—we're not torturing ourselves and stripping away any joy from our lives. In fact, the entire purpose of the process is to allow ourselves to experience our lives as completely and joyfully as possible, to be confident, to be secure, to live with progressively less fear and anxiety, to feel and be useful, and to be willing and eager contributors to the world rather than merely self-absorbed consumers and cumbersome dependents constantly on the search for elaborate excuses for our failures and creative ways to assign blame.

The point is to be able live and enjoy a life with purpose, conviction and meaning, to be at peace with our life and our choices, to remove the obstacles to success we unknowingly place in our own way. This is impossible when we're burdened by fear and anxiety, intimidated by the thought of the unknown, and overwhelmed by decisions we have no framework to make sensibly. Being tough is more than a willingness to face challenges, it's an eagerness to—not out of some unhealthy enjoyment of suffering, but because of the knowledge that the experience has unique power. The point, in the end, is simple—to not be a victim of imagined fate, but to truly enjoy meaningful, rewarding, fulfilling lives of our choosing.

FOCAL POINTS

- True toughness is defined by the four elements of character, capability, capacity and commitment: *Who are you and are you secure in that identity, what are you able to do, what are you able to withstand, and what are you willing to do?*

- Character is who we are and what we value—we choose our character and actively support it through our daily decisions and the way we speak and behave.

- Capability is a growing and broad array of abilities that allow us continually increasing self-reliance.

- Capacity is our ability to not simply survive adversity, but to use it to our advantage and thrive in its wake.

- Commitment is what we're willing to do in order to develop and enforce our character, capability and capacity, and to overcome adversity and challenges.

- True toughness isn't the absence of emotion, but the balance of it with rational thinking.

- Toughness isn't inherently a masculine quality—it's attainable by anyone willing to do the work.

- Being truly tough requires both mental and physical elements, as they're ultimately interdependent in all circumstances.

- Toughness isn't a competition, nor do the tough seek recognition or validation for their toughness.

- True toughness provides us the confidence to live at peace and achieve fulfillment.

ACTION

With all you've now read in mind, spend some time considering the following questions. It's a good idea to write them down—and an even better idea to return to these questions as you progress through the book and discover new insights and perspective. This is simply an initial evaluation to begin the process of improving your self-awareness and ability to critique yourself. This is not intended to be an exercise in self-flagellation or self-contempt. It will serve as a starting point and a guide to focusing your efforts where they're needed—keep it objective and unemotional.

- Why do you want to be tougher? What will being tougher allow you to accomplish?

- What do you think your toughest traits currently are?

- In what ways do you think you're most lacking in toughness?

- What are your ten biggest weaknesses?

- What are your ten biggest strengths?

- How do you tend to mitigate or disguise the negative effects of your weaknesses? What problems if any does that cause?

- How do you use your strengths? Do you ever abuse them?

- How do you envision your life with greater toughness? What changes? What stays the same?

CHAPTER 2
CHARACTER

Who are you? Are you secure in your identity? The first question is difficult for most of us to answer in any meaningful way—few of us have genuinely tried, even if it's ever occurred to us that we're unsure. The second question doesn't even make sense if we can't answer the first. And yet without knowing who we are, it's arguably impossible to ever be truly content and fulfilled and at peace—it's impossible to be truly tough. Most of us wander our way through life catching accidental glimpses at our own character that reveal pieces of a whole we're unfamiliar with, like an archeologist stumbling over barely exposed pieces of bone attached to an unidentified skeleton still obscured by layers of earth.

We tend to view who we are as something mysterious awaiting discovery, and let that discovery occur on its own through intermittent accidents, revealing itself to us over time as layers of that earth slowly erode under the abrasive stress of life, or more substantial chunks get broken loose by dramatic—or traumatic—events. We simply wait and glance over occasionally from the corner of our eye while we focus on what we've decided—usually mistakenly—are the more critical, pressing issues of the moment.

But character isn't something that spontaneously materializes fully-formed without our participation and lies dormant waiting for the encapsulating dirt to be scraped away. It isn't an inherent trait like eye color that we simply learn we have and accept as existing as it does. Character isn't something that happens to us—it's what we choose it to be. The problem is that few of us realize we're making the choice.

Character is the total set of distinctive mental, emotional, and psychological traits that defines each of us—what we believe, how we view the world around us and our place within it, our attitude, our values, and the way we behave and interact with others as a result of these things. In other words, our character is the complete definition of who we are—not what people see of us, not our reputation, not who we *think* we are or wish we were, but the irrefutable, inescapable truth beneath it all determining how we experience life.

An oddity of language is that we idiomatically use the word *character* as a positive description of someone we view as being ethical, honest, reliable and all of the other traits we collectively associate with being a "good" person. We can say someone *has character* to communicate our belief in their goodness, or that something *builds character* as if the only character possible to build is that composed of these same positive traits. But in fact, all of us have character—we're all composed of characteristics. The question is what kind.

That question, again, is most commonly answered largely accidentally and without particular interest or concern when it comes to ourselves. We'll invest no small amount of time and energy considering and discussing others' character, both as a rational way to evaluate the advisability of trusting or getting involved with someone, but also out of unhealthy, obsessive curiosity about others' personal lives and a related pathological aversion to self-examination. We'll offer extensive analyses of the inner workings and motivations of people we've never met, and yet respond to the question *Who are you?* with open-mouthed stares or quiet, uncomfortable laughter.

If we want to be tough, we need to do far more than discover who we are, more than know who we are, more than truly understand who we are—we need to *determine* who we are.

CHARACTER: BUILT OR REVEALED?

There may be ongoing argument about the precise nature and source of personality—how much of it is determined biologically either upon birth through genetics, over time through epigenetic reaction to our environments, or through childhood physical development, and how much is influenced throughout the course of our entire lives through our experiences and our conscious choices—but any rational observer can see that character is continuously evolving in most people through at least a portion of their lives. We can watch people transform from cripplingly shy children to confident, gregarious adults, or from joyful and lighthearted to miserable and cynical. It couldn't be clearer that character is not immutable—it's undoubtedly plastic to an extraordinary degree, even if we may retain on some level certain individual characteristics and proclivities throughout the course of development.

Not only does character change, it *should* change. What a dispiriting, depressing thought that who we are is simply fixed at birth by some unknown force, and no matter what we experience in our life, nothing about the way we think, the way we respond to situations, the way we view ourselves or the way we interact with other people, will ever change. How can our life experiences not give us at least the opportunity to determine who we are?

The related ongoing disagreement is over building versus revealing character. A given experience, some will claim, builds character; others argue that experiences don't build character, they simply reveal it. Even if we concede the use of the word character in the way it's intended in these discussions to obviously represent desirable qualities, neither position entirely makes sense on its own.

In order for character to merely be revealed through an experience, it has to already exist in a complete, fixed form. In other words, we are who we are from the moment we're born, and our life is nothing but a series of opportunities of incremental discovery of our own character—we go through life figuring out who something else has already decided we are, and our only related ability is to learn what that is through collected experiences and maybe a bit of introspection. This means that our life experiences are to a great extent without meaning because they have no influence on us—we may as well just sit comfortably at home and think about who we are.

The opposing claim, that experiences build character, makes a significant assumption: that a given experience will produce the same response—or any response at all—in any given person. Interestingly enough, the same people who will tell you that sports build character, for example, will also chew your ear off about various collegiate and professional athletes who are whiny, entitled brats. That observation alone unquestionably disproves their original claim, and yet they manage to ignore the incompatibility of the two ideas (often accompanied by the classic grumbling *kids these days* lament).

In reality, we have considerable agency in determining who we are—if we choose to recognize and employ it—*and* simultaneously, some present form of character available to be revealed. There's never a point in our lives where our character doesn't exist, and consequently any moment is an opportunity to discover and examine who we are at that time—to *reveal* our character. Those moments are very often difficult experiences or the period immediately following them because they inherently test our stability and encourage introspection as we recover and regroup.

Those same trying experiences are also opportunities for us to *build* character because they challenge our way of thinking, how we view the world and ourselves, and our mindset, leaving us with the perfect situation to reconsider all of it—how who we are affected the experience for better or worse, in what ways we succeeded and failed, and how we feel about its effects on us. When our existing character is exposed completely and mercilessly, we can best determine how we want to respond—by passively accepting our present condition and potentially allowing the experience to harm us, or by applying the lessons made possible by the experience to evolve in a way we dictate ourselves. In other words, we can choose to use the experience to build character as we see fit.

The reasonable question here is obvious: why do some of us make that choice and change positively in response to an experience, while some of us seem to simply sit and allow it to batter us without meaningful response?

It's the influence of our character at the time of the experience—are we the kind of person who takes an active role in our own lives, or the kind who watches from the sidelines? What's determined that facet of our personality prior to that point we may not know—maybe it's something it seems like we've always felt with no clear sense of its origin, maybe it's something we were taught by a parent or coach or teacher, or maybe it's something we read in a book. In any case, all that's required is enough awareness to recognize the opportunity, a belief in our own innate ability to decide who we are, a desire for self-determination, and the willingness and resilience to endure the potentially painful and arduous process of such fundamental remodeling.

Another variable in the equation is the nature of the experience itself—this interacts with and influences our choices in how we respond. Sports *can* build character—or, more accurately, sports can provide the experiences that we can use to build character. They offer opportunities for hard work, interpersonal communication and teamwork, sacrifice and compromise, discipline and will, victory and defeat, and a sense of purpose.

Arguably *purpose* is a critical element alongside our own awareness and self-determination. Hard work and drudgery don't magically produce great character—they can just as easily produce a miserable, pessimistic cynic. Your father sending you out to the backyard to dig holes every weekend that you later refill to ostensibly learn the value of hard work is more likely to do little more than make you exhausted and resentful of your father—because there is an unmistakable absence of meaningful purpose to the task itself.

Jerry Rice is widely considered to be the greatest wide receiver to ever play the game of football, and more than a few will argue the greatest player across the board. Rice's work ethic and self-imposed standards are legendary. His origin story is almost too perfect to believe, which makes it perfect to illustrate this idea. While a child growing up in a tiny rural town in Mississippi, his father was a mason who would bring Rice to work with him regularly because he needed his help. His job was ensuring his father had the uninterrupted supply of bricks he needed, and this involved Rice repeatedly catching bricks that were thrown to him.

Conveniently enough, this turned out to be extraordinarily valuable physical training for the mechanics, visual acuity, hand strength and durability to catch footballs and the physical and mental toughness to excel at the game, but more importantly, this hard work laid the foundation for his superior work ethic. This wasn't pointless misery or punishment—this was work that served a clear and meaningful purpose. He was contributing to his father's ability to provide for his family, and he very clearly saw his father working even harder than he was. Had instead his father simply sat on the back lawn and thrown bricks at little Jerry all summer, he may have learned to catch remarkably well, but it's unlikely he would have ever become the player and the man he did.

Of course, we don't have the luxury of choosing our parents or the circumstances in which we grow up, and by the time you read this book, it's a safe bet you'll already be well into adulthood. This means we may miss opportunities for such storybook-style character development at arguably the ideal age, when we're naturally most malleable and easily influenced, but it also means that we're at a stage in life at which we have greater self-awareness, more control over the content and course of our lives, and more means to create our own opportunities as we determine fit. Childhood may set us on a path, but adulthood cuts its own.

Does this mean that purposeless, miserable work or pointlessly torturous experiences don't allow us to build character? Of course not. The purpose and meaning of an experience has an influence on our response, but it's not the sole determinant. A lack of apparent purpose demands that we take a more active role and *create* purpose and meaning for our own benefit. We can choose to go two basic ways while digging and refilling holes in the backyard while Dad supervises with a beer in his hand from the porch—become victims of our circumstances and meekly put our heads through the yoke, or take control of what we can within the circumstances we cannot.

If we choose to build character, that means we can make that choice irrespective of the experience in question. We can build character digging purposeless holes, and excavating for the foundation of our next home; we can build character on the football field, the wrestling mat, or the weightlifting platform, and we can build it on the chessboard or the blackboard; we can build character in combat, and we can build character in simple, everyday personal interactions. We can build character sitting silently in the dark.

Every moment in our lives is an opportunity for self-determination. Who we are is our choice to make. We determine the lessons an experience has to teach by recognizing what it is we need to learn. We make the choice to ignore or dismiss these lessons, or to internalize and apply them.

And of course, we can choose to learn nothing at all and let life decide our fate. We have the choice to sit back and allow life to happen to us as if we're spectators instead of participants. Nothing is forcing us to play an active role in our lives beyond the most basic sense of self-preservation dictating that we ensure reliable sources of water, food and shelter; depending on our circumstances, some of us are even able to coast through life without even once concerning ourselves with that much.

The absence of participation may not be an entirely conscious choice. It may simply be the natural outgrowth of a sense of fatalism and consequent helplessness—if we believe our life is predetermined, why would we lift a finger to do anything at all? Moreover, why would we even consider it an option? We're just along for the ride. This sense of pointlessness may arise from experiences early on that seemed to prove that actions and choices had no effect on the course of life—but this is an interpretation of the facts, not the facts themselves. Typically such a conclusion is drawn not because there was no observable effect, but because the effects were not what we expected or wanted, or not immediate enough to be associated. Unexpected or undesirable consequences simply show us the choices we made were ultimately not the ones we should have—but they also demonstrate that our choices do have the power to influence the course of events. The logical response is to make the necessary adjustments to our subsequent choices, not to conclude our choices are without purpose or effect and give up the effort.

Being tough isn't simply the capacity to endure the interminable misery life decides without reason to pile onto us—it's being willing and able to endure adversity as it comes because we're aware of our power to ultimately determine the course of our lives through our decisions and actions. It is absolutely not weary resignation, but an unrelenting fight to achieve what's meaningful to us despite the obstacles.

We don't have control over everything in life, no matter how aware and active we remain. There will always be circumstances we encounter that have been determined by outside forces, whether other people's decisions and behavior, natural events, or possibly nothing more than chance. What we do have control over at all times, however, is our response to what's outside our control. We have the ability to react in ways that benefit us or ways that harm us, whether that reaction is exclusively in our minds or takes the form of overt behavior.

A failure to be active in controlling our reactions will nearly always produce undesired consequences—if not immediately, eventually. This kind of surrender to circumstances makes us progressively weaker, less capable and prone to convincing ourselves we're victims of our own lives. The more effort we invest into conscious decision-making and controlling our reactions, the more responsibility for our lives we not only accept, but take, the more power we find we already possess, and the more power we continue to accumulate.

WHO ARE YOU?

Knowing we have the ability to decide our own character isn't the same as knowing who we are. Determining who we are is an ongoing process of discovery, decision and action—a loop of discovering who we are, deciding who we want to be, and acting in alignment. The original order is inconsequential. If we first determine who we are now, we then decide who we want to be and make changes consistent with that identity; if we decide who we want to be, we then determine who we are presently to ascertain what needs to change, and then act accordingly. What matters is that we understand it goes far beyond making a single decision or evaluation—and that any decision requires subsequent related action to be meaningful.

We decide exactly who we are, but attendant to that ability is the responsibility of enforcing that identity. It's not a magical process in which we decide who we are and instantly our mindset, words and behavior perfectly reflect that character. Choosing an identity is academic; *being* someone is practical, and it's not necessarily an easy task that will be undertaken without mistakes and failure. Our identity is simply the guide to help us steer our thoughts and behavior in the direction we've chosen.

Identity is described by ideas, but defined by actions. *I'm a good person who helps others* is an idea about who we are, and as nice as it sounds, it's largely without meaning or value in and of itself. Volunteering for an organization that provides afterschool sports programs for kids without the resources to otherwise have access to them is an action that brings that idea to life—it's what actually *makes* us a good person. Believing *I'm a composed, rational person* is meaningless if we blow up and scream like a petulant child any time we find another car too close to one of the lines of the parking space we want to occupy. In the long term, an idea of identity without behavior that consistently and reliably supports it is little more than self-deception.

The solitary value and meaning of that idea is as a landmark to help us navigate through the process of reshaping our behavior. In some cases, that landmark may be very distant and require an extraordinarily trying journey in which we occasionally lose sight of it behind the natural obstacles along the trail, but in all cases, each step in its direction not followed by another back is a significant accomplishment. Without an attempt to progress toward our intentions, that landmark is without purpose.

Every day we have numerous opportunities to choose who we are, and to manifest that identity by supporting the decision with our words, behavior and mindset. We have the same number of opportunities to deceive ourselves by failing to align our actions with our purported identity. In truth, there are far too many of these opportunities to make conscious decisions practical or even possible at every step—we resolve this problem through conscientious habit building to eliminate unnecessary cognitive load without compromising our intentions. The goal is to establish over time the *routine* of being who we are—to make the words, mindset and behaviors of our chosen identity increasingly natural rather than consciously chosen each time. This, ultimately, is transitioning from *acting* like who we want to be, to *being* who we are.

SECURITY IN IDENTITY

The second element of character, in addition to knowing who we are, is being secure in that identity—this is the *knowing* part already contained within that idea, admittedly, but its importance bears distinction and emphasis, because its consequence is immeasurably vast. We may have a vision of who we are or who we're working to become, but if we're inadequately certain and confident in that identity, our decisions about our behavior are influenced remarkably easily by our circumstances. The moment we decide to think, speak or behave in a way that fails to align with our ostensible identity, we've become someone else. Being who we want to be in the absence of challenge is a start, but hardly impressive or exceptional. It's only when we're being tested that our refusal to abandon our identity is genuinely meaningful.

Understand that this is not a suggestion that intransigence is the goal. An imperative of admirable character is the willingness to change our beliefs and values when confronted with legitimate reasons, perhaps even an eagerness—it should be our continuous desire to evolve over time as we accumulate experience and knowledge and the resultant insights and understanding. To carve our identity in stone and guard it fearfully from exposure to life defeats much of the purpose of having a clear identity in the first place.

The point is that changes to our identity must be made intentionally, intelligently and rationally. Change must be a choice we make with reason, not an event that happens to us while we watch—or worse, without our noticing. The evolution of our character should be accidental only in the sense that we can't predict the experiences that will inspire us to make changes in who we are and what we believe, or even in what manner and direction those experiences may nudge us. We need to remain simultaneously open to the possibility and wary of the nature of our influences.

As creatures who are wired by nature to be social, we tend to be influenced easily by others. Survival is far easier if we fit comfortably within our various communities of every scale, and this is best accomplished through mimicry of beliefs, modes of thinking, behavior and appearance. How many times have we found ourselves unconsciously adopting the manner of speaking and vocabulary of whomever we're around? How often have we found ourselves simply nodding along to something we privately disagree with? How much do our moods shift to match an existing atmosphere? How many times have we questioned what we're doing as a result of a stranger's criticism?

This behavior is natural, understandable and entirely common—without true security in our identity and the strength of character it engenders, we're hopelessly pliant and obedient to the predominant norms. We have no inspiration or incentive to resist and endure the friction that results—why weather the discomfort to fight for something we don't genuinely care about? If we can't define who we are and describe the values that drive us, there's nothing to fight for—we simply flow through life in a molten state, taking on whatever shape minimizes resistance as we inexorably trickle toward and settle into the lowest point.

All too frequently, we unknowingly conform ourselves to the company we keep, speaking and behaving differently to impress or ingratiate ourselves to others. As an unconscious product of discomfort, anxiety or fear, this is a failure of our character to stand firmly against the prevailing winds. This kind of shape shifting itself isn't necessarily a problem—as a conscious choice as part of a strategy to achieve a clear end, it may be an effective tactic. However, care should be exercised to avoid retroactively labeling it such when no intention in the moment existed—that's nothing more than an elaborate excuse.

Security in our identity and the consequent fortification of our character is what allows us to withstand criticism of any nature or severity without allowing it to change our thinking or derail us from our path. If we know who we are, and we can support that knowledge with the confidence of genuine understanding of why we've made the choices we've made to determine our character, what we value and don't, and how integral our character is to our success and contentment, resisting the more natural urges to be swayed by the influence of others is undemanding and reliable. It is, in fact, unnecessary—the urges and doubt we might normally feel in response to even the most baseless criticism never materialize to be resisted. Criticism, disagreement and disapproval simply fade into background noise without compromising the clarity of the signal.

The truly tough recognize that not only are they capable of resisting undesirable influence from outside, but even more critically, capable of being the source of the prevailing winds that influence others. We don't have to simply fight to protect ourselves from our environment—we instead can determine to take control of that environment and remodel it as we see fit. In any group of people, the atmosphere is determined by the attitudes, energy and moods of those present, and we can decide to capitulate to those forces that seem to be naturally dominant, or we can object and *become* the dominant force—not for the purpose of controlling others, but in order to maintain the ultimate control over ourselves.

Being tough demands the ability to resist the kinds of forces that have the potential to push us into positions or choices contrary to who we are. Any resistance requires security—in the case of our identity, that security is predicated on awareness. We don't stow away our most valuable possessions and then spend the remainder of our lives simply assuming they're safe. We periodically check in on their status, reassure ourselves and fortify protections as needed. Arguably, our identity is our most valuable asset—it needs to be monitored and protected to ensure it remains safely in the form we've chosen.

This is simple conceptually. If we know who we are, and we know the kinds of thinking, words and behavior that align with that identity, *Does this reflect who I am?* is a relatively easy question to answer at any given moment even in unfamiliar situations. The most complex work has been done in deciding who we are and who we want to be—now we're evaluating whether or not the way we're living is representative of that identity, and making appropriate choices in response. This kind of self-evaluation exists on a broad scale.

We can quickly consider discrete, individual actions, and we can extensively contemplate more global views of our entire lives. What matters is that this assessment remains ongoing, frequent and sincere, and that our evaluations, regardless of how disappointing or unexpected they may sometimes be, are relied on for guiding our future choices.

VALUES

We are who we are because of what we value. These principles are what shape our identity and provide meaning to our life. We all think and behave in accordance to our values, whether or not we're completely aware of them. In order to truly understand who we are and develop security in our identity, we need to clearly define the values that shape and guide us. Without that intimate familiarity with our own internal system of orchestration, we're likely to live as if our decisions are mysterious and inexplicable—something happening to us that we have no hope of controlling. We're reduced to descriptivists, trying to explain our behavior after the fact with convoluted reasoning and convenient excuses, rather than prescriptivists actively determining each step we take with purpose. We find troubling, confounding discordance in our lives between what we do and who we believe we are, what we achieve and what we believe we're capable of, how the world views us and how we view ourselves—we find ourselves in the midst of unsettling disorder we can't quite pin down or manage to organize.

Much like we can quickly and easily answer the question *Does this reflect who I am?* to align our words and actions with our character if we're adequately familiar with that identity, when we can clearly define our values, the typical burden of making important decisions is stripped of much of its cumbersome weight. We can transform many nebulous, far-reaching philosophical questions into simple binary calculations with little demand for cognitive resources.

This doesn't mean, of course, that we'll never encounter situations that challenge our principles to their very foundations—adversity and difficulty are exactly the experiences that have the most power to shake them loose and demand we re-examine and reconsider, and in consequence decide to fortify and protect them, or remodel them in a new fashion shaped by lessons we've not previously had the opportunities to learn. Again, knowing who we are, being capable of defining our values, and being secure in our identity doesn't mean constructing an impervious wall around ourselves to prevent any possible future impact or growth—it means having the character to act in accordance to our values until the time when we willingly and eagerly consider evolving in response to meaningful experience.

SELF-EVALUATION

Throughout our lives, we evaluate ourselves frequently—most often this is an unconscious process, but our attitude, sense of contentment, and outlook on life are all influenced by the results whether or not we're aware any type of assessment is occurring. The more self-aware among us transform this natural process of self-evaluation that runs in the background into a conscious, intentional act with clear purpose—it's a way to learn more about ourselves, understand what drives us and why, and find ways to better achieve the collective elements that coalesce to create a sense of fulfillment.

The most common metric of self-evaluation, even once it initially becomes conscious, is direct comparison to others—are we stronger, faster, more intelligent, more attractive, more popular, richer, and more successful than whoever we're focused on... or not? The problems with this are numerous to say the least, and even the very foundation of the system is nonsensical—whom we choose to compare ourselves with is nearly always arbitrary, so even on its face, it's a meaningless measurement.

More importantly, evaluation by comparison is doomed to produce discontent, discouragement and a sense of failure because the reality is that there will *always* be someone out there better than us in any given metric at some point. Even the literal best in the world don't stay that way forever. An athlete who holds a world record may be elated with the achievement, but what happens when that record is broken after the athlete's career has peaked and no further chances to improve exist? If that's the individual's measure of fulfillment, it means the remainder of their life is a disappointment with no possible remedy.

In every single metric of comparison, it's not only not difficult, but impossible *not* to find someone who exceeds our own status—our minds will actively seek examples until we can find one that proves our concerns are legitimate. Worse, with more subjective criteria, if we have this mindset, we'll convince ourselves of our inferiority and failure even if it's not objectively accurate—it's the unavoidable product of this way of thinking.

Healthy and productive self-evaluation is concerned with only two metrics: our own values primarily, and our chosen goals secondarily. Do our behavior, words and character reflect and support our values or not? Are we working toward our goals actively and effectively or not? Where are we falling short in these intentions, and how do we improve? In other words, this evaluation is entirely self-contained—in no way does it consider anything beyond ourselves.

UNCONDITIONAL SELF-LOVE

The idea of self-love elicits passion from both ends of the spectrum, from those who embrace it as the ultimate solution to all personal issues, to those who rail against it as a source of excuses. Like the idea of being tough itself, at least part of the discord arises from the lack of clarity regarding what exactly self-love means and entails, and the implications attendant to its definition.

Love is simply the most profound and intense level of care we're capable of—anything beyond that is context-dependent, baggage from unrelated features of our own psychological landscape, or decoration fashioned by convention. Self-love, then, is nothing more than that intense caring for ourselves—the desire to be well, to be safe, to be fulfilled, to be content, to be secure, and to be at peace. Where it gets cloudier is when we add the *unconditional* qualifier to self-love, and this seems to be the principal source of concern and disagreement.

Unconditional means that the status is unchanged no matter what—regardless of the circumstances, whatever quality it's being used to describe is immutable, unvarying, constant, reliable. In other words, unconditional self-love means that irrespective of the situation, of our choices, of our accomplishments or failures, of our ambitions or complacency, of who we are or what we're doing at the moment, we love ourselves just as much as at any other moment. This strikes a lot of us as misguided and even dangerously forgiving—should we really love ourselves so much if we're unaccomplished, unambitious, and seemingly without purpose?

But what we have to bear in mind is that unconditional self-love doesn't mean unconditional self-acceptance as we might understandably conclude without taking adequate time to consider. Unconditional love for ourselves does not mean *accepting* what and who we are unconditionally. It means loving ourselves enough to change what needs to be changed to make progress toward our personal ambitions. It doesn't mean being satisfied or content with our current status or condition; it means caring enough about our own wellbeing to do what we need in order to be what and who we want. It doesn't mean relocating the goalposts to be closer to our present position and directly aligned with our existing trajectory. Unconditional self-love is not complacency or surrender—it's a reason to never surrender.

Think of it this way: If as a parent, our child is flunking out of school, we still love them just as much as if they were valedictorian; but that unconditional love doesn't mean we simply *accept* the situation and move on with our lives—we do everything we can to help that child resolve the problem because we love them and want them to be happy and successful. Why wouldn't we apply that same logic to ourselves?

Acceptance by nature precludes motivation to change. If we accept it, why would we want to change it? If we want to change it, why would we accept it? We have to be able and willing to recognize the objective reality of any given situation—to see it for exactly what it is without interpretation or rationalization to color it more favorably—in order to desire and commit to change. We can acknowledge the present truth about ourselves without accepting it as being fixed indefinitely.

Unconditional self-acceptance is surrender—it's resignation, acquiescence to the idea that the way we are at the moment is some kind of unalterable law of existence over which we're entirely powerless. There are such realities in life that demand acceptance—the earth is round, night follows day, rain falls rather than rises… Refusal to accept these kinds of facts is delusional—acceptance in these cases isn't surrender, it's understanding. But there are few facts about ourselves that warrant the sort of acceptance that applies to the laws of nature, and its inappropriate application is misguided and harmful, not enlightened.

Unconditionally accepting ourselves as we are isn't representative of a healthy mindset or symptomatic of attaining some buddhic level of awareness—it's a seductively reassuring misconception. If we've convinced ourselves that the healthy path is acceptance, our work is done. We have a seemingly sensible and sophisticated rationale to avoid the pain and difficulty of honest self-evaluation and the consequent interminable struggle for genuine self-improvement. It neatly wraps up every bit of possible ambition and accomplishment into a single, ultimate, already-completed achievement that renders everything else unnecessary. Unconditional self-love means that, despite everything we refuse to accept about ourselves in any given moment, we have a vision for who we want to be and the ambition to pursue it because we care, deeply and profoundly and unyieldingly. It means sincere self-assessment and the knowledge that the conclusions we draw in the process aren't value judgments. It means understanding the difference between criticism and critique, and appreciating the kind of objective measurement that results from this practice because of its utility to aid navigation through the rugged terrain of our continuing development. It means, most critically, that we care enough to bother.

Refusing to relax into the enticing comfort of unconditional self-acceptance doesn't mean we hate ourselves for being imperfect, or having failed in our last endeavor, or not quite yet entirely embodying the identity we're striving to establish—if it did, we'd invariably and indefinitely hate our own guts. We refuse to accept our shortcomings and push ahead unrelentingly because we *love* ourselves. We work every day toward achievement, no matter how minor or mundane the actions we take toward that end may often be. Unconditional self-acceptance is giving up. It's not self-love—it's self-abandonment.

CONFIDENCE & HUMILITY

Being truly tough—as the product of carefully developed character, capability, capacity and commitment—manifests as confidence. This kind of genuine confidence is integral to the elimination or extensive diminishment of the fear, intimidation, anxiety and insecurity that has the power to render us unsuccessful, unfulfilled and discontent. It is one of the essential purposes of being tough.

Confidence is a frequently misunderstood and misrepresented concept. It's simply an objectively resolute trust and belief in our abilities and values. Confidence is not arrogance or conceit or vanity—in fact, despite the persistent conflation of these qualities, genuine confidence precludes these traits. We establish confidence through honest self-evaluation producing objective metrics demonstrating our competence. In contrast, arrogance and conceit are the products of inaccurate self-assessment and the fallacious inflation of abilities in contradiction to fact. Most often, it's an outgrowth of insecurity and self-consciousness—a strategy to disguise that weakness from others and even from ourselves in order to avoid the discomfort of knowing how far we fall short of where we may want to be.

Unfortunately for the wearer, it's an unconvincing disguise. In fact, rather than assure those around us of our competence, it elicits resentment and ridicule—arguably the worst imaginable reaction for someone burdened by insecurity and the primary response their behavior is intended to deter. More critically, it's a dangerous state of mind. Unmerited faith in our abilities as a result of inaccurate—or absent—self-assessment makes us vulnerable to manipulation by those to whom we are far more transparent than we suspect, and likely to find ourselves in positions we're not actually prepared to handle.

Confidence is specific to the nature and degree of our competence and coupled inextricably with precise self-awareness. It protects us from mistakenly exposing ourselves to risks beyond our ability to successfully manage, precludes hubris from leading us to certain destruction as it invariably does, and it allows us to guard our weak points from exploitation and take maximal advantage of our strengths in order to accomplish what we intend. Finally, it guides our choices regarding what we do to further our character, capability, capacity and commitment to gradually shore up those weaknesses and vulnerabilities—and it reassures us of our ability to succeed in those pursuits.

True confidence, rather than inspiring arrogance or hubris, instead encourages modesty and humility. These are naturally occurring traits when we have no need to prove ourselves to others. Security and self-assurance negate any need for explicit approval or validation from the world around us—we can simply do and say what we believe is right without any concern or calculation regarding its appearance to the rest of the world and the resultant alterations of speech and behavior that encourages. In consequence, the kind of posturing often associated with the standard tough-guy routine is completely absent. Posturing is what prey does to create the illusion of greater strength than is actually possessed to try to discourage an imminent attack by a predator or competitor. In other words, it's nothing more than a desperate act in reaction to fear. In our world, this behavior isn't restricted to literal posture in response to the fear of death or physical harm—it can be mental and verbal as well, and can attend fear of all kinds, such as of humiliation, rejection or failure.

The kind of quiet confidence the truly tough possess is by no means imperceptible—by nature it's in fact immediately apparent, at least on an unconscious level, to all but the most pathologically unobservant. Rather than the ridiculous and embarrassingly transparent affectation of the insecure and inadequate, the truly tough move through life deliberately, unhesitatingly and willfully, both literally and metaphorically. Toughness is communicated to the world not only without effort, but unavoidably—it can only be concealed through conscious, intentional acting intended for strategic reasons to prevent discovery in certain situations.

Interestingly, the communication of toughness occurs not just through our actions, but often through our decisions not to act. The same confidence that prohibits the compulsion for posturing also eliminates the urge to react in unnecessary manners to provocation or the mere inference of it. Rash, uncalculated and excessive responses to misjudged threats or imagined slights immediately betrays fear and insecurity. The truly tough naturally and effortlessly maintain a degree of composure unmatchable even with volitional hard work by others—not just when encountering a situation they determine to not require a response, but also when confronted with a genuine threat demanding significant reaction. The confidence of toughness allows quick distinction between the two, and the self-possession to sit back and comfortably dismiss what doesn't merit reaction. The tough are always prepared and willing to respond as demanded to threats or danger, but are never the aggressors without legitimate provocation and need.

This mindset translates naturally into a lack of interest in receiving recognition and credit for what we do. Being tough strips behavior of ulterior motives because so much of what we tend to do and how we do it is intended to derive results other than the ostensible—and those results so often are related to receiving recognition from those around us. The tough simply do what they do because they've made a rational choice or have established the related habits for rational purposes—there's no intent to score points or earn rewards beyond the satisfaction of upholding their values, accomplishing their goals, or fulfilling their duties, whether self-imposed or otherwise. If we remove, through genuine confidence, the natural fear of not being valuable or having purpose in life, we're freed from the compulsion to continually seek reassurance from others of our value, purpose and success.

Unsurprisingly, true toughness also eliminates the obnoxiously common sense of entitlement that governs the behavior and colors the attitude of so many people. High levels of capability and capacity translate into independence, which eliminates much of the reliance most of us have on others to meet our needs. The ability to truly take care of ourselves doesn't just free us from that reliance on others—it tends to instill the desire to be free of it, and to disabuse us of the notion that we're owed anything by anyone. The tough develop a genuine sense of ownership and agency—exactly what the entitled are lacking that prevents accountability and creates their expectation that others be responsible for assisting them at every turn. A sense of entitlement is a crippling flaw.

Contrary to the impression many get initially when confronted with this idea—that it's a cold, lonely world out there and we're all on our own—this is actually a liberating and energizing perspective, the rewards of which grow in depth and breadth with time and investment. We're not entitled to anything from anyone, we're not owed anything, and we can't expect to be reliably supplied with our every need and desire simply because they exist. Toughness inspires an approach to life in which we feel compelled to truly earn everything we need, desire or believe we deserve, and the reward for our hard work is the exultation of genuine accomplishment many will never experience.

This attitude extends beyond what we have yet to achieve and applies to what we have already through no effort of our own. What we've been given can be earned after the fact through our choices to become and remain the kind of person who deserves what we have. The defensive hoarding of gifts we did absolutely nothing to earn to the detriment of those who did no less and yet received nothing is a perfect demonstration of entitlement that many refuse to recognize. Worse, many recipients of such unearned gifts have convinced themselves that their very existence is evidence of their merit, as if the universe has anointed them despite a complete absence of cause. We can transform what might be considered a gift into a loan we pay back gratefully with our choices and behavior—to retroactively earn what we didn't need to. This repayment is fairly comprised at least partly of our help of those who were, through no fault of their own, not as fortunate as we were through no work of our own.

EMOTION

Despite what our cinematic and literary archetypes often suggest, being tough doesn't mean being emotionless—it doesn't even mean never revealing or expressing emotion. A true absence of emotion would mean a non-functioning human being incapable of survival. As Laurence Gonzales explains in his book *Deep Survival*, emotion is the fundamental and powerful compeller of immediate action—it functions independently of cognition and its relatively slow, clumsy work of analysis, reason and conceptualization to allow quicker reactions.[1] Emotion is the physical response of the body to environmental cues—everything from flinching in response to being startled, to the knot in our stomach we can't explain with our rational mind in response to an imminent but unclear threat.

If we can bypass any (unwarranted but common) embarrassment about the topic, we'll admit that emotion is what truly provides meaning to life. We can point to more tangible or concrete things like family and enjoyable experiences like athletic pursuits or outdoor adventures as what we derive meaning from, but ultimately what we appreciate about these things is the way they make us *feel*—we're not pleasurably overwhelmed with analytical thoughts about the concepts they represent, we're flooded with ineffable sensations in response to them. Those sensations are what we all seek, consciously or not, and provide purpose to our existence. Emotion exists for good reason—but so does cognition.

The two systems—emotion and thought—simply need to be balanced in a way that allows each to operate properly, which empowers us as a whole to function optimally in any situation. Neither emotion nor rational thought can be accurately described as "better" than the other—either can be more critical at a given moment for a given task, and either can be excessive and disruptive or inappropriately applied or relied upon. We can be overwhelmed by emotion and make errors in judgment, and we can be paralyzed by over-analysis and miss opportunities or fail to act when necessary. That said, the conditions in which most of us live day to day demand very little of the kind of survival-related instant primary emotional reactions that have the power to keep us alive in the appropriate situations—aside from occasionally jumping back out of the way of rapidly oncoming traffic after stepping off the sidewalk without looking, we don't encounter these kinds of situations commonly.

Instead, we're more often dealing with secondary emotions—a more extensive array of emotions influenced by "cognitive appraisal." These are emotions created through the combination of primary emotions with some degree of cognition informing the interpretation—this allows us to recognize the difference between bungee jumping and falling off the side of a mountain in a climbing accident, for example. In both cases we experience a secondary emotion with a foundation of fear—and the immediate physical reaction with the primary emotion may be identical—but the overall experience is completely different because of the additional input from the rational mind. In one situation, we're intentionally creating the experience for a thrill and know it's a controlled environment with safety systems in place; in the other, we're very aware that we're out of control and may be about to die.

Protracted or unchecked secondary emotions are what more commonly wreak havoc on our lives. If we're startled at home by our spouse suddenly and unexpectedly walking around the corner, we immediately appraise the situation and relax. Our instantly elevated heart rate may take a minute to return to baseline, but there's no persisting effect—we don't spend the rest of the day being overwhelmed by stress hormones coursing through our blood and influencing our behavior or thinking.

On the other hand, secondary emotions like anger, resentment, shame and jealousy tend to linger and have persistent and growing influence on our thinking and behavior. This is where control of our emotions through self-awareness and our rational minds becomes imperative. Experiencing an emotional reaction is human and expected; immediately recognizing it as such, evaluating the circumstances critically, and imposing our rationally motivated will on our actual response to the situation is tough. An experience may very naturally produce anger, for example, but we have the ability to make rational calculations regarding not just our behavior in response to that emotion, but ultimately the way we think consciously about it and the precipitating event. That emotion is not stepping in through a faster neurological pathway than cognition in response to a sudden threat to save our lives—we have the ability to choose what to do with it rather than simply allow it to impose its own control.

Marcus Aurelius wrote, "It isn't manly to be enraged... A real man doesn't give way to anger and discontent, and such a person has strength, courage, and endurance—unlike the angry and complaining. The nearer a man comes to a calm mind, the closer he is to strength."[2] We can substitute *tough* for *manly* to improve the utility and clarify the universality of this idea—in truth it has nothing to do with masculinity or gender, and has everything to do with our inherent but uncommonly employed power to keep our emotions in check and working for us rather than against us. Being consumed by any emotion is a condition we allow, either by choice or by neglecting to make one. It's an absolute failure of self-control at the most fundamental level, and it's an often disheartening exposure of our actual character.

Outside of the kinds of instant emotional responses the body produces to keep us alive in sudden or imminent emergencies (over which we have no control in the moment anyway—we'll discuss how we can influence these reactions through training in the Capacity chapter), allowing emotion to dictate our behavior invariably creates problems. We have to be capable of experiencing an emotion naturally—feeling it, recognizing it, accepting it and appreciating it—without becoming a victim or slave to its influence.

It's easy to see the consequences of allowing our thoughts and behavior to be dictated by anger or hatred, but even positive emotions create problems if we allow them to overwhelm the rational control of our lives. We don't have to look any further for illustrations of this than incidents of people's lives completely falling apart as they allow themselves to become slaves to love (or at least what they perceive to be love). Being consumed by what would be universally considered a positive, beneficial emotion has led many times to everything from unemployment, divorce, school dropouts, unintended pregnancies, to the commission of crimes and deadly accidents. Even more potent fusions of emotions like love and rage lead to behavior like retributive murder and suicide.

Being truly tough demands we maintain control of our responses to people and circumstances—not eliminate emotion, which is a fool's errand, but establish a level of self-awareness and self-possession that precludes unchecked emotional reactions from harming us, immediately or in the future. It means never allowing our circumstances to prevent our making intelligent decisions that align with our character and goals, whether that means a failure to respond appropriately in a stressful situation or emergency, an unconsidered and harmful reaction to someone else's words or behavior toward us, or spending extended periods of time bathing in an emotion that interferes with our judgment.

This kind of awareness and self-control requires practice and time. We can't simply decide to no longer experience the emotional responses inherent to our nature, although the most critical step in the process is making the initial decision to institute control. We need to habitualize through practice and reflection the quick recognition of the presence of significant emotion and the immediate evaluation of the situation to determine the most appropriate response. We're essentially working to create a more refined (and even faster) version of Thomas Jefferson's classic advice: "When angry, count to ten before you speak. If very angry, a hundred." That is, we're establishing a buffer between the initial emotion and our outward reaction—a defensive zone that provides us the time and opportunity to disrupt and alter the course of an undesirable response before it's able to harm us.

Early on, there's nothing wrong with literally counting to ten (or whatever figure reflects the intensity of the emotion) to establish the protocol of imposing rational thought in the presence of overwhelming emotion. As this process is exercised increasingly over time, it will naturally organize and streamline itself until becoming nearly instantaneous in most cases. Eventually, the habit will become so well ingrained that it will be, as we intend, an integral part of our character.

SOCIAL ASPECTS

No matter our individual level of social interaction, we are by our nature and universal circumstances inextricably linked to the rest of the world. Each of us chooses how exactly this connection is expressed, employed or exploited, but that connection can't be severed short of completely removing ourselves from any human encounter by living entirely independently of any society, which very few of us are interested in, let alone actually capable of practically. Even the most isolated, off-grid, independent mountain dwellers of the world maintain periodic, if infrequent, interaction with others for various supplies. We are a piece of a larger whole, and that fact carries with it certain conditions and responsibilities.

This doesn't mean, however, that there's a requirement for any given level of interpersonal interaction beyond the minimum demanded by practical need, or that we're somehow at a disadvantage by being naturally introverted. Human beings are genetically wired to be communal, but the variation in how that's expressed and the form and extent of community interaction each of us needs is immense for myriad reasons. A solitary lifestyle has no limits to contentment for those it suits, and more frequent social interaction can prove exhausting and miserable for many.

What matters ultimately is not the quantity of social interaction, but the quality—more specifically, our treatment of and consideration for those we're interacting with. The origins of the maxim are unclear—likely because it's a fairly obvious sentiment that could have been arrived at by multiple people independently at different times—but the underlying wisdom is simple: Character can be judged by how you treat those from whom you have nothing to gain. Muhammad Ali expressed the idea clearly when he said, "I don't trust anyone who's nice to me but rude to the waiter. Because I know they would treat me the same way if I were in that position."

The nature of our treatment of people shouldn't be dependent on our potential to gain something from them. Being truly tough means that we feel no need to treat others in any other way but respectfully and considerately—

because we have nothing to prove, no concern for our appearance, and no need for posturing—unless and until someone has demonstrated our respect and consideration are unmerited. This is not to say we operate naively or are trusting to a degree of risk. Interacting respectfully with people doesn't leave us vulnerable in any way. It has no bearing on our ability to defend against manipulation, attack or anything else we need to remain vigilant against. It's a strictly outward motion.

Along these lines, we can consider ourselves as inhabiting one of two basic categories: contributor or consumer. Do we, on balance, contribute more to the world than we consume, or consume more than we contribute? We all do both to some extent throughout our lives at various times, and it's impossible to consume nothing, but the question is which is dominant, and whether we're making a conscious choice to determine this part of our identity.

Consuming and contributing each take a multitude of forms ranging from the mundane and quotidian to the dramatic and extensive. Consumption includes everything from the more administrative like relying on others for financial support or repairs, to the more psychic like demanding the time and energy of those around you for reassurance and encouragement to make it through your days. Contribution can be anything from the simplest gestures like holding doors open and always remembering your pleases and thank yous, to creating things that help others succeed or be fulfilled, or charitable acts of effort or investment.

Whether conscious or not, our decisions to not be kind, considerate or generous nearly always arise out of an inclination to protect ourselves. We often believe kindness to be a display of vulnerability that may make us appear susceptible to attack or exploitation or, oddly enough, embarrassment. The callous, aloof attitude of the classic tough guy persona is a protective measure against any potential betrayal of weaknesses. This is a misinterpretation of the signals kindness emits, of course—it in fact communicates confidence and security to anyone with a reasonably developed understanding of interpersonal interaction. Confusingly enough, even those who are reluctant to show kindness out of the fear of communicating weakness, or those who judge others' kindness as unwisely exposing vulnerability, recognize and appreciate the hero archetype, who's eventually revealed to be extraordinarily compassionate and selfless despite the incongruously hard exterior.

An essential characteristic of being truly tough is the kind of independence that can't be developed any other way, and this independence naturally eliminates much of the consumption the average person does simply out of necessity throughout a lifetime. The more we're capable of providing for ourselves, the less of what others create and provide we need to consume. Moreover, the greater our capabilities, the more we're able to contribute to the world, further weighing our ledger toward the contribution column.

The tough are independent, but not isolationists who refuse to engage in any kind of intervention beyond their own immediate personal interests. We're entirely capable of helping those in need without creating vulnerabilities that may be exploited to cause us harm. Providing assistance to others doesn't inherently create risk for ourselves—in fact, meaningful contribution creates advantages through the establishment of trust, reputation and respect. Even if we were forced to view the world from an entirely self-centered perspective, contribution would be a rational choice.

Bear in mind that none of this demands we necessarily sacrifice ourselves to any specific degree for others at any given opportunity. Possessing the capability to do something in no way means its use is required—it means its use is an option for us to consider. How much of ourselves and our own safety we're willing or eager to risk is a personal decision for each of us, and that decision is likely to be made differently at various points throughout our lives, and certainly will always be dependent on the circumstances in question. All of us are far more likely to be willing and eager to risk our own lives in order to protect our own families and friends, for example, than strangers. But being tough gives us a choice that others don't have. If we believe we have a duty to potentially sacrifice ourselves for the good of people we don't and may never know, we have the ability that allows us to choose that path.

Defense of the defenseless isn't necessarily a physical act with physical risk. It may be as simple as speaking up for someone struggling in a social situation, and it may be as complex and dedicated as participating in activism in support an entire demographic suffering systemic political and social injustice. Each is attended by risk of some nature and degree—if it weren't, we would never hesitate to step in and help. While we may not be sacrificing ourselves physically, we may be exposing ourselves to social or financial consequences. Our choices always need to be rational, but the truly tough have the confidence, security in their identities and belief in their values to make the kinds of choices others fear. In other words, they have the character to stand up for what they believe in spite of the risk.

Like the proverbial pickup truck owner always getting a call when someone is moving, being tough will draw others to us, and some of those with the intent to take advantage of us. We by nature have an inherent tendency to "default to truth" when interacting with others; that is, we have to be presented with overwhelming evidence of deceit before we determine someone can't be trusted even if we have no particular original reason to believe them trustworthy.[3] This makes people intrinsically manipulatable by those who are practiced at subterfuge, and consequently it demands vigilance against exploitation. However, vigilance doesn't mean paranoia or self-imposed quarantine—it simply means some rational consideration prior to committing to anything that may jeopardize us in the short or long term.

Even if respect and consideration for others is our default for good reason, it's by no means unconditional. It's only rational that our interactions with others be dependent on their character, behavior and choices. Continued kindness and generosity to those who have demonstrated ill will, malicious purposes or intent to harm us is senseless and potentially dangerous. Kindness and respect should be reserved for the deserving with the assumption that everyone is until they provide evidence to the contrary.

This doesn't necessarily mean we eliminate empathy or compassion for those to whom we no longer, by virtue of their own choices, extend kindness and generosity. We can simultaneously be empathetic out of the recognition of the basic human condition and how circumstances may affect people's beliefs and behaviors, and be indifferent toward them. In other words, the choice to cease being kind to someone isn't a trigger to hate or disdain them; it's no more than the elimination of the previous kindness.

Critically, this is the most beneficial approach we can take—it eliminates not just vulnerability to someone likely to exploit it, but also all time and energy investment into the person. Hatred is an active condition—because it demands our ongoing energy and time and focus, it allows its object power over us, and consequently does us more harm in many ways than it could ever do its target. Indifference, on the other hand, is the condition of absolute nothingness with regard to the object. There is no feeling, no thought, no action. Interestingly enough, this is often a far worse response than hatred or anger to its target. Very little upsets someone more than the knowledge that they're absolutely meaningless and inconsequential to the individual from whom they're desperate to elicit a response. This approach is simultaneously most protective for ourselves and effective against the other.

If the stance we default to is respect of others, and we clearly believe being tough is a respectable trait, it would make sense for us to respect the tough around us even more enthusiastically. But a final consideration, and one that's subjective to a great extent but equally critical, is the question of what people's toughness is being used for, and what values underpin their character. Do we respect toughness as a standalone quality in anyone who demonstrates it, or are the nature of the traits that compose it and its purpose inextricably linked to its merit and how, in consequence, we view it? In other words, does simply "being tough" warrant respect, or does it matter how that toughness is being applied? This question is answered in all cases by character—the character of the individual in question, and how it relates to our own. Consider an admittedly trite but necessarily extreme example to make this simple: Do you respect a Nazi SS officer's toughness? Or does the fact that his capability, capacity and commitment is applied to despicable behavior and beliefs because of his perverted values instantly render it meritless? In this instance, hopefully the verdict is straightforward and immediate, but in others, it may be more equivocal—in all cases, the question needs to be asked and answered.

Our personal choices and the manner in which we live have far-reaching effects on the world around us even in the absence of intentional attempts to influence others. The Flynn effect, named for social scientist Jim Flynn, describes the way in which individuals' improvements in their own abilities naturally drive collective improvements in the same abilities of the surrounding community. We can see this phenomenon in any number of circumstances, from global IQ increases (Flynn's original focus), to a specific team of athletes whose individual performance improvements drive increasing performance of his or her teammates through competitiveness, inspiration, methodological learning, encouragement and behavior modeling.

If our behavior and attitude influence the same of those we encounter throughout our lives, unless we're completely isolated from all of humanity indefinitely, we have to accept a degree of accountability for the state of the world. Being tough means not only recognizing and accepting this responsibility, but choosing to use it for valuable and positive effect.

MORNING JOURNAL

Despite the unfortunate impression many have that dissuades them from participating, journaling isn't the exclusive realm of aggrieved thirteen-year-olds chronicling the plight of unrequited love. We know that the practice dates back to at least almost 2,000 years ago because of the personal diaries of Roman emperor Marcus Aurelius that were later published and now known as *Meditations*. If an emperor and one of the minds that created the foundation of Stoic philosophy could manage to keep a journal without embarrassment and while running an empire through war and plague, it's fair to insist that you can get over any squeamishness about the practice and figure out how to fit it into your own schedule. It should also suggest that the practice has legitimate power, although we have abundant modern research and experience to provide evidence of that.

The morning is the ideal time for this journaling practice for a few reasons. First, and most practically, it's easier to ensure it remains in your schedule if it's first on the list. Days get away from us frequently, and if we plan to journal toward the end of the day, there's a far greater chance we'll reach the intended time and still be busy with necessary tasks, or dissuaded by the fatigue we've accumulated. By making the journal a first-thing routine, we're setting ourselves up for consistency.

Second, it's a chance for us to reset and enter the day with a freshly cleaned-up attitude and perspective. It's easier after a night of sleep having put some distance between us and the difficulties and stress of the previous day to have complete control over our outlook on life. The morning is a new start and naturally offers a sense of potential and inspiration. That additional time also gives us the ability to reflect on the previous day more objectively rather than still under the cloud of emotion that tends to hang over experiences and take some time to dissipate. This allows the second section of the journal to be done more effectively.

Finally, while we're unquestionably stretching the edges of the window, we're taking advantage of the natural pliability of the brain during altered states of consciousness. Right before falling asleep and right after waking, our minds are most open to suggestion—that is, far more willing to believe ideas that we may immediately shut down as being unreasonable or impossible at other times of the day. This is why these times are used by athletes for their visualization routines—their minds are less likely to reject the possibility of winning an Olympic gold medal at this time and more likely to allow the thought to become genuine belief.

By making this journaling a routine we accomplish first thing in the morning, we begin to expect it, and our minds will naturally reach forward in planning our responses to the prompts. This pre-emptive consideration of what we intend to write will be occurring nearer the initial waking phase than the actual writing, letting us take advantage of that unique opportunity and mitigate the limiting effects of extending that window.

Meditation of specific formats is also effective for accomplishing the goals of the morning journal, and we'll get into that recommendation later, but writing itself—by hand, with a pen or pencil, on paper—offers unique advantages over simply thinking or even meditating. We can create a compounding effect with the normal benefits of meditation through journaling because of the singular neural responses writing elicits in the brain that can't be replicated any other way.

Expressive writing—writing about our own thoughts and feelings like we will in our journal—has been shown to reduce stress, improve mood and wellbeing, lower blood pressure, and improve lung and liver function.[4,5] The physical act of writing longhand itself is the source of much of the benefit of journaling—typing fails to stimulate the same neural response. Writing by hand has been shown to improve not only the retention of what we're writing, but memory generally, the ability to think through complex ideas, and the mastery of language (which then allows better articulation of our thoughts in our journals and consequently more effective journaling).[6]

Of course, writing by hand slows the process somewhat relative to typing (for most of us), and that allows more consideration of what we're writing and more time to absorb it. This means that we're able to express what we're thinking more clearly, better understand our experiences and our reactions to them, and more effectively cement these thoughts in our minds. When we get to the third section of our morning journal in particular—manifesting—we're creating a synergistic response by combining the mental practice itself, a time in which we're more receptive, and the neural benefits of handwriting. In other words, we're optimizing the process to exploit the advantages maximally.

THE PROCESS

The key for the morning journal is maximizing effectiveness while minimizing time investment and simplifying the process. No practice is effective if it's never done or done insincerely, and minimally effective if only done inconsistently. This means stripping down a potentially bloated process of every superfluous bit possible and not only retaining but increasing the focus on the truly essential. In this way, we can create a practice that's less daunting and more easily integrated into our daily schedules, and consequently more likely to be done consistently and with genuine investment, and yet loses none of its potential effectiveness.

None of the following is truly original. The idea of journaling is ancient, the unique window for mental work of the morning is well-known, and the prompts are commonly used in some fashion or another—and are pretty obvious with a little consideration. All I've done is pare down the process to what I've found to be the most important ideas to focus on daily—what we *need* for this to be effective, and nothing more.

This process done precisely as written is going to be effective if you take it seriously, but you can also use it simply as a framework to expand from and create your own process. In other words, you can respond to the prompts exclusively, or you can use them as launching points for more in-depth consideration and writing. In any case, I suggest allowing yourself to go as far-afield as your mind carries you each day as you write—as long as you answer the prompts directly first. Be sure to do the basics, but once you have, don't restrict yourself if there's more on your mind. You may discover a new prompt that you want to include in your daily routine in the process.

In order for this to work as well as it can, you need to do it right. First, of course, you need to take it seriously. You need to put genuine thought into what you're writing. The results, like for anything else, will be commensurate to your effort—if you do it half-heartedly, you're going to get minimal benefit. If you're going to spend the time to do it at all, do it well—it takes just as much time to do it poorly as effectively, so don't waste your time.

Second, create a situation that allows you to relax and focus. Don't just jot down some notes while you're creeping through commute traffic. Get outside first thing in the morning and take a short walk if you can—walking has been demonstrated to increase creative thinking dramatically relative to sitting, and the boost it creates continues for a time after walking.[7] Get your coffee and bring it with you if you want, but otherwise do nothing else—most importantly, stay off your phone and computer. Stay away from any obligations such as work to avoid any stress or distraction that will disrupt the already fragile state of mind we need to preserve to make the activity as effective as possible. Before you go back inside or do anything else—especially check your phone or computer or in any way begin the rest of your day—find a quiet place to sit alone and do your journaling.

You don't need to commit a lot of time to this—10-20 minutes should be plenty. If you can't get even ten minutes to yourself to have a few clear thoughts every morning, you need to take a serious look at your lifestyle and make some changes. You don't need anything fancier than a cheap spiral bound notebook and a pen. If you prefer something a bit more formal, you can get your hands on a journal with pre-printed prompts at https://becomingtough.com/morningjournal.

THE PROMPTS

Following are the prompts I suggest using. For each I've included an explanation of what's intended and how to best use them, as well as brief examples whose length is not necessarily representative of what's ideal. Write as much as you feel you need for each prompt—the amount will vary day to day. As long as you respond deliberately and thoughtfully to each prompt, the length is incidental. And remember, after you address these prompts, if you have more to say, by all means continue beyond them.

I am grateful for:

Write 3-5 things you're grateful for. Do your best to come up with something new every day, but of course over time, you're going to repeat many things. However, don't get lazy here. The purpose of this prompt is to really make you take a look at your life to recognize and appreciate things you may neglect or take for granted that in fact are important elements of your happiness. Don't be afraid of pointing out tiny, specific details—these things matter too, and in fact may surprise you with their importance.

The primary purpose of this exercise is learning to find and recognize these things when they're not immediately apparent, and in the process, realizing how much you have to be grateful for even in times of frustration, discouragement or even depression. Research has demonstrated that the act of expressing gratitude actually affects our neurochemistry[8]—by beginning the exercise with gratitude, we're creating a more fertile mindset for the remaining work.

In addition to simply enumerating what you're grateful for, try briefly explaining *why*. What does this thing you're grateful for provide you? Why is it so valuable that it's worth writing down? How would its absence affect you? It's one thing to appreciate something—it's an entirely new level to understand why. Gaining that understanding is integral to your developing mindset.

Example: I'm grateful for my health because it allows me to continue pursuing my athletic goals and maintain my independence. I'm grateful for my wife and daughter because they provide meaning to my life I couldn't find anywhere else. I'm grateful for my audience, whose support allows me to earn a living doing what I love.

What did I do well yesterday? Did I live up to my standards? Where did I fall short?

This is a chance to reflect on yesterday and compare your intentions with your execution. You know who you wanted to be, what you wanted to accomplish, and how you wanted to do it all—did it happened the way you intended? What did you do well? What turned out exactly as you planned? Where did you fall short of your vision? What pushed you off track?

This is meant to be an inventory to allow you to stay on track and evaluate your daily practices and habits and continue improving your focus and mindset. It is *not* intended to be fodder for self-flagellation. Take an objective look rather than making a judgment of your self-worth, and use that evaluation to make adjustments and corrections today. If you had a rough day, don't allow yourself to be consumed by the negative. No matter how many mistakes you made, or how far out of line with your intentions you found yourself, with some consideration, you can find a few things that went well and that you can be proud of. In the next prompt, you can make reference to any shortcomings you listed here and what you intend to do differently to avoid the same problems.

Example: I completed a lot of the work I needed to by doing a good job ignoring distractions and not procrastinating, and am satisfied with the quality of the content I created, despite limited time. I maintained a good attitude and remained relaxed and composed even when exhausted and dealing with complications during 15 hours of cross-country travel. I did well not allowing that exhaustion to influence the way I spoke to my wife once I was home. I could have done a better job of organizing the rest of my day to spend more time with her after getting through my work. I need to work on organizing and prioritizing outstanding tasks to keep myself on track each day and improve my efficiency.

Who am I? What will today look like?

This is your chance to decide who you are and what your life is like today. This isn't a series of wishes or a vague sense of hope—these are *specific* things you ARE and DO. In other words, write this section as if it's a foregone conclusion—*it is presently a fact* that this is who you are and what you do. The grammatical structure is very important. It's not simply stylistic, but a tool of precision and effect.

Remember that we're rewiring our brains to function in a way that makes these things true, and, believe it or not, creates changes in our genes to improve our physical health and the tendency of our natural state of being to support these traits and abilities.

Include not just actions you intend to complete, but describe your mindset, your attitude, your energy, your outlook, your character… everything that defines the person you want to be. This is no different from the kind of visualization an athlete conducts to improve performance—the more detail and the more of the senses are incorporated, the more successful it will be. Authenticity produces belief, and that belief is what drives effectiveness.

Example: I'm energetic and enthusiastic. I'm confident in my abilities and secure in my identity so I'm not intimidated or overwhelmed by unfamiliar experiences, but invigorated by the chance to solve problems, learn and overcome. I don't change who I am to impress others or ingratiate myself to them. I work hard but efficiently by ignoring distractions and focusing strictly on my task to create the best result possible. I'm always looking for ways to im-

prove what I do and am never wed to a specific process in a way that prevents needed change. I'm a successful coach who's invested in his athletes' success for their sake, not my own, and who works hard to always find the best ways of helping them reach their potential. I'm a loving and thoughtful husband and father who goes out of his way not just to take care of my family, but to always show them their importance to me no matter how busy I am. I have complete control over my reactions to any situation and never allow myself to respond emotionally or in an unconsidered manner.

REVIEW

Periodically add a review of past entries to your morning journal routine. Pick a couple days in the past and read through what you wrote, paying attention not just to what's different about what you were focused on at that time relative to the present, but how you described yourself and your goals—how has your outlook and attitude changed over time, and how has your ability to confidently and clearly describe yourself and what you want improved?

Include these observations in that day's entry—what are you proud of having changed and improved, and what still needs work and needs to remain a focus every day? What has worked for you, and what hasn't? How are you going to change what isn't working? What is consistent over time in terms of your values? In other words, what does your writing make clear is most important for you in terms of who you are, what you do, and what you appreciate in your life? What have you moved on from after learning it wasn't as important as you may have once believed?

Use this as part of the broader process to continually refine the daily routine and reap as much benefit as possible from the practice. And always remember, the more you invest in it, the more it will deliver in return.

FOCAL POINTS

- Character is the total set of distinctive mental, emotional, and psychological traits that defines each of us—what we believe, how we view the world around us and our place within it, our attitude, our values, and the way we behave and interact with others as a result of these things.

- Character isn't a wholly predetermined trait—we decide who we are, and we continue deciding and reinforcing our decision daily with our thinking, speaking and behavior.

- We choose whether or not to use our experiences to build and shape our character, or to act like victims of fate.

- We don't have power over everything in our lives, but we always have complete power over how we react to any experience.

- A decision about who we are is meaningless without our thoughts, words and behavior supporting it.

- Security in our identity is what allows us to be who we are regardless of the circumstances and surrounding influences, and to resist undesirable change.

- Our values dictate who we are by reminding us what's meaningful to us; the more clearly we define our values, the more easily we can make decisions that align with our identity.

- Unconditional self-love isn't unconditional self-acceptance; it means we care enough about ourselves to refuse to accept what doesn't make us content, and we fight to change it.

- Confidence is the result of objective assessment of our abilities; it precludes arrogance or hubris, and instills modesty and humility.

- We can choose to be contributors or consumers, and whether or not to use our unavoidable influence over those around us admirably.

- Emotion is necessary and valuable, but needs to be balanced by our rational minds to prevent it from overwhelming us and influencing our thinking and behavior negatively.

ACTION

MORNING JOURNAL

Your first assignment is to begin your morning journal routine—tomorrow. Don't make any excuse for postponing it. You may not have a notebook on hand, but I refuse to believe you don't have access to a single piece of scratch paper and a pen or pencil somehow. Tear open a cereal box and write on the inside with the handle of a fork dipped in ketchup if you have to. It's a mistake to convince yourself you need perfect conditions to begin, and the perfect strategy to avoid ever beginning at all. You can buy a notebook in the next day or two; you can start writing immediately.

Spend a few minutes now thinking about your mornings. What, if anything, do you need to change to allow for a morning journal routine? Set your alarm ten minutes earlier, explain to your significant other that you need a few minutes of solitude in the morning, get your coffee cup ready and your brewer loaded to get you out and onto your task more quickly... It shouldn't require anything dramatic. Figure it out now and eliminate the chance for problems or excuses tomorrow.

EVALUATION JOURNAL

Get ahold of a second notebook—this will be what you use for all of the self-evaluation, planning and tracking exercises and routines that follow here and in subsequent chapters. Again, all you need is a cheap spiral bound notebook and a pen. If you prefer, you can get a journal with printed prompts at https://becomingtough.com/evaluationjournal.

IDENTITY EXERCISE

Start ruminating on this right away, either as you continue reading the book, or go about the rest of your life, and then dedicate time to sit and write about it in the next week or so. This will give you some time to prepare by sorting through your thoughts, filtering out the emotion likely associated with many of them, and allowing the ideas in this book to percolate a bit more to help you make the exercise more effective. The goal of this exercise is for you to truly determine—not discover—who you are.

Step 1: Start freeform and just let yourself spit out any responses that quickly come to mind without overthinking them to the question *Who are you?* Don't worry about any particular length or depth—just see what you get.

Step 2: From this starting point, you're going to expand. *I'm a 40-year-old man who coaches weightlifting and writes books*—this is the kind of initial answer we tend to give in response to the question *Who are you?* Of course, this tells us virtually nothing, and certainly nothing meaningful. What sport do I coach and what type of athletes do I work with? What kind of coach am I? Harsh and unforgiving, or supportive and kind? Involved and caring, or arrogant and aloof? How and why did I become a coach, and what do I get out of it? What kind of books do I write, who do I write them for, and why do I write them? Am I a crusty, decrepit, bitter 40-year-old, or am I youthful, athletic and still attacking life with new ambitions? Even directly from that simple, superficial description, we can extract enormous amounts of information with some digging.

Our initial descriptions of ourselves tend to be like a photograph of a house from the curb. You get a basic sense of it, and you can make some assumptions that may be accurate in some cases, but that doesn't tell you much. What does the backyard look like? How are the rooms laid out? How is it furnished? What about its construction? Is it a solid concrete foundation with wide footers safely below the frost line, or is it a poorly assembled and shallow rubble stone foundation that's sinking and crumbling? Is the sill rotting from unseen water damage? Are the walls plumb and stable? Is the wiring done properly, or is it on the verge of causing a fire? Do the residents neglect it, or is it well taken care of? More importantly, what happens inside that home? Who lives there, how do they interact, what do they care about, what inspires and motivates them?

Expand your description by answering questions like the following:

- *What inspires you and motivates you?*
- *What are you afraid of? What makes you anxious?*
- *What are your ambitions, small and great?*
- *How do you interact with the people around you, from intimate relationships to total strangers?*
- *Do you tend to be more emotional, or more rational? Are you easily excitable, or typically composed and self-possessed?*
- *What makes you feel happy and content? What frustrates and aggravates you? How do you express these things when feeling them?*

Step 3: Now decide who you *want* to be. Repeat Step 2, but this time describe yourself exactly as you want to be able to. Don't wish or hope or plan—literally describe the ideal you as if it's your present condition. *I am*, not *I want to be* or *I wish I were.* This is like the million-dollar check you're writing to yourself to some day be able to cash—it's the landmark in the distance you're going to use to navigate.

Step 4: Compare Steps 2 and 3 objectively. Where do they align already, and where you do fall short of your intentions or goals? Again, be objective—this isn't an exercise in self-contempt or discovering how disappointing you are. Simply note the disparities like you're calculating the difference between a pair of numbers.

Next, take the time to consider the source of these disparities—how and why do you not yet fit these descriptions? What exactly needs to change to make them accurate?

Don't let yourself get overwhelmed by the enormity of the differences that may exist at this point. Consider these disparities as potential awaiting fulfillment, not failure. If you have to walk 100 miles, you can sit and think about how overwhelming and impossible it is and remain not a single inch closer despite all of the time and energy you're investing, or you can pick up a foot and start walking—and be measurably closer to the goal with every step.

This is a critical point to understand. You may be very close already to where you want to be, but more likely, you're realizing how far off the mark you are at present. This is a process, not an instantaneous transformation— evolution, not revolution. Accept that and recognize that every step toward your landmark, no matter how small, is progress. Moreover, each step you take forward is building momentum that will propel you increasingly powerfully toward your goals. Don't wait, don't overthink, don't search for excuses, and don't allow yourself to be intimidated—without hesitation, put your head down and plow ahead.

VALUES EXERCISE

To some extent, you've started discovering your values—both current and ideal—in the previous exercise, although they're likely not articulated clearly. Now you're going to stop and think about the underlying principles that drive your decisions and your character, and whether or not they represent the identity you want to embrace. Determining and refining your values is going to be a lifelong process influenced by your experiences, just as your character as a whole evolves in response to what you experience and what you learn from it—about the world and yourself. For now, though, we need at least a reasonably firm foundation to push off of.

Take a look at who you described in Step 3 of the Identity Exercise. What values would drive that character? What priorities would be served by the decisions, beliefs, thoughts, words and actions of that person? In other words, *why* would that person choose, do, say, think and believe what they do?

There's no official format for a value. It might be a single word or a phrase, or even a grammatically complete sentence (but don't get carried away—pare it down as much as possible to get to the essence of what you're trying to say). It's whatever satisfactorily explains what you mean to *you*—no one else has to get it. This isn't a school paper, and you don't have to make anyone else understand—they'll understand what your values are as much as they need to based on the behavior you demonstrate.

Remember that values are more conditions or ideas than objects or definite things we can possess or accomplish. They're the guides for the decisions we make in life, not the objective goals we make along the way in service of those values. "Making money" or "being rich" isn't a value—that's a goal (although an unrefined one) that ostensibly matches one or more of our actual values (or it wouldn't come to mind as a goal), which could be something as misguided and destined to make us miserable as "being popular and admired" to something meaningful and worthwhile such as putting ourselves in a better position for "helping people in need."

Some examples of values might include:

- *Independence and self-reliance*
- *Health and athletic ability*
- *Creativity*
- *Productivity*
- *Broad and increasing capabilities*

Next, try to order these values based on priority. This is more an interesting exercise to get a glimpse into your own mind rather than a critical sequencing that's going to dictate your choices rigidly. There will very likely be competition for certain spots in line, and there's nothing wrong with that. I might say my health and athletic ability is a priority over broad capabilities, but there isn't much point in being healthy and athletic if you don't have anything to use it for, so in a sense, most of your values are going to be interdependent and not as easily ordered as a series of integers. It's also important you're honest here—remember that no one else is reading this, so don't write what you believe you're supposed to. For example, if you truly value creativity and productivity over family, don't reverse the order because you feel guilty. Whether or not that's something you want to change in the future is a completely different issue, and one you won't be able to successfully address if you're not sincere at this stage.

The purpose here is, like the previous exercise, to first dig in and under-stand what matters most to you and who you want to be, and second, to use these as marks on a map to guide your progress. They're not intended to be carved in stone today or at any other point, but to be as firm as is appropriate at any given time. Your values may change with time and experience, and your priorities with regard to existing values is likely to change over time.

As you move forward with this process, this list of values is going to serve as a guide to keep you in line. You can check in and ensure your deci-sions are aligning with them and your purported identity, and if not, re-eval-uate those decisions… and, equally importantly, re-evaluate those values and their priority.

EMOTIONAL AWARENESS & CONTROL

In order to develop control over our emotions, we have to first be aware of them. Make the effort every day to check yourself before responding to any situation and evaluate what you're feeling and how it's going to influence what you say and do—count to ten if you want. Recognize the underlying emotion and try to figure out what's causing it—are you upset because you're afraid? Of what? Are you upset because you feel foolish? Should you? Is the emotion even directly related to the present situation, or is it spilling over from something else you need to resolve? You don't need to have completed a comprehensive psychoanalysis of yourself by the time you finish counting to ten, but at the very least you'll be able to get enough distance from the precipitating event to allow your rational mind to intervene and better guide your response.

When finding yourself reacting emotionally, pause and ask yourself, "Is this who I want to be? How would who I strive to be react to this?" Change your behavior and words to represent your desired identity.

Keep track of these events and reactions, what you did to control them, and how well it worked in your morning journal. This will give you a way to evaluate your progress as well as discover what seems to be most effective for you.

CHECK-INS

Finally, make a plan for periodic check-ins on your progress. Part of this is handled with the morning journal reviews, but make it a habit to set aside some time monthly or so and evaluate the changes you've made and their effects. How does your behavior align with your identity? Is that identity what you've determined it to be, is it still unestablished, or is it being influenced by external forces? Which practices have you implemented and found to be helpful, and which haven't delivered the results you expected? How do you feel consistently relative to your last check-in? Are you more confident, more composed, more independent, more content? How has your perspective on life and the world around you changed?

Dedicate some time to considering these things and writing down the results in your evaluation journal. This is essentially marking your position on the map to ensure you're still moving toward that landmark and to encourage you by showing you, even if it feels like you're trudging interminably and hardly moving, that you are in fact forging ahead and closing the gap. For now, get prepared for your first check-in by deciding where and how you'll do it and ensuring you have the necessary materials, and schedule a day a month from now in your calendar to remind you.

CHAPTER 3
CAPABILITY

What are you able to do? This question should take us a long time to answer—arguably a lifetime. It should be a list that's not only extensive, but growing indefinitely. Being tough isn't the result of simply possessing a specific skill set like the physical ability to climb a mountain, survive a disaster, or defend ourselves against an attacker. Aside from toughness involving far more than physical capability, our abilities need to be much broader than what most of us initially think of when considering what it means to be tough.

Capability is a tool box—the more tools we have at our disposal, the more skilled we are in using each of them, and the more variety of the work for which we've employed them in the past, the greater our preparation to handle whatever we encounter, no matter how little it resembles our previous experiences. Tools, literal and metaphorical, all have specific intended uses for which they're built—but the combination of necessity and our own ingenuity can expand the potential use of any tool far beyond its original purpose. It's not always pretty—like pounding a nail in with the side of a crescent wrench—but it's always better to get the job done than give up because we're convinced we don't have the right tools to make it possible.

Every time we make it through the kind of experience that demands improvisation and commitment in the face of imperfect conditions and tools, we not only learn how that job could have been done better and the tools we'd prefer to have in hand to allow better preparation in the future, but we also learn more about the potential and limitations of the tools we already have, and build greater confidence in our ability to succeed through our own initiative and chip away at our tendency to be intimidated by new challenges.

Ideally much of the experience we accumulate and the abilities we develop will be driven by curiosity and its attendant enthusiasm—but we need to recognize that at least some of it will need to be accrued as a result of a practical choice to get it done out of necessity or our own benefit despite no particular interest in it. We can't artificially manufacture interest any more than we can choose what we desire in other ways—it is what it is.

Some of us are fortunate enough to have natural interest in what we need to do, but many of us will instead have to simply choose to do certain things for the sake of the role they play in achieving a greater goal or encompassing interest. For example, some people are fascinated by the process of land navigation—so much so that the sport of orienteering exists as competition to test that ability. But others are drawn to mountaineering because of its various challenges and rewards, and while having no specific interest in the use of map and compass to navigate, develop that ability to an expert level because it allows them to do what it is they actually want—climb mountains. We don't have to care passionately about every single thing we do and learn—all we have to care about is the overall process and the objectives these things eventually allow us to meet.

Having said that, it's not unusual over time for us to develop a passion for the process of learning and expanding our abilities itself, often making the specifics of what we're learning less of the focus than the learning itself. We also tend to find through the process interests and passions that would have never occurred to us to investigate otherwise—or that we hadn't previously even known existed. The tough transform this kind of discovery from accidental to intentional. A willingness to reach out beyond our current experiences and abilities is itself a critical tool for developing toughness.

The more we're able to do, the better equipped we are to solve any problem that presents itself, and the more prepared we are for any possible contingency, from the common and unremarkable to the rarest and most extreme emergencies. Our fundamental goal with regard to capability is to continuously collect *more*.

COMPOUNDING & SYNERGY

If the idea of trying to accumulate such a breadth and depth of capability is overwhelming, consider the compounding nature of learning and knowledge. It's not simply an accounting tape running through and printing a vertical column of isolated chunks of information. Knowledge is a three-dimensional structure, almost living, like the growing and interwoven roots and the ever-lengthening and thickening trunk and branches of a tree. These roots and branches interconnect and tangle with each other, they fuse together and create thicker, stronger pieces, and they stretch to pick up sunlight and reach deeper to absorb nutrients.

Knowledge compounds on itself—new knowledge not only associates with old and brings new perspective, but reshapes it and breathes new life into it, builds on the foundation of present understanding to reach higher and further than it could in isolation, and creates new applications for existing knowledge. Learning accelerates and expands, almost exponentially—every continued investment produces increasingly greater returns, and often in completely unexpected forms.

Developing new abilities doesn't simply add that new ability to the list—it actually improves our ability to develop new abilities. We not only add the specific skill or knowledge set to our aggregate capability, but we simultaneously amplify the power of the continuing process through the accumulation of new tools, improving confidence to take on new experiences that offer learning opportunities, a broader and deeper foundation of knowledge to support and make sense of new information, increasing motivation driven by previous success and gratification, and new perspectives on the world around us and the naturally following insights.

The more experience we accumulate, the less often we start something new from step zero—we're more likely to already have much of the fundamental understanding or skillsets underpinning the new pursuit, which not only accelerates the process, but propels us more reliably to a further ultimate ability. Almost as importantly, that experience means greater confidence in our ability to be successful with a new pursuit, and less intimidation by the process.

Using mathematics as a simple example, each discipline builds on previous knowledge and experience to a great extent. We learn what numbers are, then we learn simple manipulations like addition and subtraction, then division and multiplication, then more complex systems like algebraic equations, and the process continues with each new step relying on the knowledge of the previous. When we get to trigonometry, we don't start from nothing and have to learn what numbers are first. When we want to learn calculus, we don't have to start by learning what a variable is and trying to grasp the concept of that representation before we can proceed.

Learning to stand gives us a foundation to walk, which gives us a foundation to run, which gives us a foundation to jump, and eventually we can progress to remarkable feats like a gymnastics floor routine that would be entirely inconceivable to someone unable to even do a push-up, but is an everyday activity for an advanced gymnast who's invested the time and effort into the process.

Critically, these kinds of foundations don't apply strictly to a single discipline in most cases. The very nature of foundations is that they're broad and general, meaning myriad structures can be successfully built on them. Our foundation of mathematics will also support learning physics or chemistry, for example—distinct pursuits, but ones we can begin further along in the total process because of our existing knowledge. Our foundation of even the most rudimentary gymnastics movements—pull-ups, push-ups, bounding, leg raises—will allow us to more quickly and successfully pursue baseball or rock climbing. By laying foundations like a sprawling city grid that over time converges into a single extensive and continuously expanding base, we create opportunities to build any structure more quickly and easily, and reach higher into the skyline with more stability. That extensiveness and stability also means we can remodel existing structures with ease and reliability as new experiences and insights dictate.

Likewise, physical abilities are largely interrelated or predicated on others. The anatomical (increased bone density, aggregated muscular protein structures, strengthened tendons and ligaments, greater nerve myelination, increased capillary density), physiological (improved gas exchange in the lungs, more effective blood transport by the circulatory system, more rapid and thorough lactic acid buffering), and neurological (greater motor unit recruitment, increased rate coding and synchronization, GTO inhibition, and intermuscular coordination) adaptations from training allow our body to handle more physical stress and perform more varied and advanced functions.

The abilities developed from one activity or form of training can be applied to others—the bone density and connective tissue durability developed through the repeated stress of landing and taking off in gymnastics allows the structures to handle the extreme forces of weightlifting, for example, allowing former gymnasts to very quickly advance in the sport of weightlifting without needing to spend years developing such basic qualities for the sake of orthopedic health. Like learning, physical training ranges from the general and basic to the specific and advanced—and the latter must be built on the foundation of the former.

Even the process of learning itself—the effective absorption and long-term retention of information for subsequent application and association—is improved through practice like any other skill. The more we learn, the more we're able to learn, and with diminishing time and effort as our efficacy increases through our brain's physical changes along with our improving skill and understanding of universally more effective methods and systems, and more importantly, those that work best for us personally.

Our accumulating abilities also create potential for synergy—the combining of multiple elements to create a greater effect together than they would add up to acting individually. The natural and often sudden convergence of seemingly unrelated abilities and experiences when opportunities arise can surprise us with its potency. While the compounding of abilities is obvious and expected, the synergistic effects are largely unpredictable.

Twenty years ago, I taught myself website programming and graphic design because I couldn't afford to hire professionals for the new business was I trying to get off the ground from my apartment kitchen at age twenty. I'd been a writer and editor and continued to be one in various formats throughout this time. I spent my life (short as it had been at the time) in sports and training and worked as a trainer and co-owned a gym, was a competitive weightlifter, and was mentored by an accomplished weightlifting coach. Fifteen years ago, when I started the business I run now, I was able to put together an extraordinarily functional website and create quality instructional content for what quickly became the most prominent source of Olympic weightlifting information available, and to write, edit, photograph, design and publish a book that became and has remained the best selling on the sport of weightlifting in the world—all without paying a single individual, which I had no money to do.

Had I not possessed the seemingly unrelated skills I did at that time—and the confidence and willingness to try—I would have never been able to establish the business that continues to support not just me, but also my wife and daughter, and to provide me with ongoing opportunities. How exactly our abilities will interact and what combination we'll need is unpredictable, but we can know with certainty that the more we possess, the greater the probability of our being in a position to succeed when the opportunity—or demand—suddenly arises.

INDEPENDENCE & SELF-RELIANCE

Independence and self-reliance are possible only through capability—we can't achieve independence through any other component of toughness without it. No amount or type of character, capacity or commitment—no matter how strong our mindset, how much we can endure, or what we're willing to do—will magically and instantaneously allow us to be able to do what needs to be done. We depend on others to do for us what we can't do for ourselves, which means the more we can do for ourselves, the less we're forced to depend on others. This is truly the definition of freedom—being free of dependence on anyone else and able to do whatever it is we choose to do without any limitations imposed by others through their willingness (or lack thereof) to assist us or provide us the opportunities.

Children begin entirely dependent on their parents to meet their needs, from the absolute basics like water, food and shelter, to non-survival services like providing transportation, access to school and medical care, to social and developmental elements like how to speak and how to interact with other people. As children grow up, they become increasingly capable (we hope) of achieving these things on their own—they know how to feed themselves (even if it's using a microwave), they're able to drive their own cars to school or the dentist (however dangerously), they get jobs and earn some of their own money to allow them a little financial independence (or to buy alcohol), and they're adequately socialized to be able to interact effectively with the people around them (or at least not get beaten up daily). Eventually, they become functioning adults no longer reliant on their parents to meet any of their needs, save possibly for some emotional support.

But even as typical independent, functioning adults, we're still largely dependent on other people—that dependence is just transferred from our parents and diffused among a wider array of people, making it less obvious and invariably far greater than we imagine or want to believe. As adults, our reliance on those around us is generally so routine and such a normal, shared experience with those we know that it goes unnoticed—until that system breaks down and we abruptly find ourselves helpless in one way or another.

If we're fortunate, this breakdown is of a type with relatively few and minor consequences, which gives us an opportunity to recognize our precarious position and make changes to improve our condition in preparation for the next breakdown, which may not be so forgiving, without incurring much if any lasting damage. But in other cases, the first breakdown we experience may be extreme and bring with it severe consequences that have the power to forever reshape our lives—or end them. In such cases, we don't have the luxury of a warning and the subsequent chance to reconsider our approach to life to ensure better preparation in the future.

Conveniently, our minds are powerful enough to imagine scenarios and consequences we've never experienced—essentially, to run thought experiments and create models for our mindset and behavior based on our conclusions. Instead of like Einstein starting to figure out the theory of special relativity by imagining himself chasing a beam of light through space, we can imagine the consequences of various contingencies with our present capabilities. To give utility to the experiment rather than it simply being an exercise in terrifying ourselves with innumerable horrific possibilities, we can then consider how those consequences would change with different capabilities, and as a result, determine the various abilities we should be working to develop.

Through this approach, and simply an awareness of the situation (which you should now have), the natural and imposed process we experience as children of developing increasing self-reliance can be replicated intentionally by us as adults at a more advanced level. Just as we were able to gain independence from our parents over time, we can eventually diminish our reliance on the various people who replaced them.

Of course, how self-sufficient we can truly be is limited by a number of factors, and how far we want to take it is a personal choice. Being tough doesn't require we be so self-sufficient that we live in complete isolation on a self-sustaining homestead three days' journey through the mountains from the nearest hint of civilization. We can find a practical balance that suits our own requirements, and we can prioritize many of those requirements as we each see fit.

The purpose of independence and self-reliance is to be *capable* of handling as much on our own as possible without *needing* others to help us—it doesn't mean never asking for or accepting help, and it certainly doesn't mean being required to endure a hardscrabble life of solitude with no interpersonal relationships. Not being dependent on others for practical needs doesn't mean those others can't exist in our life—our capability in no way determines the nature or extent of our social interactions. Isolation is a choice independence allows us to make—it's an option, not an inherent feature. Each of us determines how our growing independence influences our lifestyle in accordance with our values—this is exactly the freedom independence affords us.

CONFIDENCE

Possessing an extensive and growing array of skills and knowledge, well-developed physical qualities across numerous realms, and the ability to take care of ourselves in as broad a range of situations possible—and knowing we do through experience—is the single greatest contributor to confidence imaginable. The confidence that capability provides us extends past the borders of our actual experience to some degree as well.

Through collected experiences of both obvious success and mere survival, in addition to the skills and knowledge we inevitably accrue, we gain increasing trust in our general ability to make it through any conceivable situation because our mindset is shaped by that history. As a result, we naturally enter into unfamiliar circumstances and face new challenges with self-assurance and the attendant commitment to doing what's demanded of us decisively. Uncertainty and vacillation in an emergency, in response to a threat, or simply in any situation in which failure carries with it meaningful risk, is the perfect formula for undesirable consequences.

A lack of confidence is the product of the fear of failure, suffering harm, exposure to others of our inability, or even private embarrassment and disappointment from discovering our own shortcomings. A firm belief in our capability, bolstered with evidence gained through experience, diminishes or eliminates that fear and allows us to confidently lean into the challenges we encounter. The more we're able to do, and the more we've already done, the less intimidating and overwhelming unfamiliar experiences are, and the less fear and anxiety they induce.

The benefit of this kind of confidence doesn't just apply to surviving emergencies or facing danger—consider how many incredible, singular opportunities in life we may miss as a result of fear or anxiety. How many irreplaceable experiences will we never have the chance to enjoy and remember because of our reluctance to face risk, whether real or perceived? How many of those experiences might we right now be looking back at fondly and with appreciation of the lessons they provided had we possessed the courage to simply try?

While capability naturally underpins confidence in a way no other trait can, we have to remain vigilant of its legitimacy. No matter how much experience we accumulate over a lifetime, no matter how capable we become through that experience and our commitment to learning, we're not infallible and we're certainly not invincible. We do have to be willing and able to recognize and acknowledge our limitations, regardless of how minimal they may become with time and work. Early on in the process of pursuing true toughness, and later down the road, we tend to be more naturally aware of our limitations—early on because we're first considering ideas that have never occurred to us and imagining situations that dangerously expose our current lack of capability, and later because our awareness and ability to accurately evaluate ourselves has improved with the aggregation and synthesis of experiences.

But there's a period of time through the middle of the process when we become particularly susceptible to self-delusion or miscalculation with regard to our capability. At this time, we've collected a decent amount of knowledge and skill, but haven't yet accumulated a commensurate number and type of experiences to genuinely test those capabilities. This allows us to more easily overestimate the quality or extent of our capability, potentially leading us to mistakenly place ourselves in situations with demands and risks for which we're not actually sufficiently prepared.

While such experiences may ultimately prove to be uniquely valuable once we make it through to the other side, they may also result in more harm than benefit, and possibly to an extreme degree—permanent injury, loss or death are not out of the question. Consequently, we have to rely on confidence for what it is and avoid inflating it unreasonably and irrationally, and this is accomplished through self-awareness and ongoing objective self-evaluation.

EMPHASIS & FOCUS

As appealing as the idea sounds, we can't possibly know and be capable of everything (although there's certainly no reason not to aim ourselves in that direction and find out how far we can make it). Accordingly, we need to find a sensible way to prioritize so we're emphasizing what we most need before we begin investing significant time and effort into less critical areas that may attract our attention by virtue of our natural interests. We can and should get to these things, both eventually and in the periphery currently, but just like we need to make sure the foundation is sound and the roof is weather-tight before we start worrying too much about picking out the perfect curtains, we need to ensure our priorities are adequately met before we start wandering too far afield.

Our lists will all vary somewhat based on factors like where we live, our profession, and the situations our lifestyle puts us in regularly—there isn't a universal catalog that applies to all of us perfectly, but we can rely on a basic formula to guide our decisions rationally.

We of course need to begin with the most fundamental and general— these things are what create the foundation that stretches out as wide as possible and allows us to more quickly and effectively build up at each point we determine necessary or desirable. This foundation is comprised of elements that may not be obviously related to our day-to-day life, in the same way we don't regularly think about the concrete structure supporting our home properly even though ultimately that's what makes that big screen TV on the wall a possibility. Our health and physical fitness (largely interdependent), basic knowledge and literacy, and familiarity with our normal environment—things we typically take for granted unless and until a deficiency is exposed through an unexpected experience or change—comprise this foundation.

The most immediately foreseeable, or reasonably predictable, demands need to be met as quickly as possible as well. This translates into the elements of our daily life—can we reliably do what we need to do in the typical day to keep ourselves alive, safe and healthy? How well can we do those things, and how much do we actually rely on others to help us with them? How much is our present success based on our ability, and how much is a result of the luck of certain abilities having not yet been tested? If for some reason we had no access to anyone else, would we be capable of producing the same outcomes, or would their absence have consequences we need to avoid? If the latter, what do we need to do in order to remedy that deficiency?

Our health and physical fitness arguably support everything else—if we're ill and deconditioned, we have severe limitations across the board not just in what we can accomplish or endure physically, but in the energy and focus we can apply to intellectual pursuits and problems, and in our psychological and emotional stability both for the sake of maintaining our daily routine and productively handling the abnormal stress of an emergency.

We can imagine for a moment finding ourselves in a survival situation—limited or no food or water, exposure to the elements, and an array of other threats to our life. It should be immediately obvious that the healthier and fitter we are, the greater our ability to endure the physical and mental strain, and the greater our ability to accomplish the tasks necessary to support our survival or escape. The advantage becomes less obvious as we reduce the extremity of possible situations we may encounter, but what we can be assured of is that there isn't a single potential situation in which health and fitness would be a disadvantage while illness and a lack of fitness would benefit us. In other words, whether or not we ever encounter an emergency or any kind of danger, health and fitness provide a critical foundation for our life and need to be a universal focus.

Familiarity with our normal environment, and the ability to successfully operate in it, also needs to take priority. If we live in Manhattan and work in an office, our needs will vary dramatically from living in rural Montana and working as a game warden in isolated wilderness areas. The survival skills in one environment have virtually no relation to those of the other. Being capable of avoiding wild predator attacks, starting a fire when it's wet, and navigating through the mountains are essentially worthless abilities on the streets of Manhattan, while the knowledge of how to escape from the 40th floor of an office building in a fire or the ability to recognize and avoid circumstances that expose us to criminal attack do nothing for us in the Montana wilderness. It makes little sense to invest considerable time and effort into capabilities that apply exclusively to environments we'll never encounter. These non-critical skills and knowledge can be reserved for the work we do on the side and after we've sufficiently mastered what's most imperative. Knowing and being capable of more than we need isn't harmful—except if it's replacing or preventing us from learning what we actually do need.

It's safe to assume a reader of this book is prepared with regard to basic knowledge and literacy—it isn't exactly Shakespearian iambic pentameter, but understanding it does require a decent grasp of the language and reasonable familiarity with an array of topics. A consideration with regard to language, however, is whether or not in our circumstances mastery of our own native language is adequate. It may be necessary to be at least passably capable in another language, either because we live outside our native country, or because the region in which we live is populated with a large number of individuals who speak another language. It's unlikely we need true mastery that allows us to understand and appreciate poetry in another language, but it's not unlikely that an ability to understand conversations and communicate in at least a rudimentary manner is useful—and in emergency scenarios, potentially life-saving.

Once we've determined what our most immediate and critical needs are, we can consider the next layer. This includes abilities that don't necessarily keep us alive and safe, but allow us to function successfully long term, such as capability related to our profession. Such capability may do nothing more than keep us employed—which, to be fair, could be reasonably connected to survival and safety as it allows us to afford the necessities of staying alive—but it may also literally keep us alive if our profession involves serious risk, such as law enforcement, the military, fishing in the North Atlantic, or being a steel worker on bridges or high-rises. This also needs to include abilities related to our lifestyle and the activities we regularly participate in. If the wildest thing we ever do is go see a movie in the theater, this is pretty easy; if our lifestyle includes rock climbing or backcountry skiing, we'll have more work to do.

Once these two foundational layers are reasonably sound—they don't need to be perfected, but at least reliably functional—we need to begin preparing for the kind of severe emergencies we can imagine encountering. When running our thought experiments for such emergencies, we need to prioritize them by probability as determined by our locality, profession and lifestyle. For example, if we live in Los Angeles, it makes a lot of sense to prepare for surviving the aftermath of a major earthquake in an urban environment with mild weather; it doesn't make sense to prepare for dealing with a historic blizzard while isolated in the mountains. Figuring out what the safest place to be during an earthquake is (at home, at work, and the places we frequent), how to shut off the gas supply to our house, how we're going to eat and get water if utilities are unserviceable and stores are wiped out, and how we're going to get in touch with the people we care about or who depend on us, should be priorities in our preparation. Learning how to survive a blizzard can wait until that's checked off the list.

Having said that, basic survival skills that apply to any environment should be learned by all of us. These are the kinds of things that we may never have to use, but it's far better to have and not need than to need and not have. Like health and fitness, none of us is going to lie on our deathbed regretting having knowledge it turned out we didn't need.

Finally, we can begin working on the rest—all the abilities that expand the reach of our capability and appeal to us for any reason while not actually applying to our daily needs or life and death situations. Maybe we've always wanted to learn how to weld, become fluent in another language, master a new sport, or learn how to program computer software. There's no limit to the capabilities we can add to the list, as long as the priorities have been satisfactorily met. This is like going out to play after our homework is done—but in this case, the game is always useful.

RESISTANCE

Most of us are resistant to the new and unfamiliar to varying degrees—we find comfort in the familiar and reassurance in what we know we're already capable of. Sequestering ourselves in our own realms provides an exaggerated sense of ability and confidence—if we're never exposed to what we're not already able to do well, it's easy for us to forget or underestimate how much of it exists. From such a position, our competence in a narrow set of skills and knowledge can be mistakenly extrapolated outside that sliver. Not only does this error in judgment limit our experiences, it sets us up for failure—potentially catastrophic—if and when we do find ourselves in a critical situation well outside our area of competence.

Being most comfortable and confident in our own particular space isn't inherently problematic—no matter the breadth of experience and ability we eventually accumulate, it's impossible to not excel in one respect over others, even if for no other reason than it having been introduced early, and it's natural to find more comfort and enjoyment there. We simply have to remain aware of our status at all times and avoid making the potential mistakes attendant to this comfort.

More insidious, and more difficult to combat, is resistance to new experiences arising from fear. The fear that prevents our venturing outside our comfort zone can assume many forms—from the fear of physical harm and death, to the fear of humiliation and exposure of our incompetence to others. Some experiences offer the entire spectrum—we may avoid skydiving both because of the fear of falling to our deaths, and the fear of appearing terrified and weak in front of the people with us as a dark spot materializes on the front of our pants while standing at the plane's open door. If we simply avoid the experience, we can avoid the potential consequences—we can often even convince others, or simply let them assume, that we have no particular concerns at all.

Many of us manage to navigate our entire lives skillfully avoiding the exposure of our weaknesses and fears, even convincingly portraying strong, fearless personas in some cases. To call this myopic and risky is a severe understatement. Aside from the obvious downside of missing out on experiences that would enrich our lives and make us more capable, it also makes us even more vulnerable to consequences. We may find ourselves in a dire situation in which our false persona has encouraged others to rely on us for abilities we don't actually have, and our failure to meet those expectations has severe, even deadly, consequences for them and ourselves.

In less extreme circumstances, the shortcomings we've worked so hard to disguise through a false persona that actually encourages belief in what we're lacking being exposed is extraordinarily humiliating and leaves a permanent mark on our reputation and psyche; had those same shortcomings been discovered in the absence of any related posturing, we likely would have simply experienced some brief, minor embarrassment, quickly forgotten by all, and moved on (ideally toward correcting those shortcomings).

A mistake in self-evaluation due to the natural comfort in our primary realm is corrected instantaneously and painlessly with recognition of its existence—but eliminating the restrictions imposed by fear demands hard work and significant discomfort. It requires a willingness to accept temporary fear, discomfort and embarrassment in order to prevent their long-term and more severe versions. Rather than tiptoeing through life hoping to avoid being tested and exposed, we can choose to proactively develop greater capability. Being willing and able to make this choice is a product of our character and security—it requires awareness and critical self-evaluation, the recognition of our limitations without acceptance of them, and a refusal to allow others' perceptions of us (accurate or not) to influence what we do. Our character, guided by our values, determines our priorities, and our security in our identity allows us to pursue them in spite of any potentially dissuasive opinions of others.

True toughness demands a change in mindset that ceases viewing challenges or the unfamiliar as threatening and intimidating, and naturally and immediately recognizes and embraces them as opportunities. We need to see them as chances for us to learn, to collect improved and more varied tools, to become more resistant to fear and anxiety, and to validate our present character, capability, capacity and commitment—and to make corrections and improvements as these experiences dictate. Intimidation needs to be transformed into eagerness.

HELPLESS TO HELPFUL

The most reliable way to eliminate a sense of helplessness is to *choose* to become helpful. The effect of this choice is instantaneous—not one of us is so incapable that we have absolutely no ability to help anyone at the very moment it occurs. It doesn't take time after making this decision to go develop a stable of skills before we can take action. Our initial offerings may not be complex or extensive if we're early on in our pursuit of expansive capability, but that's irrelevant—the one and only thing that matters in this case is the intent and the subsequent execution, not the nature of the act itself.

None of us needs to spend time studying and practicing before being able to hold a door open for someone, to carry groceries for an elderly neighbor, or to volunteer at a homeless shelter serving food. Moreover, unskilled acts of helpfulness themselves may even provide opportunities for developing abilities. Consider volunteering with an organization like Habitat for Humanity, which builds affordable housing. We need not one minute of construction experience to provide meaningful help—there is always unskilled labor needing to be done, even if it's as menial as carrying construction waste to a dumpster or sweeping sawdust off subflooring, or slightly more interesting but difficult like digging trenches for foundations or utilities.

But with enough time volunteering in such an environment with individuals who are experienced in construction, we're very likely to begin working alongside them and assisting in more skilled elements, learning those skills in at least a rudimentary fashion. And as our experience grows, so too likely will our responsibility and the complexity of our tasks, further developing our abilities. All it required was a simple decision to be helpful, an investment of time, and an attitude that showed those around us with the skills to teach that we were eager to learn and willing to work hard.

The more we're able to do, the less we're forced to rely on others. The easily overlooked corollary of this is that the more we're able to do, the more we're able to help others. Capability doesn't have to be exclusively about what we're able to do for ourselves, and arguably, it shouldn't. The tough and capable technically have no greater obligation to help anyone simply because of their capabilities, although one could reasonably argue it's the ethical use of that ability. Help is useful in a functional sense regardless of the intent or rationale, but what makes help meaningful is its being offered by choice.

In more dire circumstances, switching the way we view ourselves from helpless to helpful can actually be life-saving. Laurence Gonzales writes in *Deep Survival* that, "Helping someone else is the best way to ensure your own survival."[1] Making the decision to aid others in an emergency instantly changes the situation. Primarily, it provides an obvious and immediate sense of purpose. In survival situations, many successful survivors are driven by their desire to see family again, or even simply to spare that family the grief of their death—but that's a distant, more conceptual driver, and it also excludes any of us without family or personal relationships that reach that level of intensity. In choosing to care for others in the present circumstances, we establish a genuine purpose and a need for ourselves that's entirely practical, contemporaneous, and impossible to ignore or forget.

Additionally, it forces us to develop plans and create meaningful tasks needing to be performed, which keeps our minds focused on practical concerns to the exclusion or mitigation of the kind of emotion that can overwhelm our rational thinking, and gives us the encouragement of accomplishing these tasks to continue propelling our efforts. As Gonzales puts it, we transform ourselves from victim to rescuer.

HOW DO WE LEARN?

A fair question now becomes: How do we learn all of this? It may seem overwhelming, but in fact these days learning nearly anything is about as easy as it can possibly get. With the internet, we have access to seemingly endless amounts of information, most of it free or very low-cost. We can even access formal courses in a multitude of disciplines and areas in different formats, from text only, to pre-recorded video, to live and even interactive video, for free or at a reasonable cost.

Of course, all of the pre-internet learning resources still exist and often offer unique benefits. Books and journals, live classes, friends and family, mentors, and plain old *trying* are all valuable methods of learning. No matter the advances in technology, no experience can replace or exceed the value of working personally under a master of a craft. This is the gold standard we should seek out and take advantage of whenever possible, not only because of the extraordinary quality of the information, but because of the built-in experience with qualified supervision it entails. Similarly, live courses with expert teachers are arguably impossible to match in other formats because of the personal interaction and tailoring of presentation and instruction for the students present.

The more complex and critical the subject matter, the more important live instruction is. If we're learning graphic design, an online video or tutorial is more than adequate; if we're learning survival or self-defense skills, live instruction with supervised practice, or working with a mentor, is important if not necessary. In any case, any format is better than not attempting to learn at all (assuming, of course, the source is legitimate).

Similarly, the more complex and critical the subject matter, the more important the quality of instruction and the legitimacy of the instructor or resource become. If our graphic design instruction turns out to have come from an eleven-year-old who figured out how to use Photoshop last week and wanted to make an online tutorial for fun, the worst possible consequence is that our design abilities are limited and we need to spend some more time learning from someone else. If we learn survival skills from someone with a similarly inadequate background, we may find ourselves in a legitimate life or death situation unable to start a fire, build shelter, locate water or otherwise protect ourselves adequately—and in this case, the worst possible consequence is death.

It behooves us to invest time and effort into vetting our sources when it comes to the most important subject matters like survival and self-defense. Temporarily delaying the start of our learning of these things in order to locate and secure the best possible instruction is well worth it. In many cases, it's arguably more dangerous to learn such things incorrectly than to know nothing at all. The former too often creates a false sense of confidence that leads to hazardous errors in judgment; at best, it means unlearning bad information and trying to overwrite bad habits, both of which are much harder to do than simply learning something new or creating original habits. Do the homework—if it's worth doing, do it well, and if your life may depend on it, approach the process accordingly.

STAGES OF COMPETENCE

Martin Broadwell described the stages of competence in a way that helps guide learning and practice and has been co-opted and renamed quite a bit since it first appeared in 1969.[2] This is a useful concept for our purposes because it helps us not just more effectively approach learning in general, but to evaluate our present capabilities and determine what and how we need to learn, train and practice, and will become critical when discussing capacity training. The four stages are:

Unconscious Incompetence This is simply the state of not knowing what we don't know and what we're incapable of. It's where many of us reside outside the confines of our profession and typically narrow set of interests and experiences.

Conscious Incompetence In this stage, we've discovered what we're incapable of and don't know—that is, something has brought to our attention what we were unaware of in the previous stage. Presumably this condition applies to you at this point in the book regarding quite a few capabilities.

Conscious Competence At this point, we've learned what we previously discovered we didn't know, but our knowledge or ability is new enough that we still need to think our way through it. For a skill, this means we're likely walking ourselves through its execution step by step, cueing ourselves, or in some other way having to focus specifically and consciously on the skill as we perform it. In this stage, that ability is still very useful—we know the information, or we can accomplish the skill in a controlled environment, but we're limited in what types of circumstances we're able to apply it.

Unconscious Competence In this condition, we're able to utilize the knowledge or perform the skill without thinking about it consciously or directly. The perfect example of unconscious competence for a physical skill is walking—this is actually a remarkably complex motor skill, but we never consciously think about what we're doing as we do it. It's become so ingrained as a skill that we're able to execute it flawlessly as a background task while consciously focusing on other thoughts or even other skills simultaneously (anything from chewing gum to solving mathematical proofs).

This final stage is the ultimate goal for all knowledge and skills, because this level of competence is what's required to execute our capabilities in demanding, stressful, adverse situations. We can't have our conscious focus be split between critical evaluation and decision-making and the physical tasks we need to be accomplishing at the same time.

THE UNIVERSAL BASICS

In Appendix A, you can find a list of abilities everyone should work on developing irrespective of profession, location or chosen activities. These are capabilities and knowledge that will serve as a foundation for survival and self-protection, and as a result, the survival and protection of our loved ones and those for whom we're responsible. With luck, most of these will never be needed, but the goal in any situation is to know and be capable of more than we need—especially when those circumstances have severe consequences for inability and failure.

PHYSICAL ABILITY

Any challenge or adversity demands mental fortitude, and may or may not demand anything directly from the body, but ultimately the body is the mind's vehicle, and physical health has a direct and dramatic influence on the health and function of the brain along with our mood and attitude. An extensive and continually growing body of research (and centuries of practical experience) demonstrates the power of physical health and fitness to strengthen the mind—both through the results of the activity and the performance of the activity itself. Exercise has been shown in some cases to be as effective as the standard medication protocols in the treatment of disorders like depression, dementia and anxiety; evidence is also growing of physical changes to structures in the brain like increased hippocampal neurogenesis, which improves memory storage and organization and the processing of new information.[3]

True toughness demands the effort to develop physical capability in parallel with mental—no matter how strong the mind is, the body needs to provide something for it to work with. At the very minimum, our bodies are vehicles for our minds—a weak, deteriorating vehicle greatly limits opportunities for the mind to flourish because it limits the possibilities for experience, the true driver of intellectual and psychological growth. Premature and accelerated physical decline from neglect of our health and fitness further robs us of energy, time and enthusiasm to pursue what's meaningful to us.

In emergency or survival situations, physical capability becomes even more critical. The physical capacity to travel significant distances in difficult terrain, carry someone or something cumbersome, lift something heavy to extract someone or access an escape route, climb out of a cavity or over an obstacle to safety, defend against an attack, and other obvious abilities to manage obvious contingencies are all imperative for maximizing our chances of survival and success in any circumstances.

Less obvious is the influence our physical health and fitness has on the psychology of survival situations and emergencies. The crushing sense of discouragement of finding ourselves physically incapable of the necessary tasks in front of us is alone a potential death sentence in a survival situation—it can very easily seduce us into surrender. On a physiological level, the fitter we are in such circumstances, the less taxing the physical demands are, which means the less fatigue we incur. Fatigue and exhaustion preclude clear, rational thinking and sound decision-making in any situation—when that situation is one in which our or another's life depends on our ability to assess, analyze, and determine an appropriate course of action, any reduction in fatigue is invaluable.

Similarly, the fitter we are, the less our activity in these situations elevates our breathing and heart rates, which helps us avoid an extreme hormonal stress response, or at the very least, avoid exacerbating an existing one, and consequently ensures a cooler head to allow us to remain in control and functioning optimally. In survival conditions, the general rule is trying to operate at no more than 60% effort to minimize the demands on extremely limited resources (as well as to minimize sweating to help avoid hypothermia)—the higher our 100% is, the more we accomplish at 60%. For example, if at maximal effort we can make it 10 miles through mountainous terrain in a given period of time, we can cover about 6 miles at 60% effort; if instead our maximal effort can only get us 5 miles, our 60% effort brings us only 3 miles.

The bottom line is that regardless of our mental fortitude, intelligence, and skill set, our physical condition has a dramatic influence on the outcome of any challenge or adversity.

This doesn't mean that we all have to train at Olympic levels of time investment and athleticism. Like every element of toughness, physical capability lies on a gradient, and we all start at our present level and commit to continuing long-term improvement. Every one of us can increase our physical capabilities and capacity through training—to neglect this piece of the puzzle is a critical error in judgment that ensures potentially extreme consequences eventually.

MENTAL INFLUENCE

All toughness is ultimately mental in nature, regardless of how much the physical body is involved. Our minds are what control our bodies voluntarily, and without the necessary mental fortitude, capacity and commitment to employ them when necessary, whatever physical capabilities we possess are meaningless. A hammer can't pound any nails if we never pick it up off the workbench or can't find the nail.

Even the untrained body has stunning capabilities that are occasionally exposed in extreme situations—there are many reported instances of people lifting cars enough to allow the escape of children pinned under them, for example. It's well known that our muscles have far more potential contractile force than our nervous system accesses in normal voluntary conditions—the sport of Olympic weightlifting in a sense is built on a foundation of this feature of the human body. As a weight class sport, athletes must continue becoming stronger without gaining weight—that is, without adding muscle mass. This is done through training that elicits neurological adaptation to allow the existing physical structures to produce greater force. Women who weigh barely 100 pounds routinely lift over double their bodyweight from the ground to over their heads at the elite level. The body possesses remarkable potential that we can tap into if we choose.

It should be emphasized that this potential merely existing isn't particularly helpful. For every story of a mother lifting a sedan off her trapped child, how many others were unable to help in even far less physically demanding situations despite loving their children just as much and being overwhelmed by the same emotional forces? Do we want to simply wait for a critical moment to discover whether or not our most primitive emotions are capable of producing an extraordinary physical feat?

The *You can do anything if you believe!* mindset is misleading in its oversimplification of a complex relationship of mind and body. The body is a physical organism with mechanical and physiological limits, and those limits are influenced by what we choose and choose not to do with regard to preparation and training. There are absolutely physical limits to what any given human being can do and withstand at a given time. While the physical potential is enormous, it's far from limitless, and extending its capability and capacity takes hard work over years, not just positive self-affirmation, faith and a misguided confidence that if we believe enough, we'll simply have whatever we need when it's demanded.

Our mental strength doesn't extend our physical abilities—it determines how close to the limits of those abilities we can reach. It's imperative to understand that, while the mental side of performance is critical and needs to be trained as aggressively and consistently as the physical, it's not a magic trick that will suddenly expand our physical powers beyond what they truly are—it can only expand them beyond what we formerly knew or believed them to be.

In order to ensure our greatest chances of success in any imaginable scenario, we have to train both sides of the equation—train the body to continually extend its physical abilities and limits, and train the mind to continually be capable of accessing more of that available range when it's needed. Our confidence in being able to perform at an extraordinarily high level and withstand physical punishment that would destroy others needs to result from systematic preparation and training, not baseless faith.

SLEEP

Established facts and even lessons of personal experience seem to have oddly limited influence on decisions when it comes to sleep. So many of us have deeply ingrained beliefs about it that are completely discordant with reality, and rather than update those beliefs in the face of overwhelming contradictory evidence, we simply dig our heels in deeper—to our own detriment.

It's so common that it's become a cliché for self-styled tough guys to belittle sleep as some kind of show of weakness or lack of discipline. In their minds, sleep is nothing more than an interruption to the constant condition of being on high-alert and grinding through misery, and therefore just makes us soft. Considering the well-documented consequences, recommendations of sleep-reduction are borderline criminal in their negligence.

It needs to be first very clearly understood that sleep requirements vary broadly among individuals based on everything from genetic predisposition to the demands of their lifestyles and professions.[4] Universal prescriptions based on one individual's needs and habits are uninformed and irresponsible at best—need can legitimately range from 7-11 hours per day.[5] Ironically enough, the kinds of physical and mental demands we place on ourselves regularly in pursuit of being tough are exactly the kinds of lifestyle factors that increase our need for sleep—to deny it is to ensure reduced progress and limited ultimate development, and risk both acute and chronic illness.

Inadequate sleep has been linked to heart disease, diabetes, hypertension, reduced immune function, mood disorders, and shortened lifespan among other conditions.[6] Being tough doesn't include unnecessarily saddling ourselves with chronic illness and the threat of premature death because we feel shamed into adopting the unique personal sleep schedule of a stranger whose approval for some reason seems important, despite the reality that a chance to receive that approval will never exist anyway.

On a more immediate scale, inadequate sleep has severe consequences for mental and physical performance. Aside from the discouraging and distracting feeling of fatigue, poor mood and diminished enthusiasm, we experience a reduction in concentration, working memory, logical reasoning, vigilance, and visuomotor ability.[7] Our speed, power and strength are reduced along with reaction time, balance, accuracy, stamina and manual dexterity.

None of these conditions bodes well for successfully managing any type of emergency or survival situation. On a daily basis, these changes mean a significant reduction in productivity and progress toward our goals. In short, even considering intentionally reducing sleep below our individual demand on a regular basis is counterproductive and harmful.

The effects of sleep deprivation vary considerably among individuals like the amount of sleep needed, which is why it can be so easy for someone who functions adequately on six hours of sleep—and doesn't understand or is unwilling to accept individual variation—to recommend that amount of sleep to others. But even if the intensity varies, an individual who performs well on six hours will feel the negative effects of less than that, just like an individual who needs nine hours will be affected by less than that. The absolute time isn't the issue—the relative reduction is what matters. To apply absolute numbers to others based on our own individual experience is nonsensical, just like we wouldn't expect a 245-pound elite athlete to subsist on the same caloric intake as his 125-pound sedentary counterpart.

The effects of sleep have been studied in both directions—primarily we look at the negative effects of sleep deprivation, but we can also demonstrate positive effects of sleep extension. One study showed increased sleep improved sprint speed, shooting accuracy and vigor while reducing fatigue during training in basketball players.[8] Napping has been shown to increase performance as measured by running speed, and improve alertness and other measures of cognitive performance.[9] This is all well-known among elite athletes and coaches—extended sleep and napping are used universally by high-level athletes. It's far and away the simplest and most effective performance enhancer available.

Waking earlier in the day isn't inherently problematic—the question is whether that earlier waking is accompanied by an equally earlier bedtime that accounts for the individual's actual need for sleep. It's generally considered healthier to have an earlier sleep schedule because of the typical pattern of cascading hormone release related to sleep and circadian rhythms. Ben

Franklin famously said, "Early to bed, early to rise, makes a man healthy, wealthy and wise." If such a schedule works for us, it can be adopted. However, the reality is that, like with everything else sleep-related, there is great variability in our natural schedules. Some of us may be legitimately wired to keep later hours, and trying to force an unnatural change will fail and simply accumulate sleep deprivation in the process. Any attempts to change the sleep schedule should be done incrementally over an extended period of time, both to allow a more effective adjustment, and to avoid incurring unnecessarily excessive sleep debt in the case of failed attempts.

The human body can adapt to nearly any conditions if forced to—we can all survive for long periods of time on much less sleep than is optimal, as proven every day by most of the adult population around the world. But mistaking survival as an indicator of adequacy, or worse, optimality, is a misinterpretation laden with serious consequences.

To suggest sleeping is inherently lazy is patently absurd. Sleep is one medium through which laziness can be expressed—when we intentionally sleep in excess of what's optimal, particularly when it interferes with the necessary and important tasks and responsibilities of life, it's fair to call it laziness. Short of that, it's serving a very real and completely vital purpose. Sleep is laziness like eating is gluttony—self-proclaimed tough guys don't recommend we all starve ourselves every day because eating makes us soft, but the logic is identical to reducing sleep for the same reason. Likewise, we're not battered by advice to subsist on packaged and fast food because it's quicker and easier and frees up more time for our various tough guy activities. If we're calling sleeping lazy, we might as well call breathing self-indulgent.

Being capable of surviving and functioning well with little or no sleep when we have no choice is tough—choosing to deprive ourselves of sleep unnecessarily is a severe error in judgment.

IMPROVING PERFORMANCE WITH SLEEP DEPRIVATION

The first step in improving our mental and physical performance in a state of unavoidable sleep deprivation is driving our rested baseline abilities up.

Whatever reduction in function we experience as a result of sleep deprivation is relative to that baseline—the higher our level of normal functioning is, then, the higher our reduced level will be in absolute terms. This involves all the same work and processes discussed throughout the book.

Contradicting the longstanding consensus among sleep researchers (which was always plainly illogical), we now know that sleep can in fact be banked—that is, we can accumulate sleep now to better carry us through sleep deprivation later.[10,11] This should be extremely obvious with even the most cursory consideration—do we feel and function better after a single rough night of sleep if we went into it having been sleeping well than if it was one more in a string of rough nights? Of course.

The more well-rested we are leading into any situation in which we're deprived of sleep, the higher our level of mental and physical functioning remains, and the more quickly we rebound to normal levels with the resumption of normal sleep. This is one more reason for the importance of ensuring quality, adequate sleep regularly—not only does it allow us to function more productively and effectively day to day and continue pushing our baseline capabilities higher, it better prepares us for maximal functionality when we find ourselves suddenly and unexpectedly in a situation preventing sleep but demanding we perform.

This is not to say that occasionally enduring intentional sleep deprivation isn't a legitimate training tool—it is, just like any other challenge we create for ourselves to prepare for those challenges created for us. If nothing else, it provides us an opportunity to evaluate our performance and know what to expect when the condition is forced on us, which alone allows us to better function within those limitations. But periodic sleep-deprivation as part of an intentional capacity-development exercise being useful doesn't mean living long term in a sleep-deprived state has any merit. Staying outdoors overnight without any gear might be a legitimate and beneficial training exercise—that doesn't mean we sleep barefoot in the dirt every night.

Being capable of enduring sleep deprivation forced on us through circumstances beyond our control, and managing to continue thinking rationally and clearly, preserving emotional balance, and performing physically at a high level is an integral part of being truly tough; needlessly depriving ourselves of sleep regularly to prove ourselves to someone who doesn't understand sleep or live up to some nonsensical criterion of a poorly-formed notion of toughness and discipline is misguided and self-defeating. It's far tougher to resist that pressure and continue to do what we determine is most beneficial for ourselves.

PHYSICAL TRAINING

Physical training is a nearly limitlessly expansive subject that extends far beyond the scope of this book. The purpose here is not to provide a comprehensive treatise on exercise and training, but to establish a foundational understanding of function and movement to allow the design and implementation of training of the nature discussed here and appropriate to our individual needs. For those inexperienced with training, it will establish a solid starting point; for the more experienced, it will help guide decisions for adjusting current training to suit new considerations.

ELEMENTS OF PHYSICAL ABILITY

Trying to organize and plan training as a generalist preparing for life and its unexpected demands rather than as an athlete preparing for a specific sport with clear requirements can be overwhelming because of the enormous array of methods, exercises and philosophies and the absence of a precise objective. However, we can actually break it down relatively simply to clear out the distracting clutter of various fashions and sales pitches.

To start, we can determine the collection of fundamental abilities we need to develop. Track & field coach Jim Cawley elegantly described general fitness as competence in ten elements: Endurance, stamina, strength, flexibility, power, speed, coordination, agility, balance and accuracy.

Endurance is the ability to continue adequate gas exchange for longer duration, usually repetitive, work in order to sustain effort. This is applied in activities like running, cycling, swimming and rowing for longer distances.

Stamina is the ability to maintain continued muscular effort at a local level—that is, supplying chemical energy and buffering limiting waste products to allow muscles to continue working repetitively. This is applied in the same kinds of activities as endurance, as well as activities of briefer durations that demand repetitive motions dependent on the same muscles—for example, the hand and wrist muscles in rock climbing, or the leg muscles in running up several flights of stairs.

Strength is the ability of muscles to produce higher levels of force. All motion is created through the coordinated contraction of groups of muscles, but strength concerns the higher threshold efforts against greater resistance. This is applied to lifting or otherwise moving heavy objects or resisting significant forces; strength is also important for long term health to maintain functional independence, and helps maintain bone density and connective tissue durability.

Flexibility is the extensibility of our muscles to allow our joints to move freely through their anatomical ranges of motion. This is applied in all movement to some extent, and becomes increasingly important as movements or positions require greater amplitude, such as moving through tight spaces or reaching limited hand and foot holds when climbing; flexibility is also imperative for long term orthopedic health.

Power is the ability to produce high levels of muscular force in minimal time—often this is described as explosiveness. This is applied to movements against significant resistance that must also be fast—sprinting uphill, throwing a heavy object (or person), and jumping are examples of power.

Speed is the ability to move quickly with minimal resistance, or to repeat a motion with minimal cycle time. This is applied to quick movements against little or no resistance, such as throwing a baseball or a punch, or sprinting on flat ground.

Coordination is the ability to execute complex motor patterns involving multiple body parts and simpler movements. This applies at some level to nearly all daily human movement, such as walking; it extends to the most complex motor patterns such as gymnastic movements or Olympic weightlifting.

Agility is the ability to transition between distinct movements quickly. This is applied in any sequence of multiple basic motions that must be tied together without hesitation, such as abruptly changing directions while sprinting, or moving quickly across uneven and unpredictable terrain in which the feet must be continually moved and placed immediately outside of a pattern.

Balance is the ability to maintain the position of the body's center of mass over its base. This is applied like coordination to even the most mundane tasks like standing and walking, to far more demanding tasks like crossing a narrow log over a river or arresting a near fall.

Accuracy is precision in motor patterns to control intensity, direction, timing and location. This is applied along with coordination and agility in most cases to create maximal precision in our movements.

FOUNDATIONAL MOVEMENTS

In addition to organizing the collection of fundamental traits that comprise physical ability, we need to break down the array of basic movement patterns through which we apply these qualities. These are the movements that are foundational to everything we do, from everyday tasks to the most extreme and complex physical challenges—other movements are variations or combinations of these, and ability to perform them in different circumstances (e.g. varying durations, intensities, angles or directions, and types of resistance) will allow us to be maximally physically prepared and healthy.

Squat Squatting is one of the most basic, natural motions for the body to perform, and yet it's become inaccessible for wide swaths of the adult population through avoidance based on misinformation or simply sedentary lifestyles that destroy the necessary mobility and stability. This is simply coordinated bending of the knees and hips while maintaining balance and correct posture. For an elite weightlifter, this might be done with a barbell on the back loaded with triple bodyweight; for that lifter's grandfather, it may be getting in and out of a chair unassisted.

Deadlift The deadlift is even more basic than the squat—it's nothing more than picking something up from the ground. When done properly, with coordinated knee and hip motion and effort supported by a strong trunk with solid posture and balance, it allows us to lift enormous weights; it also supports functional independence as we age by allowing us to perform basic but extremely necessary and potentially critical tasks.

Press Pressing is nothing more than pushing something away from the body with the arms at every angle from down, to straight forward, to directly overhead, and even out to the sides. Pressing allows us to lift objects to a height above us—maybe passing an injured child to a rescuer above—to move heavy objects away from ourselves—maybe to extricate ourselves from under fallen debris, or push away an attacker—or to push ourselves up out of a hole or onto a ledge. The shoulder and upper back mobility required for sound over-head pressing preserves health in those joints long term as well.

Pull Upper body pulling is the opposite of pressing—it's moving an object toward ourselves, or ourselves toward a fixed object. Like pressing, this involves the entire range of angles and directions, from lifting something from arms' length up to our shoulders, to rowing something straight back toward our chest, to pulling ourselves up when hanging from something, to drawing something in from our side with one arm. We can apply this to the same example scenarios as pressing—being the rescuer pulling the child up out of the hole, pulling debris up to extricate a victim, pulling an attacker in to establish neck control or a grip on the body, or pulling ourselves up out of a hole or a ledge. Like pressing as well, the mobility and strength for overhead pulling (such as pull-ups) creates and maintains the health and stability of the shoulders and upper back.

Run/Walk Running and walking of all speeds and durations gives us mobility in the geographic sense without reliance on vehicles of any kind. This mobility allows us to do anything from escaping a dangerous location or individual, to locating help, to reaching someone who needs our help.

Jump Jumping provides us access and mobility like walking and running but on a smaller scale. It allows us to access something above our standing reach, whether to bring it back down to ourselves, or to grab onto it to lift ourselves up, and to cover horizontal distances larger than our walking strides that don't offer support, such as holes, unstable structures, or water.

Carry Carrying combines running and walking with some kind of burden—the difficulty of that burden may be based on its weight, shape, size or all three together, along with how we're able or forced to carry it. This might be one or two burdens in our hands at our sides, something slung over our shoulders, something on our backs, or even something held overhead—anything from critical equipment or supplies, to an injured and immobile person.

Drag/Push Dragging and pushing might be considered variations of carrying—either when a burden prevents carrying due to its weight, size or shape, or if we've determined it's the more effective or efficient way to move it. This may mean moving something or someone over a large distance and long duration to escape danger or find help, or a very brief but extremely high-effort movement of an obstruction.

Climb Climbing combines multiple fundamental movements in an essentially infinite array—pulling, pushing, squatting, running and jumping. The surface, length and composition of what's being climbed will determine the method, but in any case, the ability to climb is a basic but critical ability. This may mean climbing a rope, tree, pole, wall, or rock face, or scrambling up piled rock or debris.

Heart & Lungs A consideration that merits inclusion here despite not actually being a fundamental movement is monostructural endurance work—we can think of it as fundamental movement of the heart and lungs. This includes running, walking, cycling, rowing, swimming, cross-country skiing… anything in which we're performing simple repetitive motions over long durations that relies primarily on cardiovascular endurance. We can achieve cardiovascular endurance training using any of the fundamental movements, particularly repeating sequences of them, but monostructural work offers a unique and simple method.

Accessory Finally, it's worth mentioning that in addition to the primary movements and exercises, we need to include accessory work to accomplish objectives not adequately covered otherwise. The most important category of accessory work is trunk strength—direct training of the abs and back to both protect the spine against injury and improve performance through control and stability. The kinds of exercises we're performing absolutely improve trunk strength and stability themselves, but the importance of the trait warrants specific training above and beyond the collateral.

Accessory work also includes minor exercises that can be general to all populations or specific to individual need, including dedicated grip work or joint-specific stability work, such as for the shoulders. Again, these things will be naturally trained to a certain extent with our selection of primary exercises, but in many cases, they require additional direct work.

SCALING

While the fundamental traits of physical ability are used in every level of activity to some degree and always in combination, the specific expressions vary dramatically—coordination, balance, power and accuracy for a young gymnast might mean the execution of a back flip on the beam; for a 95-year-old grandparent, it may mean simply being able to reliably and confidently step up onto a curb while walking, or safely navigating the uneven ground of a hiking trail. This relativity is important to understand. Every type of movement and ability exists on a spectrum of difficulty, intensity or complexity—they're all completely accessible to anyone at some level or form.

For a young, healthy athlete, pressing strength work might be a barbell press with a couple hundred pounds, while for a formerly sedentary middle-aged insurance broker with poor shoulder mobility, it may initially be pressing a broomstick as close to overhead as possible. One individual might do farmer carries as fast as possible for a few hundred meters with handles loaded to over a hundred pounds each, while a grandparent might work up to carrying a pair of heavily loaded grocery bags twenty meters to the kitchen for the first time in years without assistance. An athlete may squat a heavily loaded barbell, while someone else may have to start simply sitting and standing from a chair while assisting the motion with the arms holding onto a table. With a little thought and creativity, variations of every fundamental movement can be created to suit the present ability of a given individual.

SPECIALIST ATHLETES

While athletes of any discipline and level are undoubtedly at an advantage over any sedentary, untrained individual, they're also disadvantaged in certain respects dependent on their sports. A competitive weightlifter is extremely strong and powerful, but has very limited endurance and stamina—she might be able to lift some debris to free a trapped friend, but she can't run away from a threat for three miles. On the other end of the spectrum, a marathon runner has great endurance and stamina, but very little strength and power—he can run away from a threat all day long, but his friends better hope they're never trapped under anything heavy.

In most sports, the more advanced we get, the more specialized and limited our abilities become. This is a compromise we make in pursuit of specific goals because the body can't develop maximal capacity in physiologically and structurally contradictory abilities. Sports provide us straightforward rules and consistent environments and demands that allow us to perfectly tailor our training to suit them while ignoring anything that doesn't directly support those needs. Life is less predictable and offers infinite contingencies.

Competitive athletes will have to decide how much they're willing to sacrifice in either direction—that is, if they're willing to reduce their top end in sport for the sake of more breadth in ability, or if they're willing to sacrifice some of that breadth to excel maximally in sport. In any case, it should be a rational decision based on individual priorities. No athletic career is indefinite, so any decision is temporary.

TRAINING TEMPLATES

In Appendix B, you can find three training templates that provide examples of how this kind of training can be assembled into practical application for different levels of experience and ability.

FOCAL POINTS

- The more we're able to do, the better equipped we are to solve any problem that presents itself, and the more prepared we are for any possible contingency, from the mundane and quotidian to the rarest and most extreme emergencies.

- Developing new abilities doesn't simply add those new abilities to the list—it improves our ability to develop new abilities.

- Our accumulating abilities create potential for synergy—the combining of multiple elements to create a greater effect together than they would add up to acting individually—and prepare us to succeed in unexpected circumstances.

- Capability is what allows self-reliance and independence.

- The development of capability should prioritize the needs and possibilities of our profession, lifestyle and locality.

- Adequate sleep isn't laziness or a lack of discipline—it's a critical element of health and performance.

- Physical ability and the training that develops it is an integral part of being tough—neglect of this element creates potential for severe consequences.

- Physical health and fitness support mental and emotional health and cognition.

ACTION

This is the time to get organized and get started. The to-do list you compile is going to be extensive and not something you're going to complete anytime soon (or ever if you stick to the philosophy described previously), but there's nothing preventing you from starting immediately. Keep your priorities in mind and avoid getting distracted by the more peripheral at the expense of the more critical. Don't make the mistake of waiting for a "good time" to start—begin chipping away immediately. A journey of a thousand miles begins with one step, you eat an elephant one bite at a time, and you expand your capabilities incrementally as well. Start now.

Use your evaluation journal for the following exercises.

INTROSPECTION

- What are you afraid of and how is that limiting what you do? What experiences or abilities might alleviate that fear?
- How confident are you in your abilities? Take a moment to critically evaluate that confidence—is it truly supported by your abilities, or has it swollen in the absence of those abilities being tested?
- Is your perception of your identity supported by your capabilities? What is missing?

DAILY ABILITIES

- List what you absolutely need to be capable of in your daily life. Now consider if you're not up to speed on any of those things and what you need to do to get there.
- List what you currently depend on others for that you can reasonably learn to do yourself, both short and long term.
- List everyone (or the type of person) you depend on for anything at all, then what it would take to eliminate that dependence, and if that's possible or practical (for example, you likely depend on

an auto mechanic periodically. Few of us can reasonably become expert car mechanics, but if you live way out from civilization and that's your only lifeline, you need to be able to keep your vehicle working on your own).

UNIVERSAL BASICS

- Get started on the Universal Basics list in Appendix A. List all skills or items you don't presently possess and organize them into categories: purchases, skills you can learn on your own through books or online, and skills you need to learn live from an instructor or mentor.
- Plan, schedule and budget for each.

CRITICAL INCIDENTS

- Critical Incident Thought Experiment: As discussed earlier, spend some time imagining some worst case scenarios—natural disasters, medical emergencies, accidents, criminal violence, airplane crash, being lost in the wilderness… anything you can come up with.
- Consider the possible experience and consequences with your present capability, then how those consequences would change with different abilities. Use this to determine what you need to work to develop.

EXTRAS

- List non-critical skills you've always wanted learn. These can be simple or extraordinarily ambitious. Don't leave anything out for fear that it's impractical or you're not talented enough—write it all down. This is your list for your downtime time while accumulating your critical abilities, and after achieving a reliable baseline for those critical abilities.

TRAINING

- Get started immediately with a training program—see examples in Appendix B. Use the *No Excuses* template if necessary, but don't put it off. The longer you wait, the more intimidating and overwhelming you'll convince yourself the process is. Any training is better than none, so start now and improve and perfect as you go.
- Start a training journal. Write down each workout with notes on how you felt both physically and mentally. This information will be immensely valuable over time to allow you an objective measure of your progress.

CHAPTER 4

CAPACITY

What are you able to withstand? This trait is typically described as *resilience*: the ability to not simply survive, but to recover subsequently to our previous condition. But a return to our original condition after a challenge or adversity should be considered the bare minimum measure of success—being truly tough not only means we survive, but we *thrive* as a result of adversity. Rather than simple resilience, we want work-hardening—we search for and demand improvement, strengthening, learning and growth not just in the wake but as a result of difficult experiences by exploiting them to our advantage in any and every possible way. In other words, we don't just remain tough through an experience, we get *tougher* in response to it.

Capacity understandably seems to be the quality most commonly associated with toughness. We're enthralled and inspired by stories of extraordinary fortitude and endurance through extreme trials. But this natural attraction to tales of triumph allows us to forget about the far greater number of stories of failure in the face of similar or even far less dramatic challenges. We can argue about the tendencies of human nature, but adversity produces widely varied experiences and results with different people—while some will demonstrate incredible strength of will and succeed, many others will crumble and give in, never fully recovering from the psychological damage incurred. Our goal is determining how to fortify ourselves to ensure our ability to handle even the most extreme adversity, and then applying this to rational, systematic preparation.

Through our mindset, intentional behavior and training, we can prepare ourselves to contend with adversity of any nature more successfully. Our character and capability contribute the necessary attitude toward adversity and the physical and mental tools to perform in these circumstances, and commitment provides the structure and guidance—the development of capacity prepares us in its own unique way to allow these attributes to be applied productively.

Prevailing in the face of adversity requires proactivity over reactivity—while there's no question we can learn and adapt contemporaneously in the midst of a challenge to improve our ability to cope with it (and always should), the more tools and preparation we've accumulated and the fitter our minds beforehand, the greater our chances not only of survival, but of being able to harness the power of the experience for our long term benefit—the tougher we are going in, the tougher we're capable of becoming on the other side.

A challenge should invigorate us with the unequivocal knowledge that it's an opportunity if we determine to make it such. Possession of this mindset doesn't mean an otherwise miserable experience is magically pleasant—it means simply that we're better able to endure the experience and ultimately benefit from it because of a sense of purpose and meaning; it means the ability to transform the power of the experience from destructive to constructive in spite of the suffering that persists.

In his book, *Man's Search for Meaning*, concentration camp survivor and psychiatrist Viktor Frankl quotes Fyodor Dostoevsky as saying, "There is only one thing I dread: not to be worthy of my sufferings." Continuing about those who had died around him, Frankl wrote, "the way they bore their suffering was a genuine inner achievement. It is this spiritual freedom—which cannot be taken away—that makes life meaningful and purposeful." It's unlikely any of us will ever encounter adversity of a nature and severity that can be fairly compared to that experience, but his point can be applied to any challenge we face: Adversity creates an opportunity for us to make a choice—we can choose to surrender and become victims of our circumstances, or we can choose to fight—physically, mentally, emotionally and spiritually—and force the challenge to ultimately allow us to develop and discover strength, purpose and meaning. This, as Frankl says, is an ability that can't be stripped from us by anyone or anything but our own decisions.

SURVIVING VS. THRIVING

The capacity element of true toughness is more than the ability to merely survive an experience—it's the ability and intent to thrive through and after it. Human nature tends to cling relentlessly to life of any kind, even the most miserable, unfulfilling, purposeless, and seemingly hopeless existences. This may in some cases not even be out of any kind of appreciation of life itself, but simply in response to a fear of the unknown fate presented by death.

Each of us has to ask ourselves what value life has to us and why, and it's up to each of us to determine the quality and quantity of that value for ourselves. Friedrich Nietzsche wrote, "He who has a why to live can bear almost any how." If we expect to be able to thrive in the wake of suffering rather than be destroyed by it, there has to be some kind of purpose and meaning to fuel our will and drive an unrelenting and possibly protracted fight. There's arguably little point in surviving an experience if the result is being completely and permanently broken psychologically and emotionally as a result—to simply exist rather than live.

This is not to say that no retroactive effort can be made to recover and become tougher in the wake of an experience for which we were totally unprepared and devastated us as a consequence. There is always the possibility of using any experience at any time to develop toughness—but the more temporally distant the experience, the more difficult and less effective the process will be. We need to prepare for both the experience and the aftermath of any situation. There are experiences that leave indelible marks on us—our intent is to ensure those marks are empowering rather than crippling, even if that transformation takes years of hard work to complete.

Adversity doesn't inherently make us tougher—it can just as easily break our spirits and transform us into fragile cowards who desperately avoid risk and completely relinquish all sense of agency over our own lives. Nietzsche's now unfortunately trite line, "That which does not kill us makes us stronger," is typically regurgitated with little or no thought to practical experience. There's no shortage of stories of survival with not only an absence of such redeeming amelioration, but of absolute psychological crippling—this may in fact be the more common scenario. Nietzsche also wrote, as a convenient but less-often cited complement, "To live is to suffer, to survive is to find some meaning in the suffering." The experience of suffering alone doesn't inexorably produce strength—we must choose to act in response to that suffering to gain from it. In truth, that which doesn't kill us—*and of which we determine to actively harness the power*—makes us stronger. It's not the suffering itself, but our mindset, decisions and actions in response that produces the result.

RESPONSIBILITY & ACTION

There's a relentless and powerful current flowing below the surface of toughness—action and responsibility. Being truly tough demands we assume responsibility for ourselves entirely, and we exercise that responsibility through action, even when that action in some cases involves no outward expression. We accept this responsibility not as a burden, but as an empowering ability.

Martin Seligman, the psychologist who developed the theory of learned helplessness and pioneered work in depression and optimism, discovered the pessimistic explanatory style as being a primary source of depression. This is the habit of explaining the cause of bad events as being "personal, pervasive and permanent."[1] In other words, the individual with this mindset blames themselves for anything negative that befalls them, believing it to be not just the result of their own flaws or failures (personal), but that those flaws and failures will never change (permanent), and moreover, that these things are the source of every possible problem in their life, not just the one currently being experienced (pervasive). It's not hard to see how that would create depression, and by extension, a lack of ambition and success, and an absence of fulfillment.

With this apparent contradiction in mind, it's critical to distinguish a pessimistic explanatory style from the idea of assuming complete responsibility for ourselves—the former is crippling and imprisoning, while the latter is enabling and liberating. By not just accepting, but *seizing* responsibility for ourselves, we're realizing our power to influence our own lives—to determine the way we think, the way we view ourselves and the world, the actions we perform or abstain from, and ultimately, the outcomes of our experiences. This is not soul-crushing blame we're grudgingly imposing on ourselves— this is power we're granting ourselves. We're ruthlessly asserting control rather than submissively surrendering to our presumed immutable nature and inevitable fate. Blame is a door closed quietly in despondent acquiescence; responsibility is a door kicked violently open to boundless potential.

Seligman's early work demonstrated that a sense of helplessness—not just in a specific, current situation, but as a personality trait persisting into the future and applying to unrelated experiences—is likely to be developed as a result of a negative experience over which we're convinced we have no control. If we believe that no matter what we do to try to change a situation it remains miserable, we learn in consequence to simply give up trying and accept that we have no way of influencing our circumstances—we simply sit and wallow in our misery like victims. Note that the word *believe* above is important—it doesn't need to actually be a fact that we're unable to exercise control over a situation for this phenomenon to occur, we only need to be convinced that we can't. That belief can be established and cultivated in our minds in many ways, often in spite of evidence to the contrary.

In the experiments Seligman conducted, he concurrently found that learning we do have control over the negative experience built a mindset that continued to naturally exercise that sense of control in future, unrelated negative circumstances. In other words, once we genuinely *believe* we can influence our circumstances to effect positive change—that we're not, in fact, helpless—we possess a mindset that applies that conviction to any situation we encounter, whether or not it resembles the experiences in which we first discovered this ability.

With this in mind, it's easy to understand why adversity can produce such a broad spectrum of results in different people, and why Nietzsche's *that which does not kill us makes us stronger* idea isn't inaccurate, just incomplete.

Psychologist Angela Duckworth, when discussing Seligman's work in her book *Grit*, explains, "Experiencing trauma without control can be debilitating."[2] The most obvious form of control, and the one used in Seligman's early learned helplessness research, is physical action. If we're being shocked, and we move to another location and the shock stops—a simple physical action produces an immediate and complete positive physical change—the lesson is clear and direct. But what about circumstances in which there isn't a possibility of executing a physical action to effect change, or in which the negative experience itself isn't even physical in nature? It may be a more complicated process, but it's fundamentally the same—all voluntary physical action begins in the conscious mind with a decision, and those decisions are made only if there's a belief in the ability to execute the action.

In any situation of any nature, we have the ability to make a critical binary choice—to surrender and accept it, or to fight and change it. This decision is the foundation of capacity—the conscious, willful determination to resist succumbing to the far easier path of acceptance and surrender, and instead to employ any and all tools in our possession to create positive change. Being tough means *choosing* to take control in any situation, no matter how bleak it may appear, or in fact be, and no matter what the exact form that control can possibly take.

There are circumstances that are truly inescapable—situations that are impossible to change in any physical sense. Viktor Frankl experienced such a situation in a concentration camp—he survived by virtue of the timing of the Allied victory, while others succumbed through no psychological failure of their own to starvation or outright murder before this chance for release.

But as he pointed out, even those who perished were capable of determining *how* they experienced a physically immutable situation psychologically and emotionally, and this itself was a triumph. Frankl, through his own determination, was able to live successfully and meaningfully afterward in spite of the unimaginable horror he experienced. Both he and at least some of those who were unable to continue took control of the situation in the only manner possible—they chose to channel the power of the experience into strengthening themselves mentally, gaining insight and edification likely impossible to attain any other way, and improbably, to find an internal peace.

This choice is an action, in spite of the absence of physical motion we commonly associate with the idea. This means that, irrespective of our circumstances, we have the ability to take action—a situation in which it's truly impossible for us to act doesn't exist. We have the power to assert control, even if that control is exclusively of the way we think, and consequently, we are never incapable of responsibility and action. The ability to recognize the possibility of this choice and to trust in its power to influence our circumstances is tempered with conscious repetition like any other skill until eventually ingrained to a depth of indomitability.

Our sense of responsibility for ourselves is the engine for action, but it's also critically a source of infinite hope and a steady focus for faith. The Stockdale Paradox, named for Admiral James Stockdale based on his descriptions of his experience as a POW in Vietnam, explains the danger of indiscriminate optimism and misplaced hope eclipsing the acceptance of reality and encouraging inaction. After witnessing the most optimistic prisoners succumb to death first, he concluded that, "You must never confuse faith that you will prevail in the end… with discipline to confront the most brutal facts of your current reality…"[3]

In any adverse circumstances, a belief in our ability to overcome and prevail is imperative—without such a belief, we have no reason to do anything but surrender to our presumed fate. The source and nature of that faith, and the way in which we view our relationship to it, is equally critical. If we rely exclusively on faith in some kind of external force in the universe—no matter what we call it or how we envision it—to solve our problems, we've

given away our agency and the attendant power and left ourselves completely exposed and vulnerable. Every moment this unseen force in which we've
placed the entirety of our faith fails to save us, our conviction is chipped away
and our hope inexorably withers. This phenomenon is played out starkly in
experiences like Admiral Stockdale's, but can be seen in the full spectrum of
life experiences, including the most mundane.

If instead we take responsibility—direct our conviction and trust internally to our own ability to take control and influence our circumstances—as
long as we're alive and conscious, we possess an infinite source of hope that
can never abandon us. We know unequivocally that we have the chance to
prevail through our decisions and actions, and we will respond accordingly.

This doesn't, as it may initially appear, necessarily negate a belief in a
higher power—it simply defines our role in any relationship with it. Lying
back and awaiting something else to save us—even the divine—is defeatist
and fatalistic. It's not impossible to simultaneously believe in a higher power
that intends us to be successful, and believe in our need to play an active role
in that success. It seems reasonable to assume that any higher power would
appreciate a little hustle. Some may interpret this as a limit of faith in their
chosen higher power, but it can just as easily be interpreted as the grateful use
of the faculties such a higher power has provided us for exactly this reason.

Our attention needs to always remain vigilantly on the "brutal facts" as
Admiral Stockdale referred to them. Chris Pascoe interprets a rule from a
book written in 1503 by Desiderius Erasmus to provide guidance to knights
as, "The enemy you ignore most is the one who conquers you."[4] Few of us will
find ourselves threatened by corporeal enemies, but our enemies are arguably
more insidious in their intangibility, and our inaction in response to them
can in fact be just as catastrophic.

Psychologist Henry C. Link wrote, "We generate fears while we sit. We
overcome them by action." To some extent, action provides distraction from
fear and anxiety—we feel a reduction in them simply by virtue of our focus
being directed elsewhere rather than allowing it to remain concentrated on
these feelings and magnify them as a result. While the underlying source
of that fear and anxiety is unchanged by it, or possibly not even addressed

at all directly, that doesn't mean distraction is unhelpful or misleading. Regardless of the method, alleviation of fear and anxiety allows clearer, more rational thinking and decision-making, and these in turn are precisely the tools necessary for resolving sources of fear and anxiety. Further, action reassures us of our ability to influence our circumstances, reinforcing our sense of power and diminishing the perceived magnitude of the threat, making it more manageable.

In any event, surrender and inaction can be confidently relied upon for failure at all scales, from life and death emergencies, to the often seemingly inconsequential choices we make daily that in fact collectively determine the course of our lives.

A fire in a London tube station in 1987 killed 31 people in a tragedy that exemplifies the consequences of inaction and a refusal to respond appropriately to reality—passengers and employees ignored growing smoke and flames until it was too late to contain, unwilling or unable to believe the gravity of the situation. Dr. John Leach, a professor of psychology at Lancaster University who witnessed the event, later wrote about it, "Denial and inactivity prepare people well for the roles of victim and corpse."[5] Such events are compellingly illustrative because of their severity, but it can be easy to compartmentalize because of that severity and fail to recognize the associated lessons' application to all circumstances.

Outside of a life-threatening emergency, a failure to take responsibility and act is unlikely to have sudden consequences as patently extreme as death or permanent injury, making such failure easy to ignore—yet that failure can and absolutely will result in dramatic consequences, whether or not they're immediately manifest or even obviously directly related. Our lives are steered overwhelmingly with a continuous series of incremental changes in course, often immeasurably small in the moment, but which collectively determine our direction and destination. Every fractional abdication of our responsibility and ability to act means our bearing remains fixed through mindless inertia until periodically influenced by the weather created by the people and events that surround us—forces entirely unconcerned with our wellbeing, ambitions or intentions. Over time, these imperceptible course changes deliver us to an unexpected destination that finally captures our attention when we run aground on the shores of its undesirability—often finding ourselves stranded and unable to escape without extraordinary effort and commitment.

PERSPECTIVE

We observe life from a perspective impossible to be genuinely shared by anyone else, no matter how vigorously and sincerely we endeavor to describe it. Arguments will persist indefinitely over what truly constitutes reality, but we can say confidently that our way of thinking influences the way we view the world around us—how the collection of objective facts are assembled to shape a more complex picture of life. A single experience shared by multiple people will produce wildly varied assessments on all levels, from which details of the occurrence were most significant, to its underlying meaning as a whole. Undoubtedly the clear recognition of individual facts with objectivity is a required foundation for any rational thought and decision-making, but views with a wider lens allow for—and even demand—interpretation. How we interpret those collected facts and experiences is what creates our perspective and the mindset that dictates how we function.

"It's not what you look at that matters, it's what you see," wrote Henry David Thoreau. This succinctly describes the phenomenon of the influence of individuals' perspective on how the world appears, and emphasizes the need for thoughtful consideration rather than careless acceptance, but it also unintentionally depreciates the importance of *what* we look at, which itself has intrinsic value.

Not all experiences offer the same potential for insight and edification—even with a common aim, we can't replicate the value of certain experiences with others. Adversity and challenges in particular provide the possibility of lessons that simply can't be learned in comfort and security. Even when those lessons are communicated to us directly by those with the personal experience, the value and effect is diminished through that transmission—reading a book about climbing a mountain is not climbing a mountain; reading a book about surviving a disaster during that climb is even further from the experience.

We have immense power within ourselves to imagine and ruminate and produce stunningly consequential ideas as a result—Einstein's notorious thought experiments prove this. But we can stoke our imagination and provide more fodder for rumination with actual experience. Roman philosopher Seneca is quoted often as saying, "A gem cannot be polished without friction, nor a man perfected without trials." In fact, it would be so unrecognizable to us without such preparation that a gem could be argued to not even truly exist without the effects of friction. Likewise, life itself could be argued to be largely devoid of meaning without its share of difficulty.

Adversity of all natures, from the briefest challenges to the most protracted hardships, shapes our perspective with greater clarity and depth than comfortable, tranquil thought or communication of others' hard-earned wisdom can ever match. These experiences ineluctably draw out the truly important from the muddy furrow of the trivial and sharpen the focus of an ever-broadening lens. The ability to distinguish the meaningful from the inconsequential liberates us from the chains we find entangling us with the kind of petty nonsense that robs our life of time and purpose. The perspective afforded by the experience of adversity and the eagerness to learn from it bestow us with the wisdom to decline the inessential and frivolous, and the time and energy to invest our efforts in what matters most to us.

MINDSET

Mindset is a broad and somewhat nebulous term that's typically defined most simply as our attitude, but that's arguably somewhat oversimplified—essentially our mindset is the fusion of every element that influences the way we view ourselves and the world around us, and how we process and react to that information. We could reasonably view the contents of this entire book as discussing mindset and its various facets—it's more than simply being positive or negative, fixed or growth-oriented, or any of the several binary or multinary sets of mindset types various sources have presented that by limitation of their rigid structures preclude the true degree of natural variance that can exist.

What we can simplify easily is the purpose of mindset—to provide us the best possible tools and mental environment to accomplish what we intend and feel fulfilled, content, secure and at peace. Any extant feature of our minds that limits us, distracts us, discourages us, or otherwise prevents our achieving whatever it is we've determined is necessary and desirable needs to be eliminated or remodeled to suit that overarching purpose. The world provides us, with its complete indifference to our existence, more than enough difficulty without our creating or preserving unnecessary internal conflict and limitations.

To be clear, this isn't a weekend project like cleaning out the attic for a fresh start—this is likely an entire lifetime of consistent work toward this end, potentially with the assistance of a mental health professional in some cases. Like everything else we're doing, though, the task doesn't need to be complete for it to be valuable—every forward step in the process is beneficial and, like the momentum and encouragement gained as the attic begins to open up, the total effect is continually amplified as each step accrues.

In *Paradise Lost*, John Milton wrote, "The mind is its own place, and in it self can make a heav'n of hell, a hell of heav'n." This ability of the mind to transform circumstances beyond the material facts is borne out continually around the world—we often see those with nothing to speak of who work hard and struggle daily just to eat filled with joy and gratitude, and those with every known luxury, advantage and privilege miserable, hateful and bereft of meaning or purpose. Our minds can't transform the objective facts of reality, but we can create, as Milton describes, "A mind not to be chang'd by place or time"—that is, a mind that determines independently of its uncontrollable circumstances how to view the life existing within them. As Mihaly

Csikszentmihalyi wrote, "…those who take the trouble to gain mastery over what happens in consciousness do live a happier life."[6]

POSITIVITY & OPTIMISM

Positivity and optimism as concepts have, like the idea of being tough, been transformed with misrepresentation or poor implementation into what many of us have relegated to the silliness of unaccomplished people desperate to create a sense of contentment out of nothing. That is, we dismiss them as somewhat of a joke that no truly serious person bothers with—it's just something that lotus-positioned new-age goofballs pontificate about over weak cups of tea in their discussion groups before writing some checks from their trust funds. Instead we believe that committed, driven, accomplished people are cynical and pessimistic—or, as we like to think in support of those traits in ourselves, realistic. Of course, all of these things are true to an extent, making it even harder for us to determine what's effective.

Setting aside for a moment any preconceived notions of what optimism looks like in practice, we know a number of things about it generally. Optimistic people tend to have better functioning immune systems, experience less stress and pain, recover faster from medical procedures like surgery, have higher survival rates from illnesses like cancer and HIV/AIDS, and generally live longer.[7,8] Optimists are also more likely to find effective solutions to their problems, tend to encounter fewer problems in the first place because they're more proactive[9], have more and better personal relationships, and recover from setbacks more quickly and effectively. Optimism and positivity unequivocally provide measurable advantage. The only questions are regarding justification and implementation—that is, what allows us to be genuinely optimistic and positive (rather than simply acting like it outwardly), and how do we apply those qualities in a practical sense?

Optimism is simply the belief that our future generally or the outcome of a current situation specifically will be successful. This belief in and of itself isn't particularly absurd—any potential absurdity is attached to the rationale or the source of that belief. The most absurd rationale for belief in a successful outcome is one that doesn't exist at all—that is, a completely baseless trust that we'll be taken care of by some invisible benevolent force of the universe that for some unknown reason is personally invested in our success simply because that's the outcome we'd prefer. This becomes even more absurd when we consider that in at least some cases, this trust is possessed with equal fervor by two opposing individuals—combatants in a war, fight or even a sporting event—who are equally convinced that their outcomes will be successful for equally absent or ridiculous reasons, and who may be matched in worthiness of success in the most obvious practical ways.

For optimism to make any sense at all, and to be a way of thinking (and feeling) that's reliably successful, it needs to have a legitimate foundation supporting it. The only foundation over which we have true control, which will always be present in any circumstances, and consequently in which we can trust entirely, is our self. If we ourselves are the basis of our belief in our success, we have a source of belief that will never abandon us, and with whose capabilities and commitment we're intimately familiar. When we fail, we have the ability to find new avenues of success; when we're set back, we have the ability to reframe the situation and determine how to use it to our advantage.

With an unknown or external source of hope, in times of failure or crisis or setbacks, we're often left doubting or questioning that power—why has this force that we believed would take care of us abandoned us to pain, misery and failure, what have we done to deserve this punishment, or, even more unsettling, have we imagined its existence entirely and in fact we're just meaningless, inconsequential biological accidents whose lives are completely dispensable and interchangeable? We're left not only waiting for an indeterminate period of time for something else to resolve the problem for us, we're crushed with a sense of helplessness and existential uncertainty. In no conceivable circumstances does this condition prepare us for success or even survival.

Al Siebert concluded throughout his lifetime of work on what he termed the *survival personality* that, "The every day habits of life's best survivors include... feeling completely responsible for their lives working well, and learning how to influence events to result in good outcomes."[10] Martin Seligman wrote, "Your way of explaining events to yourself determines how helpless you become, or how energized."[11]

When we believe in the power of our own character, capability, capacity and commitment, we possess a stable, reliable sense of agency. We don't have to continually scramble emotionally and psychologically in search of any possible precarious foothold on a crumbling mountainside in order to feel secure or trust in successful outcomes—we become our own solid base on which to stand firmly and avoid that inexorable tumble into a depthless existential void that awaits those who surrender to unwarranted hope in the external and inevitably find it annihilated on the rocks below the cliff of experience.

Our belief in our own ability to influence the events and outcomes of our lives is an infinite source of forward drive. It compels us to continue the fight through failures and setbacks because we know there are always more options when others have been exhausted unsuccessfully—we know those options are limited only by our willingness to work hard to discover, create, imagine and attempt. The only option it eliminates is quitting.

Positivity isn't a state of mind created by ignoring the negative or desperately trying to convince ourselves it doesn't exist—it's an approach to accepting and dealing productively with the negative. Belief in our control over ourselves means our natural response to the negative is eagerly and confidently determining solutions rather than cowering helplessly and surrendering to its influence.

The tough aren't optimistic and positive because of a vague, baseless sense that everything will somehow work itself out, and therefore can be ignored while we lounge around and attend to other business—the tough are optimistic and positive because we know without equivocation that we'll work those things out ourselves. It's the sober realization and willing acceptance that the world at large owes us nothing and doesn't care or even know we exist, and feeling no concern or objection to that state of affairs—because we don't need it to.

It's often said that what allows us to continue through hard times is hope. But hopefulness is an entirely passive condition—it's nothing more than an expectation—or merely a desire—that everything will be fine. Hope works well until it's truly challenged—that is, hope will sustain us until it's actually pitted directly against a genuine threat. It's then that we discover how fragile and fugacious it is.

François de la Rochefoucauld said, "Hope is the last thing that dies in man; and though it be exceedingly deceitful, yet it is of this good use to us, that while we are traveling through life it conducts us in an easier and more pleasant way to our journey's end." This quote is evidently used by many to prop up their trust in hope, but a more critical reading of it exposes the trouble with hope. It *deceives* us into believing all will be well somehow if we simply continue clinging to it desperately like a rope stopping us from a fall. We grip relentlessly and hang on its frayed end *waiting*, assuaging our fears and misgivings with the reassuring texture of the fibers in our hands, making that perilous wait "easier and more pleasant"—until that rope is cut against the sharp edges of true adversity and we plummet, still frantically clutching that useless piece of disconnected rope, to "our journey's end." In other words, hope changes nothing about the circumstances—it merely distracts us from the precariousness and palliates us into the comfort of surrender.

The tough believe—truly, completely, unwaveringly—that they will prevail. They withstand hard times and triumph over challenges because they know—not hope—that they can and will succeed through their own choices and actions. Henry Rollins wrote, "Hope is the last thing a person does before they are defeated." When we believe in the power of our own character, capability, capacity and commitment, we eliminate any need for hope—we replace wishing with knowing and hoping with acting. We're positive and optimistic not because we believe everything will work out, but because we're confident in our ability to *make it* work out. Rather than simply dangling from the end of that rope until it breaks, we climb it until we find solid ground.

NEGATIVITY & PESSIMISM

Having negative feelings occasionally and temporarily doesn't make one a negative person—according to Al Siebert, it actually demonstrates "excellent mental health." A need to artificially enforce only positive thoughts is a sign of mental and emotional fragility—an inability to cope with life outside a "protective environment."[12] This is the model of positivity described previously that many of us envision—delicate, weak, adult-sized children afraid of being exposed to anything negative out of the conscious or unconscious knowledge of their inability to handle it, and this is why the idea is often so repellent.

A degree and type of negativity and pessimism is valuable to the point of being critical in many cases when implemented properly and at the right times. This is not the kind of indiscriminate negativity that without justification smothers everything with the proverbial wet blanket. It's absolutely not complaining—the self-indulgent wallowing that never in its long and storied history has helped anyone. Complaining exacerbates any problem by redirecting and flushing away the energy and focus that could be applied to discovering solutions. It's a symptom of a weak mind that surrenders to and obsesses over problems as if they're monolithic obstacles to happiness against which we're completely helpless. Worse, it's the selfish burdening of others with our personal struggles and failures, an attempt to flatten life to the level of our own misery rather than lift ourselves up toward its peaks—a drowning man pulling his rescuer under with him.

The moment we feel the bitter sting of complaint on our tongues, we can choose to swallow it back and consider what we can *do* to change the source of our compulsion to complain. We may be incapable of resolving it immediately, but discovering a solution exists—or even simply recognizing or remembering we have the power to find or create one—draws our attention to the absurdity of complaining and cuts off its fuel.

A universal sense of negativity or pessimism—the all-shrouding wet blanket—immediately extinguishes any sparks of motivation, enthusiasm, creativity and ingenuity before they're able to establish the flames necessary to create the steam that drives us forward. It crushes the sense of possibility and the willingness to attempt bold action. Alex Osborn, in his book *Your Creative Power*, discusses two types of thinking: judicial and creative. Creative effort generates ideas and possibilities, while judicial effort evaluates, rejects and selects.[13] Universal negativity or pessimism are in part characterized by exclusively or overwhelmingly judicial thinking—critically evaluating ideas, compiling reasons they won't work, and dismissing many out of hand before they're even fully formed.

An adverse situation often demands solutions that lie well beyond the boundaries of tradition or convention. Desperate survival situations in particular often leave us stripped of the tools and materials on which we're typically reliant and have rarely had to consider closely in terms of construction or functionality. Steven Callahan survived alone on a life raft in the Atlantic Ocean for 76 days after his boat was destroyed—he built a sextant with a pair of pencils he happened to have on hand, and managed to use a fork to help fix a leak in his disintegrating raft.[14]

This level of ingenuity, made absolutely necessary by the circumstances, is impossible to access through the stiflingly heavy fog of pervasive negativity and its dominantly judicial thinking—no judicially-thinking person even entertains the possibility of repairing a leaking raft with an object that we normally associate with creating leaks itself. We have to be able to allow creative thinking to flourish, even to the most ridiculous extent, to supply us with options we can then judiciously whittle down. We absolutely need that judicial thinking to play its role—but we have to keep it in check until that role is contributive in culling the extraneous, impossible and determinately unfeasible rather than disruptive in preventing the necessary accumulation of possibilities.

In his book, *Learned Optimism*, Martin Seligman points out that optimism is unsuited to certain circumstances, and that optimistic people actually need an appropriate dose of pessimism for practical reasons. Optimists, he writes, tend to "overestimate their abilities" and "distort reality" to suit their needs or desires, while pessimists tend to more consistently see these things accurately. In consequence, he argues that the inherent capacity for pessimism developed through human evolution serves a legitimate purpose—namely, keeping us out of trouble and ensuring we don't invest ourselves in ridiculous impossibilities. It pulls "us back a bit from the risky exaggerations of our optimism, making us think twice, keeping us from making rash, foolhardy gestures."[15]

While this is clearly wise in the sense that we of course want to avoid being rash and foolhardy, the premise assumes that our optimism is of the fundamentally flawed type described previously—universal and baseless. That is, we're optimistic for no particular reason, or, more accurately, we're simply *hopeful*. As discussed, this is absolutely a dangerous attitude that positions us for exactly the kinds of miscalculations—or failures to calculate at all—that Seligman argues an appropriate amount and type of pessimism prevents.

Whether or not we term it *pessimism*, it's critical we preserve a firm grasp on reality and a sense of objectivity at all times. Arguably this is more the product of properly cultivated and maintained optimism, not a balance of optimism and pessimism. That is, optimism without foundation is what's dangerous—it's a nebulous sense of hope that tenuously supports our confidence, judgment and decisions without reason. In stark contrast is the type of optimism built solidly and reliably on an objective evaluation of our own character, capability, capacity and commitment, the lessons of our experiences, and the resultant trust in our ability to influence outcomes in our favor, along with the confident willingness to accept without worry what's beyond our control. Our sense of optimism, then, is entirely justified, and has rational boundaries.

Equally importantly, this kind of optimism doesn't cloud our judgment or allow us to misinterpret situations in a way that pushes us to take unnecessary chances that aren't explicitly accepted benefits that we've objectively determined are worth particular risks. We don't look at a gaping canyon before us and believe optimistically that we can fly over it to arrive safely on the other side simply because that's where we want to be; we consider what we know about our pertinent abilities and how closely they match up to the challenge, and then weigh the likelihood of success against its necessity or benefit, even if this calculation is unconscious and virtually instantaneous.

Believing we're capable of clearing the gap, then, isn't optimism in the conventional sense of the word, but confidence; believing we're not capable of it isn't pessimism, but an acceptance of a reality that the demand exceeds our ability. And if we don't believe we're capable of making the leap, our optimism fuels our continued search for a solution that *is* possible, because we know we're capable of discovering one.

When we continually develop our character, expand and deepen our capability, forge greater capacity, and fortify our commitment, we're building the qualities that physically, psychologically, and emotionally underpin confidence. This process creates growing optimism—a belief that everything will work out—while preserving our necessary objectivity. We develop what we might call tactical optimism and pessimism rather than strategic—each is applied according to the given circumstances to achieve a clear objective, neither as a universal policy.

POSITIVE SELF-AFFIRMATION

Even more acutely than positivity as a policy, positive self-affirmation as a practice is often a source of laughter among those of us who consider ourselves practical and realistic—and, arguably, with equally good reason. Even Martin Seligman, the author of an entire book on optimism, writes in it that, "We have found over the years that positive statements you make to yourself have little if any effect."[16]

This isn't at all surprising considering the conventional approach to positive self-affirmation—repeating positive, encouraging, self-nurturing mantras every day... and then waiting for change to materialize. This method is rendered ineffectual by a structure lacking action in the same way that simply proclaiming that we will do something—no matter how many times and with how much conviction—doesn't get it done. Standing in front of the bathroom mirror each morning, puffing up our chests and saying, "I'm tough!" is nothing but a childish fantasy without related action—we might as well tuck a towel into our collars to fashion a cape and then make flying noises while our moms cut the crusts off our sandwiches.

But this doesn't mean positive self-affirmation is useless and without value—it simply means that the method of implementation determines its effectiveness. It's first imperative to recognize what this kind of autosuggestion actually is. It's not an effect or a result or in any way a realization—it's *potential*. We're rewiring our brains to unconditionally and categorically believe a given possibility, and in consequence, to allow us to commit to pursuing it rather than being tugged back with the reins of doubt and fear. If we believe something is impossible, or even impractical and unlikely, we're unable to invest ourselves into attempting to achieve it. This is a reasonable protective measure if we view it rationally—we believe we can't fly, so we avoid jumping off of cliffs to try it. It only becomes a problem when we allow that system to exceed its threshold of utility and begin prohibiting what is in fact possible, however improbable, difficult or ambitious.

If we reconsider that metaphorical jump over the gaping canyon to the safety awaiting on the other side, unqualified belief in our ability to make it allows us to fully commit to the attempt, channeling every available bit of the necessary resources into it. If instead we continue harboring doubts about its possibility, we'll fail to commit and find ourselves without access to the leg power we need—and falling. The purpose of positive self-affirmation is to eliminate that crippling doubt or uncertainty and free us to reach what's in fact our true potential. Again, however, no matter how robust our conviction in that potential, it's meaningless if we never make that jump.

Interestingly, the psychologist who introduced the world to the practice of autosuggestion in the early twentieth century, Émile Coué, believed that what might seem to be the most obvious and effective way to manifest what we desire is not only ineffective, but counterproductive. He wrote in *Self Mastery Through Conscious Autosuggestion* that in a battle between will and imagination, imagination invariably wins.[17] That is, when we try to force ourselves to do something with willpower, without a genuine belief in its possibility, we not only fail, but likely arrive at the opposite result.

Consequently, the composition of autosuggestion is critical—it needs to be focused on *believing* something is possible rather than telling ourselves we *will* perform a specific action. Returning again to our canyon-jumping challenge, if we repeatedly tell ourselves, "I will jump over this canyon," we're likely to fail because we believe the jump is impossible and are simply trying to *will* action in opposition to that belief—and that belief, or imagination, will impose itself forcefully as we make the attempt, preventing our commitment and leading to our fall.

Instead, we need to establish the belief in the possibility—and the inevitability—of the outcome in question. Arguably, this is often better accomplished through visualization than the repetition of a linguistic phrase. It's often more difficult to generate such a phrase than to vividly imagine ourselves in the condition of having achieved something—for example, viewing ourselves on the other side of the canyon, feeling the exhilaration of success, the relief of safety, and the satisfying physical residue of a difficult feat. More about visualization later.

We can also consider the effects of *priming* and how that phenomenon—a kind of indirect suggestion harmonious in principle with Coué's ideas—can play a role in the efficacy of positive self-affirmation. Essentially, priming is the creation of unconscious expectations that influence how we experience an event, how we behave or speak, or how we perform.

Research has repeatedly demonstrated the influence of priming on our subsequent reactions and behavior. Something as simple as reading a list of words with a certain theme will cause people to have completely different perspectives on the same event, to react differently to a situation, and even to perform better or worse. For example, in one experiment, two groups completed an exercise of unscrambling letters to create words—the first group's words included *aggressive, intrude, annoying* and *rude*; the second group's included *polite, sensitive, honor* and *considerate*. In a subsequent setup, these same subjects moved to another room to perform their next unknown task, where they found a researcher pretending to unsuccessfully explain that task to another researcher posing as a fellow subject. The first group interrupted to ask what they were supposed to do almost twice as fast as the second. Even reminders of stereotypes that involve ideas about certain abilities or tendencies prior to objective testing has been shown to influence the subjects' performance in that testing in alignment with the stereotypes with which they were primed.[18]

This is a powerful tool if we're able to apply it intentionally to ourselves. If we prime ourselves with the expectation of success, we're far more likely to achieve it—not through mystical forces, but through the natural response of our minds to perform in the manner that supports that achievement. The specific words we use in our self-talk have power, not just the meaning or intent of what's being said, demonstrated by how the seemingly arbitrary words in the unscrambling exercise influenced those research subjects' subsequent behavior. More on self-talk later.

Simply stated, positive self-affirmation has the potential to be dramatically influential when we understand how to use it, or a complete waste of time if we don't.

COMPOSURE & STRESS

An instantly recognizable mark of the truly tough is composure—the air of self-possession they exude in even the direst and most demanding and stressful circumstances. Even if we can't articulate it or don't identify this quality consciously, we all know it when we see it, and this is consistently reflected in the hero archetype across the spectrum of cultures and time—we don't see hero characters who in the face of a challenge are panicky, indecisive or flighty, although we may see them with any number of other character flaws or histories of failure.

This quality of the tough is intimately and directly related to the source of our optimism—our rationally borne confidence and our willing acceptance of the circumstances' reality without surrender to them. Marcus Aurelius wrote, "Be like the rock that the waves keep crashing over. It stands unmoved and the rage of the sea still falls around it." This is a vivid metaphor to illustrate tranquility in the midst of chaos, but it's worth keeping in mind that the same rock that stands unmoved is also slowly eroded by the pounding of those waves and is reshaped to some extent according to the ocean's force. The state of calm we maintain is in fact possible in part because we recognize and accept this influence—we understand that the experiences of life's challenges change us. By being aware of and accepting this rather than expending endless energy on ineffectually fighting an indomitable force, we're able to determine the nature of that change—to harness that same force and direct its power in order to ensure the inexorable changes we experience fortify our character rather than dismantle it.

An increasingly fashionable refrain is that there is no such thing as a stressful event, just stressful reactions. This is nothing new, of course—Epictetus wrote almost 2,000 years ago that "It isn't events themselves that disturb people, but only their judgments about them." This sounds delightful and so consummately stoic, but it belies the fact that certain circumstances are objectively stressful, and in those cases, believing otherwise is more self-deception than stoic mastery of our emotions. Having our house burn to the ground and with it all critical financial records and identification is objectively stressful—it creates practical difficulties for us that can't be eliminated through any degree of composure. Remaining calm as you watch these things burst into flames doesn't prevent their destruction and the subsequent demands to recover from the loss.

Of course, reacting emotionally to this or any other event, whether we can reasonably categorize it by its nature as stressful, does nothing more than remaining calm to change the facts of the situation. Screaming and crying at the flames won't cause our birth certificate and the deed to the house to rematerialize, or alter the necessary steps to recover from the loss. Moreover, this kind of emotional reaction creates its own additional problems by preventing clear thinking and rational decision-making, compounding the difficulty of an already trying experience. It simply adds misery, extends the duration of the experience, and discourages useful action.

The only way to be truly without stress or concern over any event in our lives is to care about absolutely nothing. If we drive by a totaled car in a stranger's driveway, we have no reaction at all with the possible exception of curiosity; if we get a single scratch on our own car, we're likely to experience stress in response. Remaining calm and not reacting emotionally to events because we're in control and maintain perspective is entirely different from feeling no reaction because we don't care. The goal is not to convince ourselves that everything is meaningless, but to recognize what's truly meaningful and what isn't, and to understand how our responses to events shape our experiences so we can avoid self-destructive reactions.

Remaining composed and in control of our secondary emotional reactions in the face of adversity needs to be not the product of deceiving ourselves into believing a legitimate problem isn't a problem, but of the acceptance of the circumstances for exactly what they are objectively while believing resolutely that we have the ability to survive and recover—that is, to accept the problem as a problem and remain confident that we can solve it. If we avoid believing what's truly happening to be happening in a direct effort to remain calm, we're simply delaying the process of recovery. We create a moment of slack during which we simply watch and wait rather than beginning to work toward the solutions necessary to push us through the storm and emerge safely from the other side—and when the inexorable and gathering motion of the event violently takes up that slack, we're jerked abruptly into a vulnerable position in which immediate response is necessary but far more difficult to execute because of our lack of preparation.

Our composure instead needs to be a natural outgrowth of our confidence in our toughness—our trust in our abilities, resilience, and mental fortitude to carry us through. In other words, being tough makes us calm; being calm doesn't make us tough.

Few of us ever experience an event as trying as losing our homes to fire, and yet many of us go through our days as if our life is a perpetual house fire, in a nearly continuous state of emotional tension punctuated by sudden outbursts in reaction to the slightest perturbations of our delicately homeostatic elevated stress level. Missing a traffic light cycle, having to wait an extra three minutes in line for a $7 cup of coffee, or not having a strong enough WiFi signal to watch an overly-produced video of a stranger's life on Instagram shouldn't elicit the kind of reaction more appropriate to losing a home or a job.

The first step to gaining composure throughout any given day and avoiding this ridiculous and unnecessary level of stressful reaction is to be aware of our condition. Often we don't realize what we're doing until we've done it—and while in retrospect we may regret it and be embarrassed, that doesn't rewrite history. Until we can develop the presence of mind to catch ourselves as we're about to take that first leap into such a reaction, we'll simply repeat the cycle of responding with overblown emotion and wishing we hadn't once we see the damage. This can only be achieved initially by setting out each day with the conscious intent to remain vigilant, and nurturing this into habit. Part of our morning journal routine should be evaluations and reminders to ourselves about this as needed, and we'll discuss more tools for it later.

A final consideration here is the act of worrying, the most debilitating and unnecessary form of stress imaginable. Worry takes the problems of exaggerated emotional reactions to actual events and applies them to events that haven't even happened yet… and likely never will. Mark Twain wrote, "Worrying is like paying a debt you don't owe." It's about as useful and rational as writing monthly checks to the bank to pay a mortgage on a house that doesn't exist—we continually lose the money without ever even having the benefit of a home. We're creating problems to solve but never solving them because there's no solution to an imaginary problem—we establish an unrelentingly torturous condition made interminable by the impossibility of alleviation.

Legitimate anxiety disorders requiring professional intervention aside, we eliminate or avoid worry through conscious practice of how we direct our focus and evaluate our circumstances. Ultimately worry takes hold not because our imaginations spin out of control creating worst-case scenarios that terrify us, but because we lack the confidence in our ability to manage those imagined scenarios. It might be exhausting for our minds to be continually fabricating elaborate storylines, but the existence of those stories doesn't in and of itself result in worry or anxiety. No differently from actual scenarios in our life, worry is an outgrowth of a lack of trust in our ability to solve a problem or otherwise handle the circumstances. If we feel confident in our ability to effectively manage any imaginable scenario, worry ceases to exist, and we simply have a hyperactive imagination and some spare material for a novel.

Admittedly, it's somewhat silly to share the observation that worrying is pointless—no one fails to grasp that obvious fact. But if we can understand rationally why it arises, remain vigilant over our reactions, and continue striving to develop our capability and capacity in order to support our confidence, we can begin to eliminate it. We learn to accept without surrender what we're unable to control or influence, that concerning ourselves over it accomplishes nothing, and remain composed and unworried because we have no doubt in our ability to effectively handle whatever we encounter.

TRANQUILITY

The ability to create a sense of tranquility within ourselves amidst chaos and tribulation is an invaluable skill that demands considerable practice. We have a finite amount of psychic energy in any given period of time, and without intelligent regulation and distribution, we burn through it quickly and haphazardly and leave ourselves vulnerable with a short supply when we suddenly encounter a situation that demands a large input.

We need the ability to voluntarily regulate our mental processes and to make wise choices about our investment of our limited resources so we avoid inadvertently enfeebling ourselves. The ability to shut out distractions and focus our attention is already one of the natural primary jobs of the mind— it's continuously regulating what of the overwhelming environmental data cross the liminal threshold and reach our consciousness. Without that function, we'd be reduced to drooling, paralyzed lumps unable to keep up with the information processing demands.

Even with this natural barrier, however, we can become overwhelmed into near uselessness by allowing our attention to ricochet wildly without restraint. The natural order of the mind is in fact disorder, which is the underlying reason we so consistently seek continuous distraction through entertainment—to avoid the often negatively-spiraling thoughts that overwhelm us in the absence of external stimulation providing a point of focus.[19] Practice is necessary to learn control over our attention and refine our ability to distinguish signal from noise—and to prioritize distinct signals.

The first step is to regularly experience environmental tranquility—to intentionally place ourselves in an intrinsically peaceful atmosphere and allow its serenity to influence our mental state. This time is both a rest for our mind from its continuous battle against overstimulation and distraction, and a chance to consciously familiarize ourselves with a model to internally mimic outside of such environments.

The next step is something even more potentially repugnant to the self-styled tough than optimism and positivity: meditation. Like optimism and positivity, meditation is easily misrepresented and misunderstood—and similarly often poorly executed, misapplied and ineffective. It has nothing to do with hanging upside down in the forest in the lotus position wearing nothing but a cloth diaper.

Before we dismiss the practice out of hand with a disdainful scoff, we need to consider what the research shows—we don't have to simply trust what various practitioners claim. It's been demonstrated among other things that meditation improves an array of mental performance qualities, from situational awareness, critical evaluation, decision-making, problem-solving, focus under stress, attention span, optimism and overall productivity; physiologically, it's been shown to have effects like reducing heightened levels of circulating stress hormones, diminishing systemic inflammation, lowering blood pressure, mitigating chronic and acute pain, improving sleep, and increasing our resilience in the face of stressful experiences.[20,21,22,23]

To ignore a tool of this potential without legitimate evaluation for ourselves is negligent at best. The task is to determine exactly what protocol is most effective for each of us individually, and then to commit to consistent, long-term practice. Individual sessions may provide relatively minor benefit in the moment, but the cumulative effects of regular meditation are far more extensive and significant.

Wading through the array of different meditation protocols is overwhelming and unnecessary. We can rely on the universal principles to derive the benefits without having to become yogis or monks, or having to commit much time at all.

The two overwhelming priorities are simple: de-excitation of the mind and the nervous system as a whole, and control over our attention—calming down and getting focused. Controlled breathing alone takes care of both to a great extent; add to that a mantra of some kind and we have an effective meditation protocol without years of deprivation and study on a misty mountaintop.

To be clear, a mantra isn't some mystical incantation—it's nothing more than a simple, repetitive word or brief phrase that creates a single point of focus for our mind. It can quite literally be anything—it doesn't even have to be a word, but merely a sound that's easily replicated consistently in our head. The one possible mistake is using a word, phrase or sound that's distracting because of its associations or intrinsic ridiculousness. We need to choose something simple and free of connotations unless strictly advantageous to us, such as a word that reminds us of a quality we want to embody.

For five to fifteen minutes every day, we simply need to sit comfortably and without interruption, breathing deeply and slowly while repeating our chosen mantra—passively allowing arising distractions (of which there will be a seemingly unending series) to pass by without concern or forceful attempts to clear them away. More details about controlled breathing follow later. For more information and a complete and effective but simple and low-investment meditation protocol, see the book *Stress Less, Accomplish More* by Emily Fletcher.

Setting aside time every day to intentionally create this tranquility isn't pretending the world around us doesn't exist or doesn't matter; it's not deceiving ourselves into believing our problems have disappeared or that we have no further concerns in life. It's not irresponsibility or fearful escapism—it's simply a tool for temporarily redirecting our attention and diminishing the extreme and unrelenting demands on our minds in order to improve our capacity and capability for more effectively managing the various challenges life presents us.

AWARENESS

Awareness is our conscious connection to both our external and internal environments. Like most conscious processes, in the absence of our intentional control, it will be naturally determined according to the pertinent criteria presently existing in our brains, which can be shaped by myriad influences to produce extreme differences among individuals. Naturally, some of us notice extensive detail about locations, events or people, while others continually leave cabinet doors open after accessing their contents without the slightest recognition of the incompleteness of the behavior; some of us tend to be more focused internally, while others' focus is primarily external. In any case, we can learn through practice to determine what we're aware of and when in order to improve our ability to function effectively in the spectrum of experiences, from the dullest and most typical content of our lives to the most extreme and demanding circumstances we encounter.

One of the most frequently cited mistakes of awareness is the inability to truly reside mentally in the present—to be invariably occupied with rumination on the past and concern for the future to a degree that we fail to genuinely experience our lives as they play out around us. This condition is well-used fodder for regret and the inspiration for countless musical ballads.

In response to this evident failure, advice to "live in the present" is broadcast widely and largely indiscriminately, tinged with a sense of disdain for the past and future as if they're villainous thieves of our true life. This may be a poetic and seductively romantic notion, but from a practical perspective, it's misleading and incomplete. The past and future are critical and irreplaceable sources of guidance for our decisions—ignoring them imperils the very present in which we're striving to exist. A refusal or failure to consider the future is an unsustainable existence unless our every need is being managed by a caretaker—this is the condition of early childhood, the attempted replication of which offers clear drawbacks in any number of ways. Shutting out the past robs us not just of the experiences we rely on to learn, practice and create the foundation for our decisions today, but of the joy of our good memories.

Effective awareness encompasses all three temporal regions to extents and durations appropriate for the given moment and task at hand. In no way is it impossible to sincerely experience and appreciate the present in its fullest detail while also learning from the past and planning for the future—it simply requires intent and conscious control. Ambition and goal-orientation don't intrinsically rob the present of meaning or enjoyment. It only becomes a problem when, as Mihaly Csikszentmihalyi writes, "people are so fixated on what they want to achieve that they cease to derive pleasure from the present."[24]

In other words, the pursuit of goals and progressively demanding mental and physical challenges itself isn't the problem—the way in which we approach it is. We simply need to transition our attention according to the demands of the moment—relishing the nostalgia of childhood memories is a poor choice in the midst of an emergency; failing to give attention to the future when choosing a course for our lives and instead simply enjoying whatever immediate pleasure exists now ensures short-lived enjoyment and a very abrupt and shocking end to the reverie when the rent is suddenly due—metaphorically and literally.

Even within the present moment, we have continual decisions to make about the objects and purpose of our attention. We often believe we possess the ability to pay attention to a wide array of incoming information, but our focus is actually quite limited. We demonstrate this every time we become truly engrossed in a particular task—hours later we may realize we've forgotten to eat, missed an appointment, or have to make up with the angry spouse we didn't hear talking to us. Our attention provides us a wide range of possibility, each end with its tradeoffs—on one end, we can be somewhat aware of many things; on the other, we can be completely aware of one thing. The latter can become extreme in dire circumstances—it's not uncommon for those who've experienced a lethal fight to report near or total auditory exclusion and tunnel vision, for example, and to have no memory of surrounding events or many details that seem impossible to have missed to others present.

Our goal is to establish and reinforce ideal situational awareness as our default state—our awareness of as much about our present environment as possible without becoming fixated on anything in particular, all while being capable of experiencing and enjoying the present. That is, we want to avoid becoming paranoid wrecks unable to enjoy the moment because we've convinced ourselves that we need to be constantly and furiously assessing every detail of the room in search of potential threats like Jason Bourne. Varg Freeborn best describes this condition in his book *Violence of Mind* as "focused on your environment in a relaxed but actively scanning manner."[25]

This skill has also been well described as "looking at, not for." In other words, rather than compiling a list of specific items we want to notice because we believe they would represent a threat or some other kind of imperative data, and then scanning the environment in search of them, we instead simply observe what's around us with a moderate level of attention. By creating specific pre-existing targets for our focus, we're reducing our ability to notice potentially critical information that isn't on our list—we're restricting our focus and creating mental tunnel vision even if physically we still possess vision of the periphery. "This is what will allow you," Freeborn writes, "to relax and enjoy your life, while you run a constant background scan for *abnormalities* in your environment."[26]

This is an ability like most others that requires practice to develop and refine. Every day is an opportunity to practice if we consciously make the choice. We can also set aside time specifically for this skill to accelerate our learning. One method is referred to as using a "sit spot" by Jon Young, founder of the Wilderness Awareness School. In his book, *Extreme Wilderness Survival*, Craig Caudill describes this practice as choosing a place to sit and observe the environment each day—to take in as much of the information as possible, and to begin to see the patterns and order that actually exist in apparent randomness. He suggests you note your observations and make sketches to improve retention.[27]

This practice can be applied to any environment, not just the natural. Sit in a coffee shop. Stand on a city sidewalk. Ride the train or bus. Observe how people behave and how they interact with each other. Note patterns and oddities. Not only is this good practice in directing the focus and controlling the depth of our attention, it's creating a mental library of experiences that provide varied information for later association and in total establish a more accurate "normal" baseline. This improved and more detailed sense of normal is the framework for our determination of the kinds of abnormalities Freeborn discusses as potential signals of danger, or at the very least, necessary targets for closer assessment.

With this understanding and these practices, we can become increasingly able to remain safe, productive, goal-oriented and present in the moment.

PREPARING FOR ADVERSITY

True adversity by nature descends upon us without warning—the unexpectedness and unfamiliarity amplifies the challenge by forcing us to respond without the luxury of planning and direct preparation. But being tough means always preparing with the expectation—and the certainty—that adversity will find us eventually. This is a theme that runs consistently over many centuries throughout philosophy, sports and war. Seneca wrote, "It is when times are good that you should gird yourself for tougher times ahead." In sport, a common philosophy is to push so hard in training that competition itself is easy: Jerry Rice, renowned for the intensity and relentlessness of his training, said, "Today I will do what others won't so tomorrow I can accomplish what others can't." And General Norman Schwarzkopf concisely rephrased an ancient idea when he said, "The more you sweat in peace, the less you bleed in war."

The absence of hardship at a given time isn't a sign that hard times are over—it's an opportunity to prepare for the inevitable hard times to come. Recognizing the potential value of adversity, and being willing to endure it for the sake of its power to help us, doesn't mean we wait idly for it to arrive. Challenges may simultaneously be opportunities, but opportunities are meaningless if we fail to actively take advantage of them—it's our own mindset and decisions and actions that determine whether a challenge crushes us, or we exploit it for our benefit.

Dr. Al Siebert, in his book *The Survivor Personality*, explains that the "best survivors" respond to "disruptive change" as if it's welcomed and desirable."[28] This shouldn't be misinterpreted to suggest that we actually desire disruption and hardship—it describes the attitude we apply when such disruption is unavoidable in order to fortify our resistance. Preparing for adversity isn't eagerly inviting it. We're neither wishing desperately to avoid hardship, nor hoping it finds us—we're simply preparing mentally and physically for the unpredictable and difficult to ensure that we're capable of withstanding whatever we encounter with confidence and success. The attitude of welcoming adversity robs the challenge of much of its potential destructive power, which is manifest overwhelmingly in our own mental struggles rather than in reality.

A primary objective in the midst of any adverse circumstances is to countervail the negative effects of fear. This is not to say that fear should be (or can be) eliminated—a true absence of fear is dangerous. Fear is a natural state that inspires heightened awareness and efforts at self-preservation, and in proper dosage and timing, it assists our efforts rather than detracting from them. We're counteracting the potential paralyzing effect of unchecked fear with the composure and confidence gained through our preparation and resultant ability to maintain clear, rational thought in the presence of a threat. Cus D'Amato, legendary coach of Mike Tyson, said, "The hero and the coward both feel the same thing, but the hero uses his fear, projects it onto his opponent, while the coward runs. It's the same thing, fear, but it's what you do with it that matters."

Fear and anxiety actually increase energy, physical ability and mental acuity—they stimulate the sympathetic nervous system, which causes the release of hormones like epinephrine (adrenaline) and norepinephrine that increase breathing, heart rate and blood pressure for improved circulation to better supply oxygen and glucose as needed; glucagon and glucocorticoids to liberate energy stores for immediate use; and endorphins and enkephalins to diminish the sensation of pain.[29]

That energy and ability can be transformed into destructive or constructive forms depending on our decisions and behavior in its presence. The US Air Force conjures the image of "hugging the monster" in its pararescue school to convey the importance of embracing fear rather than running from it, to capture and harness its power. It's a mistake to pretend fear isn't present, or worse, that its current source doesn't exist. While we can attenuate the negative effects of fear and anxiety through action, we can magnify the efficacy of that action if we're able to channel the inherent power of fear by accepting it and welcoming it.

The exact nature of true adversity is typically impossible to predict before the experience—this inability to prepare for the unknown is a primary contributor to fear and the difficulty of the experience. Compounding the problem, our response to a given challenge is difficult if not impossible to accurately predict, and our responses can vary dramatically depending on the nature, severity and duration of the experience. Further, we may even respond differently to similar situations at different times.[30] This variation can have several possible causes, such as our present level of fatigue or our unrelated emotional state preceding the event in question. We can of course reduce that variability through attempting to maintain consistency in our condition through taking care of ourselves physically to avoid unnecessary exhaustion, and through moderation of our reactions and emotions generally through our rational mind. In any case, we shouldn't make the mistake of expecting and relying on identical natural responses to all adverse situations.

If we're experienced and comfortable in the mountains, but have an extreme fear of the ocean, we're going to naturally react to being stranded overnight in the mountains with inadequate equipment much differently than being stranded overnight in a raft in the middle of the ocean, and the differences in our psychological and physiological responses have the power to influence the decisions we make, which will impact the outcome. Maybe we can gut through twenty-four hours of just about any type of intense mental or physical suffering, but what happens when that suffering or hardship stretches into months? Years? A lifetime? Do we have the physical and mental fortitude to continue fighting, and the necessary tools to cope with the effects?

While we may be unable to perfectly predict our natural response to a given unfamiliar situation, we can dramatically improve the predictability and consistency of our responses universally with training and experience. In athletic training, we can prepare the body to be capable of the entire range of fundamental physical qualities, and those qualities can then be applied in any possible combination and format even if we've never previously experienced that exact demand, just as we can learn letters and phonemes and be capable of reading or pronouncing words we've never seen before, or by learning individual words, be capable of understanding or constructing complex sentences we've never encountered previously.

In other words, the intention is to collect the tools and practice their use, temper the metaphorical hands (and the literal body) through that work, construct universally applicable strategies for solving problems through extensive and varied experience, develop a mindset unperturbed by adversity, and the confidence to stand against it. The elements of true toughness are interdependent—our capacity is predicated on our capability, character and commitment, and built through both intentional and inadvertent experience along with well-designed training. The process as a result is both systematic and organic, and the elements naturally combine and compound.

TRAINING & PREPARATION

If experiencing adversity isn't inherently beneficial to us, it follows that developing capacity requires more than simply intentionally exposing ourselves to it. It's not difficult to be uncomfortable and unhappy—we can dive into an alpine lake in the middle of January, pick a fight with someone we're confident will obliterate us, or not eat for a week. The possibilities are limited only by our imagination. But without a clear purpose and carefully considered goals, adversity is largely just an unpleasant experience, that like all reasonable people, we won't feel any particular interest in repeating. Our preparatory experiences need to be meaningful and thoughtful training exercises, not senseless torture and misery. Flailing around searching for arbitrary challenges or hardship isn't a way to develop toughness—it's simply mindless self-abuse, or worse, a desperate plea for attention and recognition.

Capacity training will assume many forms, and not all of them will involve the kind of challenges the bulk of the following discussion evokes. Many will be minor daily tasks or even strictly mental processes—we'll get to those details later.

We have two fundamental goals with capacity training. The first is to improve our physiological response to stress, both by reducing the severity of the natural reactions, and by developing conscious control of the processes to the greatest extent possible. The purpose is straightforward: to prevent deleterious effects of an excessive stress response by our sympathetic nervous system. In this way, even during exposure to extreme stress we're able to maintain a reasonable heart rate and breathing rhythm, optimal auditory and visual acuity, normal manual dexterity, maximal motor skill and physical abilities like strength and power, and full cognitive access. In other words, we're working to avoid becoming trembling, weak-kneed, hyperventilating, tunnel-visioned, partially deaf, witless, swooning messes in the face of extreme adversity.

The second fundamental goal is to preserve complete access to our higher order cognitive functions, which involves the ability to subdue the influence of emotion on the thought process. Higher order thinking includes processes like the objective evaluation of circumstances, rational decision-making, organization, creativity, adaptability and resourcefulness—in short, it's the cognitive abilities that allow us to respond appropriately and effectively to unfamiliar and stressful situations. Maintaining these faculties is impossible in the presence of the mental and physiological effects of extreme fear and anxiety.

The ultimate objective mentally is, rather than panicking and blowing the situation out of proportion until it's completely overwhelming, to be capable of reframing any adverse circumstances as a practical problem that can be solved with rational thought and attendant action—and beyond this, a problem that we *want* to solve, and the resolution of which will not merely help us survive, but will provide gratification and allow us to appreciate the experience. This is the source of opportunity in adversity.

ARTIFICIAL ADVERSITY

Because a considerable amount of the difficulty of an adverse experience is a direct result of the unpredictability of its timing, duration, nature and composition, it should be apparent that we can't artificially create true adversity for ourselves. Any situation we create by choice is largely predictable and under our control to at least some degree—we know when and where it happens, what we do and don't have access to, how prepared we are mentally and physically, and exactly what the risks are. More importantly, we're far more likely to have a way to relatively quickly and safely exit the situation with a simple decision to do so.

This is not to say that such situations aren't valuable training exercises—they absolutely can be, and they of course will have to be if we want to proactively prepare (otherwise we're simply left to wait hopefully for a tough situation to arise). What it means is that we have to be very aware of the way we construct these exercises to ensure maximal utility, and be cautious of becoming overly confident in our progress if poorly designed preparation is giving us a false sense of challenge and accomplishment because of its predictability and our control over it.

The most obvious workaround is to engage in exercises designed and administered by others. In this way, we still choose when we participate and have at least some ability to prepare mentally and physically, but we don't know the exact nature of what's coming, and we're not in complete control of the process. Additionally, we're far more likely to feel obligated to continue and motivated to perform when in someone else's exercise, and a decision to quit or modify the situation to reduce its difficulty is going to carry more severe consequences—we no longer have only to contend with our own feelings of disappointment or frustration, but now also embarrassment and guilt. In this way, we remove the ease of bailing out on a whim and enforce greater commitment to the process.

Military training is replete with exercises that both test and train the abilities of candidates, especially when it comes to Special Forces units. Former member of US Army 7th Special Forces Group and founder of the Tactical Games, Tim Burke, shared a story of his time as an instructor of Green Beret candidates that perfectly illustrates the value of not having control over your own preparation. In a final exercise, candidates had to complete an extremely difficult ruck (carrying a heavy pack and gear on foot) over unknown terrain for an unknown long distance. Failure to complete the ruck meant disqualification from the selection program. Burke, during his supervisory patrolling of the course, encountered one candidate with his pack off, sitting back against a tree, who swore he was unable to continue, even when, against protocol, Burke provided the slightest bit of encouragement. Finally, refusing to continue, the candidate threw his pack and himself into the back of Burke's truck and took an extremely brief ride to the end of the course—which turned out to be a mere few hundred yards away.

Had this candidate been familiar with the course ahead of time, he would have known, as Burke did, how close he was to the end, and seeing how spryly he managed to pick up his heavy pack and jump into the truck, would have been able to gut through to the finish. Instead, because of his complete unfamiliarity with the course and his lack of control over the exercise, his decisions and actions were based entirely on his abilities and mindset as they would be in an authentic adverse situation. In his case, it meant failure in the selection process, but for our purposes, this means not just effective training, but an incredibly valuable opportunity for evaluation of our condition, which then allows the reconsideration and adjustment of our preparation strategies.

Few of us have access to this kind of training and these kinds of instructors, but this is the type of scenario we want to mimic whenever possible in our higher-level exercises. In addition to the obvious benefits already outlined, there are some potential neurobiological benefits from this kind of experience that may not be possible to stimulate in other intentionally created situations. Psychologist Steve Maier believes—while emphasizing that more research needs to be done to understand the process—that the connection of the conscious mind and the limbic system (parts of the brain that control physiological responses related to emotion) can, through certain experiences, be wired together in a way that allows us to manage adversity more effectively through better regulation of physical reactions and a mindset that recognizes our ability to influence our situation. His research was specifically about these effects in adolescence persisting into adulthood, so there may be a question of whether or not the same level of neuroplasticity exists in adults to allow these same effects to occur to the same extent. In any case, Maier makes the point that in order for these changes to take place in the brain, the experience must be "something pretty potent", not just "minor inconveniences."[31] Research has also demonstrated that we retain information (at least as measured by 24-hour recall) learned while under stress better than when in the absence of stress[32], and better remember more "emotionally arousing" experiences.[33] In other words, lessons we learn during higher-intensity experiences tend to better cement themselves in our memory.

The goal for at least some of our training, then, needs to be to create high enough levels of intensity to allow for these additional potential benefits of neurobiological adaptation and memory. This means minimizing our control over a reasonable portion of our training exercises to maximize the unpredictability and therefore the "potency" of the adverse experience.

If we don't conveniently have Special Forces instructors available to create and conduct training exercises for us, how do we manage this? The simplest and most universally accessible method is through organized competition— generally as individuals rather than in teams, but not necessarily exclusively depending on our circumstances. We can find ways to compete, under someone else's control, in a multitude of disciplines, not just traditional sports. If we want to primarily train and test physical ability related situations, we can participate in athletic competitions like weightlifting, powerlifting, track and field events, triathlons or marathons (all of which have age categories for masters athletes to compete against older athletes of similar age); if we want to focus on more mixed-modal situations, we can compete in obstacle course racing, adventure racing, or something like the Tactical Games; if we want to work on more skill-specific situations, we can compete in things like orienteering, climbing or shooting; and if we want to focus on profession-specific competition, there are options like the Firefighter Combat Challenge, and various tactical police and SWAT competitions.

Competition provides two critical elements of effective preparation that we can't generally produce outside of it: it removes much of our control over the situation, creating at least a degree of the unpredictability we need for more intense experiences, and it adds greater pressure to perform and more severe consequences for failure, which diminish our willingness to quit on a whim and create more authentic conditions for us to work on optimally functioning mentally and physically under stress.

None of this of course is to imply that preparation outside of competition is without value—when properly constructed and executed, it's immensely valuable, and fortunately so because it will for practical reasons have to account for the majority of our training.

FAILURE

If we're creating adversity for ourselves as a method of preparing for the real thing, and our intent is to ensure that at least some of that training is at a very high intensity level, inevitably we are at some point going to fail in our intended tasks. This is a critical piece of the puzzle to contend with, as failure presents a number of psychological possibilities that we can't allow to proceed unmanaged. (Note that this discussion of failure is specific to capacity training—how we need to consider it varies somewhat it other contexts. We'll discuss failure further in the Commitment chapter of the book.)

Our primary goal with regard to failure in our capacity training is to prevent it—most of the time. This may seem to be an obvious point, as by nature we tend to avoid failure, but this kind of preparation offers far more opportunities for it than standard daily life, and its general avoidance for our purposes is more imperative—it's an issue of efficacy and long-term psychological development, not just disappointment or embarrassment. If one of the overarching objectives of our training is to develop confidence in our abilities that translates into more successful decision-making and performance, the most obvious concern is that continual failure in our preparation is counterproductive—it teaches us we aren't actually capable of what we intend to be, which means doubt, ambivalence and hesitation in real situations that demand decisiveness.

Martin Seligman's learned helplessness research is also important to keep in mind when considering failure. If we set ourselves up to repeatedly fail, the very simple and clear conclusion is that we don't have control over the outcomes of various situations, and by extension, of ourselves and our lives. We have to at least *believe* we have control—that's impossible without self-delusion if we accumulate a considerable number of failures, or if our failures are more dramatic, consequential and memorable than our successes, which they tend to be by nature. The earlier we are in our development, the more critical it is for us to establish and reinforce confidence in our abilities and control over our circumstances. If we build a strong foundation, we'll be able to endure more and greater unavoidable failure later—if we start out overwhelmed by failures, it's likely we'll never set that foundation and be capable of reaching an unbeatable level of resilience.

The general avoidance of failure in training shouldn't be achieved through arbitrary and excessive reduction in the difficulty of the challenges we create for ourselves—swinging the pendulum to this other extreme is equally, if not more, dangerous. The proper method of minimizing failure is the intelligent design of our preparation that correctly aligns the nature and intensity of the exercises with our present abilities. This is no different from the most fundamental physical training concepts—if your best back squat is 150kg, your training program shouldn't prescribe 200kg for the back squat. If you have no experience in placing protection, attempting to lead a climb of El Cap is not an intelligently designed challenge. If the farthest you're able to run is 400 meters, registering for a marathon next week is ill-advised. Your first camping experience shouldn't be a two-week solo backpacking trip through the Alaskan tundra. In other words, we avoid failure not by avoiding truly challenging experiences, but by ensuring the challenges are appropriate for our present level of development—and if properly designed, those challenges will increase in difficulty commensurate to our level of development over time to continue forcing us to extend that level.

This doesn't mean that we should expect to never fail in anything we attempt. We will fail at some point because we're bound to make mistakes, both in the performance and design of these tasks, and because we're naturally creating the risk of failure through challenge. But failure should be relatively infrequent, and overwhelmingly the result of pushing our boundaries and extending ourselves to stretch into the next level of development—not the result of making stupid decisions that put us in positions that all but guarantee failure.

Confucius said, "Our greatest glory is not in never failing, but in rising every time we fail." This can be easily misinterpreted or misrepresented to suggest failure is beneficial if that's the belief we're looking to support, as some have been known to. But in reality this piece of ancient wisdom isn't encouraging failure at all—it's encouraging the mental fortitude to not give up in the face of the inevitable.

Knowing with certainty that we will fail, it's critical we possess a mindset capable of dealing with failure constructively. In any failure, just like in any adverse experience, there's opportunity for learning, developing new capabilities or improving existing ones, and fortifying ourselves to better cope with future challenges. It's a chance for objective evaluation of our methods and strategies in handling specific circumstances and challenges in general, and to subsequently determine how to increase their efficacy and where to focus our future time and efforts. If we're able to use periodic failure productively in this way to accomplish the overall goal of the process—increasing capacity and capability, further developing our character, and cementing our commitment—then in a sense, it's unfair to consider it failure, at least in absolute terms. But let's not get in the habit of making all of our exercises impossible to accomplish successfully for the sake of education...

SPECIFIC TRAINING & UNIVERSAL STRESS INOCULATION

The potential variation and unpredictability of adversity makes entirely specific preparation essentially impossible—if we don't know exactly what we'll encounter in the future, we can't create training exercises to perfectly simulate and prepare for it, and the number of possibilities would create an infinitely long list even if we did. We can create probable scenarios based on history or recreate historical scenarios if we're working in a specific field— such as law enforcement or military conducting an exercise that mimics an actual engagement with a criminal or enemy to better prepare for the likely encounter of the same situation in the future, or a pilot in a flight simulator responding to certain types of equipment failures or weather events that are known to be the most likely to occur—but the broader our focus is, the more impossible that becomes.

Specific experience and training will always be superior for preparing to handle the exact same situation in the future—beyond training, it becomes an actual rehearsal. This in fact is common practice for military and law enforcement—rehearsing an operation prior to beginning—because it's so effective. Fortunately, an inability to train completely specifically for every possible contingency by no means leaves us helpless or unable to prepare extremely well.

In any given situation, we can organize our response into three primary categories—the actual actions we take, the physiological response to stress, and the cognitive activity that develops, determines and dictates our actions based on the demands of the circumstances. The first includes physical skills and qualities—the larger portion of our capability—the next includes how our bodies react physically—things like breathing, heart rate, tension and visual and auditory acuity—and the last includes everything else, from our intelligence and knowledge, to our mindset and attitude, to our ingenuity and resourcefulness.

Specific training provides us with the ability to learn and apply completely specific physical skills—for example, building temporary shelter with the exact materials, terrain and weather conditions in a certain location at a certain time of year—and the completely specific knowledge that applies to that exact scenario—for example, how rainwater drains off of that exact shelter and over that exact topography with the wind moving in that exact direction and speed. Having had that experience, we'd be extremely well-prepared and confident if we ever happened to repeat it—we could simply replicate our decisions and actions from the first time we managed it successfully. Being able to engage in this kind of training for every single contingency would be extremely convenient, but of course it's not remotely possible.

Specific skills and knowledge are all based on underlying principles—fundamental and universal information and ideas. We can create an effective shelter in that specific situation without ever having experienced it previously because we know how various structures withstand the elements, how to determine the direction of prevailing winds, how water behaves, and what's necessary to keep us dry and well-enough insulated. Similarly, specific physical skills are based on general physical qualities—we don't need to have practiced specific physical actions to figure out how to do them (if we did, we'd be incapable of any physical action at all) and we can combine basic motions to create more complex ones.

If we truly understand the principles and become capable of the fundamentals, we can manage any specifics, familiar or not. This is the difference between being a master and a technician. Technicians don't understand the principles in their entirety—they simply follow algorithms created by someone who does. In other words, they rely on step-by-step procedures and if/else logic: I do this, then this, then this; if this happens, I do that, but if instead that happens, I do this. Their dependence on procedure leaves them largely helpless if a scenario diverges from the possibilities the established procedure covers—and if we know adverse situations are unpredictable, one thing we *can* predict is that they won't follow a limited set of predetermined courses that would allow for the successful preparation and reliable application of rigid algorithms.

Masters, on the other hand, have genuine understanding of the principles from which the technician's algorithms are derived. They know what the ultimate objective is, why each action is taken in response to each event, and what effects that action will have on future events. This means that a master can respond effectively to essentially any novel situation because they can determine appropriate actions to produce the desired outcome, and continually adjust as necessary to unexpected changes as the process proceeds.

It should be obvious, then, that our goal is seeking the mastery of principles over the simple rehearsal of algorithmic training. This doesn't mean that quality algorithms should be discarded by the master—they can and should be used to minimize cognitive load when possible, but we have to always remain aware of their limitations and be immediately ready to abandon them when the need arises. To that mastery of the fundamental, we can add layers of specificity determined by the probability of our needs as a result of our profession, lifestyle and locality.

In addition to skills, knowledge and physical abilities, we need to consider our mental and physiological responses to stress—if these are poorly developed, they can easily prevent or diminish the implementation of any of our skills and abilities. If we're a trembling, hyperventilating, tachycardic mess because of an excessive stress response in a high-pressure situation, it doesn't matter if we know how to tie a thousand different knots—in the moment we need that skill and knowledge, we don't have the manual dexterity to tie a knot properly or even the presence of mind to determine which knot from our repertoire is the best choice for that application.

Fortunately, there's both research and practical experience that suggests stress inoculation has a degree of universal application and transfer rather than being confined exclusively to the specific circumstances in which it's originally trained[34]. We can train ourselves to respond more effectively mentally and physiologically to stress in a general way rather than needing it to be entirely case-specific. Without a doubt, incident-specific training will produce superior results in this respect just like it will with regard to skills, but again, because specific training has considerable limitations, we need to rely primarily on our ability to train our general stress response and apply it to novel situations.

We can revisit Steve Maier's research in this context as well, which suggests that learning that we have control over a "potent" adverse situation wires our brain together in a way that establishes a continued ability to cope with unrelated adversity in the future. The bottom line is that we can very effectively improve our stress response by engaging in purposefully stressful experiences and learning how to cope effectively with them in multiple respects (skill, physiology, psychology) through the greatest method of improvement ever created—plain old practice.

Stress inoculation is perhaps not the best term to describe this training despite its ubiquity, as inoculation refers to disease-specific measures—a measles vaccine won't be effective against polio, for example. It makes more sense to think of it like an immune system involving general mechanisms that can be strengthened with the proper materials and practices, and antibodies that can be developed through exposure to specific elements, that operate in concert to keep us functioning at maximal capacity. We strengthen the system's universal operation through general training, we aggregate specific resistances as we accumulate specific experiences, and we supplement with vaccinations for predictable conditions. In addition to the stress response element, we of course can train conscious psychological coping skills and rational problem solving in a universal manner like we learn to use any tool. If we know how to use a hammer, we can pound in a nail in any unfamiliar situation—as long as we're aware, composed and rational.

In short, the intent is to develop a mastery of principles and fundamentals, engage in general training to strengthen our stress-coping system overall, and create specific training when possible to address the most likely scenarios and needs of our profession, lifestyle and locality. Being tough isn't the spontaneous, magical condition of being imperturbable—it's the possession of and confidence in—through purposeful training and practice—the knowledge and capability necessary to productively deal with any situation we encounter.

METHODS & PRINCIPLES

Capacity is our ability to withstand and thrive through adversity. But this is not passive as it may appear with that description—it's not the act of simply huddling quietly and hopefully waiting for the hard time to pass over us like we're riding out a storm down in the cellar. Succeeding through hardship and challenges means *doing*—it demands some kind of action, determined by the nature and severity of the situation. In other words, it requires we apply our capability to achieve some objective, even if that objective is as basic as staying alive.

This being the case, improving our capacity largely involves the training and practice of various skills—physical and mental—in an extensive spectrum of situations. These situations need to range from the simple and quotidian—that is, consciously and actively practicing our mental and physiological strategies when dealing with all the minor inconveniences and difficulties occurring naturally in our daily life—to the most extreme challenges that we create for ourselves. There are a lot of moving parts, and the overall picture is going to be different for all of us based on our background, experience and requirements. Part of our ongoing task is to use our knowledge of the fundamentals and principles to continually evaluate our needs and devise and revise our training to meet them.

The following are the primary objectives to keep in mind for capacity training practices and exercises:

- Practice with our tools daily in even the simplest, most minor situations to accumulate a high volume of repetition and establish good habits.
- Design exercises of the type and intensity appropriate for our present level of development.
- Prioritize training that aligns with the demands of our profession, lifestyle and locality.
- Increase the difficulty and variation of challenges incrementally over time to push our development.

- Ensure overwhelming success—without unnecessary reduction of difficulty—to reinforce our sense of control and confidence.
- Avoid failure due to poor exercise design; expect and accept occasional failure due to pushing boundaries.
- Respond productively to failure by using the information to contribute to advancing the overall task and goal rather than to draw negative conclusions about ourselves and our abilities.
- Maximize potency of periodic exercises by reducing predictability and control.
- Emphasize learning fundamentals and principles and how to apply them to specifics.
- Improve universal qualities with more general situations, and improve specific qualities with exercises related to the demands of our profession, lifestyle and locality.
- Develop unconscious competence of capabilities and demonstrate it under stress.

RELATIVITY

A critical point to bear in mind at this stage is that challenges and adversity are largely relative. What may be a significant challenge for one of us is a daily occurrence that doesn't even require attention for another. In our endeavor to improve capacity, we need to begin at our own starting point, regardless of how that compares to anyone else's—all that matters is our progress relative to our own present condition. For some of us, controlling severe anxiety well enough to simply get to the grocery store may be a demanding task; for another, a significant challenge may be attaining a single pull-up; and for another, it may be summiting an 8,000 meter peak (Interestingly, those three challenges might be legitimate for the same individual because the nature of the demands are completely different and one doesn't directly influence another). Others' present abilities should never be used to diminish our own hard work and commitment, and just as importantly, shouldn't unduly influence the design of our own capacity training beyond providing inspiration.

PROGRESSIVE OVERLOAD

The concept of progressive overload is a tenet of strength training—by introducing the body to incrementally increasing demand, we develop increasing ability in response. In the most basic terms, if we lift slightly more weight each time we train, we get slightly stronger as the body adapts to be capable of handling not just that exact level of resistance, but adds a margin on top as it recovers from the stimulus. Beyond the beginner stage, designing and timing stimulus gets considerably more complex, but that underlying principle never changes. However, if we exceed the body's ability to adapt by applying excessive levels of stimulus, e.g. trying to lift too much weight too soon, we not only don't progress, we actually regress.

This same principle can be applied to capacity training. Rather than the resistance of weights being lifted, our stimulus is an exercise or task that challenges our abilities. If the type of task and the degree of difficulty is appropriate, we'll adapt by becoming more competent and confident, and over time, we continually ratchet up that stimulus to drive progress. If we try to accelerate the process beyond our ability to adapt by engaging in exercises far beyond our present capability and capacity, we may learn a thing or two (the hardest possible way), but overall the experience is likely to set us back through the negative effects of failure, such as a reduction in confidence and the chipping away of our mental fortitude, not to mention the potential for physical consequences like injury. In short, we need to properly progress the intensity of our exercises to maximize the benefit.

One of the ways we moderate this "loading" is the level of control and intensity of the environment or circumstances. With any capability, we need to initially learn and train it in isolation and a controlled environment—in other words, we work on that skill on its own and in relative safety to graduate from conscious competence to unconscious competence. As we're reaching unconscious competence, we need to begin training and testing that capability in more demanding environments and in combination with other skills—that is, we need to learn to do it, and ensure we can, under stress of increasing levels of intensity, and while also having to simultaneously manage other concerns.

A simple example is capability with knots. We first sit in the comfort and safety of our living room learning and practicing tying an array of knots. Once we reach a reasonable level of competence—not necessarily complete unconscious competence, but approaching it—we then take that capability to a more demanding environment. Maybe this means rock climbing, or creating shelter for a night of minimal equipment camping. We then might progress to training rope rescue scenarios with artificial time limits or in poor weather conditions to increase the difficulty and level of distraction. Our ultimate capability with knots might be expressed during an over-the-edge rescue, in which we need to establish an anchor at the top of a cliff, secure an injured patient in a litter at the bottom, connect ourselves to a line along with that litter, and accompany the patient back to the top of the cliff, all while under the pressure and time constraints imposed by that patient's life-threatening medical condition. If our training is effective, we'll accomplish such a task without ever having to slow down and consciously work our way through deciding what knots to use and how to tie them.

ACCOMMODATION

A related principle is the idea of accommodation. The body adapts to novel stimulus—a heavier weight than we've lifted before is the simplest example of novelty. If instead of increasing the weight we're lifting over time we simply lift the same weight indefinitely, the body becomes accommodated to that stimulus and no longer responds in any way. Similarly, if we repeat only the exact same exercises in the same way with the same number of repetitions and sets, there's no new stimulus to compel the body to adapt. This means that we have to periodically introduce different training exercises or methods to avoid accommodation and continue pushing progress.

In the same way, if we have no variety in our capacity training, we become stale and progress slows. There's a practical limit to the intensity of training exercises. We can't launch ourselves into space to practice knot-tying in a zero-gravity, zero-atmosphere environment with a rapidly dwindling oxygen supply, for example—and if we could, what would be the next step? But what we can nearly always do is introduce novel situations with unfamiliar distractions, demands and constraints in which to practice and train the same skills.

This is largely the realm of the unconscious competence level—a large volume of simple repetition during the conscious competence stage is in fact the best method. Sitting on our couch and tying an alpine butterfly knot over and over every day for a month is going to cement that skill extremely well and help move it to the level of unconscious competence. As we're reaching that stage, and once we've achieved it, variation becomes imperative to continue driving progress.

The benefits of continual exposure to new experiences and situations extends well beyond the competence of physical skills. The unfamiliar is intimidating and frightening and forces us to implement our various mental strategies and stress-reduction tricks in new ways, and the accumulating experience fortifies our confidence and leaves us entering each novel experience more prepared, which means more composed and more successful. Additionally, training given skills or tasks in varying situations is an effective way of learning or better understanding the underlying principles through the recognition of the connections between different experiences. This means not just the improvement of the skills being implemented in those situations, but new insight into how to improve other existing skills subsequently, and how to better manage the mental and physiological elements that influence our performance.

STRESS INOCULATION/EXPOSURE TRAINING

In the 1980s, Donald Meichenbaum formally developed a cognitive therapy protocol he called Stress Inoculation Training.[35] The principles were adopted and the procedure slightly modified, then often referred to as Stress Exposure Training (SET), by organizations looking for ways to improve performance under stress, such as the military. The process is comprised of three stages:

The first is to learn and understand the various physiological effects of acute stress and how they influence our thinking, behavior and performance in order to prepare to experience them without surprise or panic (rapid heart rate and breathing, trembling, tunnel vision, auditory exclusion, reduced fine motor control, etc.).

The second is to learn and practice the implementation of tools to mitigate those stress responses to keep them under the threshold of performance and cognition disruption (rational thinking to combat emotion, breathing and relaxation techniques, etc.). This stage also includes learning and practicing the skills and tasks we expect to need in stressful circumstances (specific to our profession, lifestyle and locality)—this is where we're largely aiming to achieve unconscious competence in our skill sets.

The final stage is the implementation of these tools and skills in training exercises that introduce progressively greater levels of stress and difficulty. This application stage is not just practice, but also an opportunity for evaluation of our present abilities to determine our needed points of focus in future exercises, or possibly a need to invest more time in the second stage for certain skills or tools.

To beat our knot-tying example to death, in the first stage we would learn that under stress, we'll be tense, breathing rapidly, have an elevated heart rate, experience reduced manual dexterity, and have trouble focusing clearly on our task and environment; we may also be overwhelmed by a feeling of fear and consumed by thoughts of self-doubt. In the second stage, we'd learn cognitive and physiological tactics to reduce those effects, and we'd learn and practice in a controlled environment the various knots we expect to be using. In the third stage, we'd conduct exercises that induce appropriate and increasing levels of stress to allow us to employ our physiological and cognitive control tools in order to successfully tie knots in high-pressure situations.

This process is not strictly linear—we'll cycle between stages two and three repeatedly as we're developing new skills, or to refine existing ones we discover are not yet adequately mastered—it's fairly easy to overestimate our level of competence in the absence of genuine stress, so it may require initial stage three exercises to get a more accurate assessment of newer skills. Likewise, we may discover we need more education or practice with the cognitive and physiological tools outside of the full-stress environment.

This basic structure should guide our capacity training exercise design. The first stage has largely been accomplished if you've read to this point. The specific skills of the second stage will be determined by your own requirements; physiological and cognitive control tools are discussed below. The final stage has been discussed throughout this chapter.

EXPOSURE THERAPY

Exposure therapy is a psychological practice used to help reduce fear and anxiety that can take a number of forms. In essence, the process is used to prevent the inevitable magnification of fear that occurs with complete avoidance of its source, and to diminish that fear through repeated and progressively more intense exposure to the source of that fear while in (at least initially) a controlled environment.[36] While this is typically a formal therapeutic procedure for severe anxiety, phobias or PTSD, the principles can be easily applied to our self-directed capacity training. Simply, we identify the types of situations that create the greatest fear for us, and create exercises to expose ourselves to them with incrementally increasing levels of severity and duration.

There are two imperatives here: First, the dosage needs to be appropriate at any given time. This is our progressive overload principle. If we exceed a reasonable dose, i.e. too much too soon, it's possible for us to actually regress—to have the existing fear reinforced rather than reduced. For example, if we're afraid of heights and we decide our first exposure exercise is going to be rappelling from a hundred-foot cliff when we've never before practiced the skill in more controlled, less extreme circumstances, and as a consequence of our inexperience, we free fall the final twenty feet to a painful landing, what did we accomplish? We learned that we were absolutely right to be terrified of heights because they're dangerous. We took a fear that was likely based originally on nothing but our imagination and bolstered it with legitimate evidence.

Second, we need to implement coping tools during these exercises. This isn't meant to be simply curling into the fetal position and allowing ourselves to be battered by our fears until the experience mercifully stops once it's run its natural course. It's an opportunity to experience a dose of fear and then practice combating it and controlling it with cognitive tactics and intentional actions that diminish the physiological components of fear. In other words, the goal isn't to simply force ourselves to endure fear and hope our survival of the experience dismantles the power that fear has over us, but to train our ability to mitigate its effects and develop an awareness of our control over ourselves and our circumstances.

TOOLS & TACTICS

While the exact nature and extremity of capacity exercises will vary for all of us based on our individual needs, there are tools and tactics that can be applied across the board. The same tricks that will help us get through the most extreme challenges will also help us maintain composure and control when dealing with even the lowest-grade problems we encounter day to day. The practice of these tools daily with the minor inconveniences, frustrations or problems we inevitably encounter is the only way to accumulate the volume of practice necessary to be adept at their use in more extreme adversity—this is essentially our stress inoculation training stage two classroom.

CONTROLLED BREATHING

The most effective tool for maintaining or regaining composure and focus, mitigating the problematic physiological responses to stress, and preserving the function of our higher order cognition[37] is also conveniently extremely simple and requires virtually no skill—controlled breathing. Intentionally rhythmic, deep, slow breathing has powerful physiological effects through the stimulation of the parasympathetic nervous system to counteract an excessive sympathetic stress response. Additionally, it provides a natural distraction from the source of stress or panic by creating a new and continuous point of focus.

There's a multitude of specific breathing prescriptions and names—tactical breathing, box breathing, square breathing, 2-1 breathing, 4-7-8 breathing, equal breathing, etc.—but the critical elements are universal. First is the depth of breath. We typically breathe shallowly into our chests. With any breathing technique, we need to ensure full diaphragmatic breaths to maximally fill the lungs. This means relaxing the abdomen to allow it to expand and create space for the diaphragm to contract and push downward, and longer inspirations—there's a limit to the rate at which we can get air into the lungs, so we need to extend the time we're inhaling to allow the full volume.

Next is the control of our expiration—extending the time we take to exhale rather than pushing the air out as immediately as possible, and ensuring maximal emptying of the lungs rather than inadvertently returning to shallow breathing by keeping the lungs partially filled.

Most breathing techniques also involve breath-holding after both inspiration and expiration. This further reinforces the completeness of our breaths, and breath-holding itself reduces heart rate and blood pressure.

Finally, effective breathing techniques involve a deliberate count to maintain the prescribed breathing rhythm. The act of counting itself creates a synergistic effect along with the physiological influence of breath control by creating a point of focus aside from the source of stress and has a calming effect on the conscious mind in the same way a mantra does during meditation.

A reliable and simple prescription to start using is what Mark Divine named Box Breathing—a four-second inhalation, four-second hold, four-second exhalation, and four-second hold.[38] This is also referred to as square breathing or tactical breathing. Note that the time isn't magical—we can know this confidently because our ability to count perfect seconds is poor and inevitably varies at different times, and the technique still remains effective.

It's important to keep in mind that many of the adverse situations in which we'll most need to employ breath control are going to involve physical exertion, possibly to extreme levels. Even if we had the innate timing of a metronome, the gas exchange demands of a physically active body are going to supersede our voluntary breath control to an extent commensurate to the level of exertion and our relative fitness. If we're engaged in a fight, straining to climb a difficult pitch on the side of a mountain at high altitude, or running away from a threat, there will be a limit to how close we can get to a perfect breathing tempo. Understanding that this is expected and natural and that our efforts to get as close as possible in the given circumstances are still going to be effective will prevent further panic or stress arising from being incapable of breathing perfectly. In the most extreme cases, aim to simply inhale as deeply and slow your exhalations as much as possible.

This breath control technique should be practiced daily, both as a way to combat acute stressors in the moment, and as a standalone exercise to both become more comfortable with it and to benefit from its general calming and focusing effects. Create a habit of performing at least 5-10 sets of box breathing each morning and evening—if you can stretch it out to 5-10 minutes, even better. This is a perfect habit to couple with your journaling routine—perform your breathing immediately before beginning your journaling. This will help put you into a better mindset for effective thinking and writing, and is a simple way to reinforce a new good habit.

When practicing or performing before journaling or any planned intellectual work, close your eyes; in a capacity training exercise or true adverse situation, keep your eyes open as needed to remain adequately aware of your environment. Simply:

- Relax your abdomen and inhale for a count of four, feeling your abdomen and chest expand.
- Pause for a count of four—not by closing your epiglottis to lock your air in, but by actively maintaining the expansion of the abdomen and chest.

- Exhale under control for a count of four, intentionally relaxing your face, shoulders and hands as you do.
- Pause for a count of four by completely relaxing the chest and abdomen in their collapsed state.
- Repeat, focusing on the sensations of breathing and on the numbers you're counting.

Box Breathing can be easily combined with our meditation protocol to amplify the effectiveness of both. Rather than actually counting one through four, perform the breath count by repeating your mantra four times for each phase—four is a small enough number to easily keep track of without relying on the explicit number sequence. This allows us to simultaneously maintain the ideal breathing rhythm and de-excite and focus the mind.

PHYSICAL RELAXATION

When experiencing stress—either extreme and acute or low-grade and chronic—we become tense. This tension bridges the physical, mental and emotional, but the physical is the simplest to feel and understand, and the easiest to manipulate directly. Because these three elements are interdependent, controlling one influences the others—by intentionally reducing physical tension, we can reduce mental and emotional tension.

Simply take a few moments to intentionally relax the typical locations of physical tension—the face, the shoulders and the hands. Unfurrow the brow and stop squinting, let the jaw hang loosely, allow the shoulders to drop and let the hands open—even spread the fingers or shake them out. Combining the relaxation of each area with extended exhalation is even more effective.

Like our breathing exercise, this can be done very quickly in the midst of an adverse situation in which we find this tension accumulating and restricting our rational thinking and the fluidity of our actions, and it can be done regularly as a way to both practice the technique and maintain appropriately low levels of tension in the absence of acute stressors.

FACIAL EXPRESSIONS & HUMOR

We can influence our mental and emotional states with voluntary physical actions like breath control and the relaxation of tense muscles, but physical influence actually extends even further. An increasing volume of research is demonstrating that our facial expressions can influence our mood, not just the other way around—we can actually produce the emotions a given facial expression represents by forcing that expression voluntarily.[39]

Our facial expression even has measurable effects on our athletic performance—relative to frowning and no intentional expression, smiling or relaxing the face has been shown to increase running economy and reduce the perception of effort.[40] Another study showed that humor, and in particular the act of laughing, actually diminished pain.[41]

While of course these effects aren't powerful enough to completely eliminate pain or emotions resulting from genuinely intense causes, or suddenly bestow upon us Olympic caliber athletic ability, any reduction in negative emotion or pain and improvement in our physical capability during an adverse experience in which our success demands optimal rational thinking, decision-making, confidence and physical performance is immensely valuable and should be exploited. Combined with breath control and broader physical relaxation, the synergistic effects can be dramatic.

In short, it turns out that "laughing in the face of danger" is actually a legitimately effective tactic, not just a mark of questionable mental stability.

POSITIVE SELF-TALK

Less effective and far less universally accepted than breathing and relaxation techniques, positive self-talk should still occupy a space in our toolbox. As previously discussed, many of the disputes over its effectiveness are arguably the result more of misguided application than the practice itself generally.

As an isolated, unsupported technique in a vacuum, positive self-affirmation does in fact have little to offer. Like with defining character, saying something, whether to ourselves or aloud to anyone else, means little or nothing if it has no supporting behavior attached to it. Positive self-talk needs to be a starting point or a single element of a larger whole, not a self-contained technique.

The primary purpose of positive self-talk here is to regain or prevent the loss of control of our rational mind, our confidence and our commitment to whatever process we're involved in, and a reminder to re-engage in the actions we need to be executing when we've been knocked off track. It's not a standalone, nebulous blob of positivity we're trying to use like a bandage to simply hide a gaping wound rather than actually treating it.

Positive self-talk is largely just a reminder of our objective abilities and a way to stop our minds from spinning out and catastrophizing or obsessing over doubts, or our emotions from dominating our decision-making, while dealing with adversity. In other words, we're not feeding ourselves positivity as self-deception or to try to magically create previously non-existent capabilities in the moment they're needed—we're reminding ourselves what we already know we're capable of, preventing doubt from limiting our performance, and keeping ourselves focused on the necessary tasks. Really it's little more than ensuring our rational mind remains in control rather than being overwhelmed and subdued by our irrational imagination, fears and insecurity.

Self-talk is also an opportunity to define our position and role in a situation. The most negative mental posture we can adopt is that of defense—this is the role of victim, and is reactionary in nature. That is, we view ourselves as having been attacked by a challenge, or saddled with a burden, and then grudgingly respond to its effects as we experience them. Instead, we can formulate our self-talk to position ourselves offensively—to bring the fight to the challenge and always be acting first rather than reacting later. This puts us in control and generates momentum to push through the heaviest obstacles we can be sure are coming.

Keep self-talk straightforward and honest—don't look for elaborate strategies or elegant deliveries. Instead, think of it like coaching yourself through an athletic performance. Use simple, positive cues to maintain focus and forward momentum, and to deny negativity any territory to occupy, by clearly defining simple actions and highlighting pertinent capabilities. Positive, offensive words like *can* and *will* need to take the place of defensive, doubtful words like *try* and *might* or even *should*. *Take five more steps*; *I've worked harder than this in training*; *I can withstand anything I need to…* It doesn't take anything fancy.

VISUALIZATION

Visualization is an extremely effective technique when it comes to performance and confidence, which is why it's used nearly universally by elite athletes of every discipline throughout the world. It's last here not because of a low ranking in efficacy, but because it's more of a tool of preparation than mitigation in the moment like breathing, relaxation, facial expressions and positive self-talk.

Visualization allows the mental rehearsal of performances to establish tactics and confidence. A convenient feature of the human brain is that in essence, it can't distinguish between an actual experience and one we've imagined with adequate authenticity. A simple demonstration of this is that if we visualize a frightening or exciting experience, our heart rate and breathing accelerate—there's clearly no need, and yet the brain initiates the same physiological response that would be appropriate and necessary in the actual scenario. Research has shown remarkable results, such as significant physical strength increases, with nothing more than the visualization of a specific exercise.[42]

This effectively allows us to practice what we're unable to in real life. We can't physically practice making the clutch gold-medal-winning clean & jerk at the Olympics beforehand so we're ready to do it when the chance arises. But we can rehearse it mentally in such detail that our mind experiences it authentically enough to believe we have, so that when the moment actually occurs, we have the confidence and composure of an athlete who's already done it thousands of times.

One limitation of visualization is its need for specificity in more complex scenarios. In order to genuinely rehearse something, we need the details, just like an actor relies on a script when rehearsing a scene. If we're preparing in a general sense for unknown adversity, we're limited in what we can accomplish because the details are impossible to know.

However, we can visualize specific skills separate from a broader context and still benefit. We can rehearse tying those knots of ours to secure a litter; we can rehearse establishing our grip and attaining site focus on a firearm; we can visualize individual boxing strikes or parrying motions—these things will all remain the same in essence regardless of the encompassing details.

We can also visualize imagined scenarios we've determined are common or probable for our profession, lifestyle and locality. These are unlikely to ever be perfectly replicated in real life, but the mental practice still contributes to our capability and confidence, just like accumulated experience from a series of mountain climbing expeditions all contribute meaningfully to capability and confidence for future climbs on completely different terrain and conditions.

In addition to this type of mental rehearsal, we can also use outcome visualization, which eliminates the process and focuses exclusively on the results. This is useful for visualizing the achievement of specific goals, such as winning that Olympic gold medal, to build confidence and create the kind of deep-seated, unwavering expectation of success that underlies true dedication to an objective. While useful, this should be considered only supplementary to rehearsal—visualization of the process is more effective.

In any type of visualization, realism and thoroughness are imperative. The greater the level and breadth of detail, the more convinced the brain is of the experience's authenticity. This means incorporating all five physical senses—what we see, hear, smell, taste and feel during the experience—as well as the critical but typically neglected emotions that we feel. Visualization should be done from our own perspective—that is, what we would actually see in the experience—rather than from an outside perspective—watching ourselves like a spectator. We don't want to watch ourselves clean & jerk from the audience—we want to watch our feet jog up the stairs to the stage, see our hands plunge into the chalk bucket and then grip the bar, and finally see the three white lights from the judges illuminate as we've fixed the bar overhead.

We also need to feel the various emotions that accompany these actions—the emotional element is what truly creates authenticity for the brain. We want to feel the nervous excitement as we approach the bar, the confidence and determination wash over us as we take our final composing deep breaths, and the joy and exhilaration as we successfully complete the lift. We should notice and incorporate the physical responses to our visualization—changes in our heartbeat and breathing, certain muscles contracting, our foreheads prickling with the hint of sweat, and the unique feeling of specific facial tension created by expressions that naturally accompany the emotions we're experiencing in the process.

Like any skill, visualization requires practice, and its effectiveness will improve in step with our experience with it. We can practice visualization daily in two simple ways: First, it's a good practice to incorporate rehearsal or outcome visualization focused on major goals just before going to sleep every night. Second, we can practice process visualization with daily tasks, beginning with brief and simple and progressing over time to longer and more complex—for example, beginning with a single training exercise in the gym and graduating over time to an entire training session or competition process. This ensures we have a well-established ability with the tool when we find ourselves faced with hardship or a challenge that demands all of our resources.

FOCAL POINTS

- Capacity is our ability to withstand and thrive through adversity.

- The experience of adversity alone doesn't inexorably produce benefit—we must choose to act in response to adapt productively from it.

- Being truly tough demands we assume responsibility for ourselves entirely, and we exercise that responsibility through action, even when that action in some cases involves no outward expression.

- Not all experiences offer the same potential for insight and edification—we can't replicate the value of certain experiences with others. Adversity and challenges in particular provide the possibility of lessons that simply can't be learned in comfort and security.

- Being tough means always preparing with the expectation—and the certainty—that adversity will find us eventually.

- Capacity training will assume many forms, from minor daily tasks or even strictly mental processes, to difficult exercises and major challenges.

- Stress inoculation can and needs to be done both generally and specifically to our profession, lifestyle and locality.

- Capacity training is relative—we all need to start at our present condition and work to become better relative to ourselves rather than others.

ACTION

INTROSPECTION

Take some time to look back at your life and write down in your evaluation journal any situations where you've panicked or in any other way found yourself unable to do what was needed or to perform at the level demanded by the situation. This can be anything from a physical challenge, an emergency, not finishing something you started, or even speaking in public.

Identify in each situation what the problem was. Did you not actually possess the ability to do what needed to be done? Did fear prevent you from staying focused and making clear decisions? Were you overwhelmed by emotion and unable to think rationally? Did the pressure of being responsible for others make you doubt your abilities or fortitude? Try to distill each problem into as simple of a description as possible, ideally a single brief phrase. For example: *Realizing others depended on me in an emergency made me question my qualification and the adequacy of my preparation.*

Finally, see if you can identify any common themes that tie all or some of them together. What if anything about these situations or your condition was consistent or similar? Any recurring issues should be prioritized in your work toward improving your capacity—history is telling you that this is either a pervasive problem that applies to many possible circumstances, or that a particular type of situation is something you're likely to experience more frequently than others (for example, circumstances that your profession places you in relatively commonly). This is where you need to prioritize your investment of time and energy.

RELAXATION & CONTROL

At least twice daily—once in the morning immediately before starting on your morning journal, and once in the evening before starting your evaluation journal work—perform at least 5-10 sets of box breathing. If you have the time, you can extend this to 5-10 minutes, or combine it with another meditation or relaxation protocol. Be sure you're including the intentional face, shoulder and hand relaxation during your breathing.

At any point throughout the day when you notice yourself becoming wound too tightly or overreacting to a stressor, immediately employ at least one technique to calm down and reset mentally. Force a smile and hold it until it actually becomes genuine; think of something that reliably makes you laugh, whether it's an old inside joke or a scene from a movie; intentionally relax your brow and eyes (ideally as you smile), let your shoulders sag comfortably, and let your hands open and hang loosely.

REACTIONS

Make it a goal each day to pay close attention to your immediate reactions to adversity of any type or intensity. Do you naturally respond emotionally or blow minor inconveniences out of proportion, wasting time seething and complaining rather than taking action to resolve the problems? Practice catching these kinds of stress-multiplying reactions as quickly as possible and reframing the situation into an objective problem that you now have an opportunity to solve with composed, rational thinking and suitable action. As part of the process, employ the breathing and relaxation techniques above to regain control. Make notes of these in your evaluation journal to assess how well and quickly you're catching yourself and turning things around.

AWARENESS

Set aside some time to practice observation and awareness in a "sit spot"— even once monthly is better than never. Daily, practice stopping what you're doing periodically and observing as much around you as possible, looking *at*, not *for*. Notice, understand, file—don't spend time formulating judgments.

CAPACITY TRAINING

Finally, it's time to plan and execute some capacity training exercises. Remember that your chosen challenges need to be appropriate in nature and intensity for your present condition. Especially right out of the gate, it's important you not overshoot and end up simply beating yourself down and getting discouraged. Don't be easy on yourself, but make sure you're appropriately set up for success—there will more than enough opportunity down the road to get as extreme as you want as you progress through the process.

You may want to keep a separate journal strictly for your capacity work, but you can also combine it with your evaluation journal, which you can be using also for your goal setting and evaluation (more on that in the Commitment chapter). In any case, write your ideas and plans down—don't just daydream. You may initially have some ideas that you're not quite sure about, or will require some research—getting them written down will let you come back to them later as you get details squared away.

DAILY CHALLENGES

Starting tomorrow, do at least one thing in the course of your normal daily life that you find difficult and that tests your composure, makes you uncomfortable or anxious, or in some way is a challenge you would normally find ways to avoid. These challenges will be very personalized—they may not be challenging at all to someone else, but don't let that dissuade you.

They can take all kinds of forms—parallel parking on a busy city street, starting a conversation with a stranger, taking the stairs, not eating or drinking that thing you know you shouldn't, parking farther away from your destination, finally starting an odious chore you've been putting off, or even just going out of your way to take the trash out before your wife has to ask you to a dozen times. Don't limit yourself by thinking something is ridiculous or easy for everyone else—if it's something you have to force yourself to do because it's uncomfortable, difficult or even simply inconvenient, it's a good choice.

Because the point here isn't just to make yourself miserable, practice the composure skills from this chapter with each little challenge—box breathe before and during as needed, visualize the process and outcome, intentionally relax, smile or laugh, and/or give yourself a positive cue to stay on track. Equally important, pay attention to what you can learn from it afterward—

primarily what these little challenges have to teach is that you have far more control over your circumstances and reactions than you imagined. This is also a simple way to teach and remind yourself that things don't have to be perfect, ideal or easy for you to be successful and content.

If this all seems silly, remember—if you can't even handle such little things and maintain control and composure, how do you expect to handle the extreme, unexpected challenges that you'll inevitably face? If you're not willing to create and deal with some minor inconvenience and discomfort, what makes you believe you'll be up for the serious challenges that seem more meaningful? Think of these as the incremental exposure to a poison that over time creates immunity to an otherwise lethal dose.

STRESS EXPOSURE CHALLENGES

Now to the more exciting work—planning and executing your big challenges, i.e. your SET Stage 3 exercises. Again, remember that "big" is a relative term—these are major challenges for *you*. If you've never hiked before, don't plan an expedition to Everest—start with a nearby three-mile loop with minimal elevation change.

Remember your priorities based on profession, lifestyle and locality. This is the best place to start rather than dreaming up some arbitrary challenge just for the sake of it being challenging—challenging *and* related to your own life is far more valuable.

Determine your first challenge and put it on the calendar now. Minor adjustments can be made later if needed, but don't make the mistake of not cementing a schedule right away—that's a reliable way to somehow manage to never get around to it. Having a known date gives you structure to help in your preparation and helps keep you on track, just like an athlete preparing for a specific competition. An easy way to do this, of course, is to actually register for a competition—that gives you both a date and some skin in the game by way of financial investment. If you really want more accountability, share your plans with people so you have even more motivation to not back out—or you can even recruit some teammates to participate with you if the nature of the exercise is suitable.

Once you've determined and scheduled this first challenge, lay out a simple plan for your preparation. What do you need to do in order to be successful? What skills do you need to learn and practice, how do you need to train physically, what mental tactics should you invest some extra time in? You don't need to have every single detail recorded, but give yourself a clear structure and guidelines to keep yourself on track.

Soon after you plan this initial challenge, get to work on the next ones. Lay out a loose schedule, such as 3-5 of these yearly depending on how big and involved each is. The more of a beginner you are with this, the more frequent these challenges can and should be, because they'll be less demanding of time and resources; the more advanced you are, the more these challenges are likely going to require some legitimate logistical work and investment. Of course, at any level, not every challenge needs to be the same degree of difficulty, duration or complexity. Once you've summited your first 8,000 m peak, it doesn't mean the only challenge left is to climb an 8,001 m peak.

In the long term, keep a running plan a year or so out, even if it's simple notes and ideas initially. Collect those ideas as they arise—you can always scratch them off or modify them if by the time you get to them, they're no longer challenging enough, or you find better ways to implement them than you'd initially imagined.

CRITICAL INCIDENT PLANNING

Use the lessons you've learned through your capacity training to proactively prepare for potential critical incidents—figure out contingency plans for emergencies before they happen. Just like an athlete visualizes successful performance, this kind of planning can provide composure and confidence when an emergency actually occurs and allow you to take full advantage of your abilities and execute your plan. Look back at the Critical Incident Thought Experiment from the Capability chapter for ideas, read the news for others, and simply use your imagination for more. Again remember to prioritize based on probability related to your profession, lifestyle and locality.

CHAPTER 5
COMMITMENT

What are you willing to do? This simple question that underlies the element of commitment is both expansive and unfathomably deep in its implications. Commitment encompasses the other three elements of being tough—character, capability, and capacity—and either fortifies their development and invigorates their expression, or starves their growth and chokes them into submission. Our commitment is what continues breathing life into all facets of being tough, fertilizes the soil that allows them to thrive, clears the space for them to expand, and builds the network of pathways that carry us through the process. Without commitment and the action it induces, the other traits become meaningless fantasies—little more than self-serving fairy tales we tell ourselves to prop up our egos in the absence of good reason.

Commitment is also its own critical element of being tough that contributes just as much unique value as character, capability and capacity. The mental and physical acts of commitment are where the true demands of life lie—this is what allows us to push uphill, against the wind, and through the depths that threaten to hold us down, drive us off track, or drown our intentions. Commitment is what translates our ideas and plans into action and results and allows us to become who we intend to be.

Hannibal, legendary general of Carthage during the second Punic War, is credited with the phrase, "Aut inveniam viam aut faciam"—*I shall find a way or make one.* He demonstrated this ultimate commitment by doing what was presumed impossible, even by his own officers—marching his army, replete with elephants, through the Alps into Italy in order to defeat the Roman army. The expressions and results of our commitment may never reach this level of historical significance, but they unquestionably have the potential to change our own lives just as dramatically.

MOTIVATION

Ultimately every decision we make, from the most minor to the most consequential, is a product of our motivation—some underlying reason induces the choice. Those reasons are not always evident, even with intentional introspection, but they exist nonetheless. No matter how capricious or haphazard it may appear superficially, nothing we do is actually arbitrary. In order to truly determine the course of our own lives and establish control over ourselves, we need to discover and better understand our motivations, which are intimately related to and interdependent with our identity and values. It's impossible to be driven by motivations that contradict our values—it's only possible to be unsure of what one or both actually are—just like it's impossible for an event to defy the laws of nature, only for it to exceed our present level of understanding. In other words, if we find ourselves motivated to do something out of character, in fact it's only our understanding of our character that's out of line.

Unlike the laws of nature, we have influence over our character and values. If through the discovery of motivations that seem contradictory to who we are we realize our values are not actually what we believe or want them to be, we have the ability to change—to determine our identity and its attendant values, and realign our motivations accordingly. To believe otherwise is to believe we're helpless to change and must resign ourselves to forever being and doing what we've always been and done. This demands a high level of awareness and vigilance, and a willingness to perform continuous and often difficult self-evaluation—to become the proverbial curious child relentlessly asking *Why?*

The common usage of the word *motivation* has effectively conflated the idea with *enthusiasm*. The two are not in fact the same, but an absence of enthusiasm is typically interpreted and treated as a lack of motivation. Motivation is nothing more than the reason or reasons we do what we do—any relation to excitement or enjoyment is incidental. As an obvious example, many of us work jobs for years that we're not only unenthusiastic about, but that make us miserable. But we continue to get up each morning and trudge our way through the day because we're motivated to do so—primarily by the need and desire to earn the money that we support ourselves and our families with, to live up to the basic social standard of being productively employed, and to meet the demands of our personal pride. In this case, understanding the *why* behind the behavior is easy, and it clearly has nothing to do with the thrill of it. We're motivated by the product of the behavior, not the behavior itself—it's delayed gratification, which requires a long-term perspective and commitment to bridge the gap between acting and achieving the desired results.

If everything we needed to do were exciting and pleasurable, there would be no need for commitment—we'd be continuously driven to the behavior by the rewards it offered directly and immediately. But the reality is that arguably the majority of what we need to do in a given day or lifetime is demanded by future need rather than encouraged by immediate pleasure. Without commitment, then, much of it would fail to get done.

This is not to say that everything we do should be expected and accepted to be dreary, depressing, Dickensian drudgery. The ultimate goal is to change the course of our lives to find work and circumstances that stimulate and gratify us directly—but even achieving that idyllic situation doesn't completely eliminate all possible unpleasant necessities, and in the meantime, we need to be capable of plowing forward through the rocky soil along the way. It's critical that regardless of the circumstances, whether temporary or permanent, we remain on course for our particular ambitions, find meaning and a sense of purpose, and derive gratification in some way or another. This depends on our mindset as a product of our character and capacity.

Motivation is about understanding and remembering *why* we're doing what we're doing. Only if that underlying drive is clear and remains present in our minds is true commitment to the process possible. Without it, every obstacle, unusual difficulty and distraction draw us easily away from the path leading to our objectives because that path is too indistinct and rugged to be convincingly reliable. The clearer and better established that path, the less easily we can abandon it with the rationalization that it's not working—the less easily we can reassure ourselves that a move off the path is a wise course correction rather than simply giving up. This kind of misguided quitting is what keeps so many of us continuously discontented and unfulfilled—our motivation remains while our progress toward accomplishing its goals ceases. The less we move with it, the more the unrelenting pull of that dissonance cuts into us.

Enthusiasm will inexorably wax and wane with everything we do in response to myriad factors—how successful we are in the present stage, how content we are with the rest of our lives at the moment, our level of physical and mental fatigue, who we're surrounded by, or the weight of unrelated obligations. Understanding that enthusiasm doesn't necessarily represent or even parallel motivation, we can avoid the mistake of believing our motivation has diminished along with our enthusiasm at the moment. We can remind ourselves that as long as our *why* persists, our path remains, and its destination awaits—and through commitment, we can remain dedicated to the path that will bring us there.

THE SOURCE

Neitzsche wrote, "He who has a why to live for can bear almost any how." The missing piece here for most of us is knowing that *why*. We're more likely to seek out external motivators and incentives and inducements to push us to begin or continue on a particular path than to turn inward and search for a more powerful source of drive, or to gain understanding about what led us to this path originally.

The true source of our motivations is our character and values—this is what determines what's meaningful to us and consequently what we desire and are willing to work to pursue. If formal education isn't meaningful to us, we're never going to be truly dedicated to schooling and will require external motivators to persuade or force us to do what needs to be done to achieve whatever objective has been determined for us by someone else; if, on the other hand, our values include that kind of education, we'll be willing to spend our nights taking classes and studying after long days of working multiple jobs and taking care of our kids in order to earn a degree.

School is a perfect illustration of this—how many kids are labeled "unmotivated" by teachers, administrators and parents because of an obvious lack of interest in formal education, while outside of school, they're passionately dedicated to something else, whether it's a sport or even an unrelated intellectual pursuit? Motivation isn't some blanket quality that applies to every aspect of our lives—it's entirely specific. In order to be "motivated," we have to discover what it is in our identity that we truly care about, what our basic internal drives are, and how we can access and apply those things to accomplish what needs to be done in a way that satisfies those deep-seated desires.

Motivation must be intrinsic to drive us successfully long term. It's impossible to artificially create desire—we either have it or we don't. Motivational advice to "want it more than anything" is accurate in the sense that that's what's required to succeed to the greatest extent, but is utter nonsense in its implication that we can simply decide to want something, or amplify how much we want it. We feel what we feel and want what we want—all we control is what we choose to do in response.

A simple analogy here is sexual attraction. We're attracted to certain people or types of people inherently—it's impossible to decide to be attracted to anything or anyone else. We can make the decision to date someone we're not naturally attracted to, but that doesn't create physical attraction where none exists, and that lack of attraction unavoidably results in an absence of passion. If we hate the color red, painting our house red doesn't make us love it—it just makes us miserable having to look at our disgusting red house every day. We can choose to do things we're not motivated to do, but we can't create passion for those pursuits simply through their mechanical performance or creative rationalization.

The obvious and possibly discouraging conclusion here is that throughout our lives, we're going to have to force ourselves to do things we're not passionate about. But this isn't for the sake of self-torture—it's with purpose to achieve what we *do* care about. We don't brush and floss our teeth because we find the activity immensely pleasurable and our basic internal drive is to experience the sensation of cleaning our teeth—we do it because we care about our health and wellbeing, and that's one of the many steps to achieving and maintaining it.

Elite athletes rarely enjoy every minute of their arduous training, and are even less likely to enjoy the various restoration and recovery modalities, strict nutrition and sleeping practices, and lifestyle restrictions demanded for optimal performance. The successful ones consistently engage in these things because they have a clear understanding of their ultimate motivation—whatever underlying need they believe being a great athlete will fulfill—and use this focus to remain committed to the daily tasks that support achieving the goal. The world is littered with extraordinarily physically talented athletes with incredible potential who never achieve anything of note because the genuine motivation to achieve great things in sport is absent, and no coach or teammate can create it for them, no matter how desperately they may try.

While others can't genuinely create passion for us where none exists, they can indirectly drive us toward certain goals. This is the dangerous territory of unhealthy motivations—reasons we push ourselves toward an objective that we don't sincerely care about and that will ultimately fail to fulfill us. These reasons can range from a compulsion to please someone or receive their approval and validation, to seeking some kind of vengeance or proving someone wrong. Motivations like these can undoubtedly produce great achievements in an objective sense, but they also produce the type of people who seem to have it all and yet remain miserable. There's no real mystery about it—they've dedicated their lives to achieving things that aren't meaningful to them and in the process have displaced what is, or have never even given themselves the opportunity to discover what is. Being unfulfilled and discontented is unpleasant enough itself—having to spend a lifetime of hard work to the exclusion of enjoyable and meaningful pursuits to earn that condition is far worse.

Lao Tzu wrote in the *Tao Te Ching* around 2,500 years ago, "Care about people's approval and you will be their prisoner." Much like literal prisoners often become reliant on the structure and consistency of the experience after many years and consequently struggle to orient themselves and find purpose upon release, when we're motivated primarily by the demands or approval of others, once we achieve the goal in question and are released from the process, we're left lost and without a sense of meaning—and without the true feeling of fulfillment that accomplishment normally delivers.

Allowing ourselves to be motivated by external sources of any kind will never in the long term leave us fulfilled, because our actions and choices simply won't align with what we truly value. The most phenomenal achievements will fail to satisfy us or make us feel content if they have no intrinsic meaning to us. Avoiding this trap is only possible if we're intimately familiar with ourselves and our values, have examined our true motivations, and continually verify that our choices remain in harmony with them.

FINDING A REASON

In order to remain committed, we need to discover and understand our intrinsic motivations through the same kind of self-examination we use to determine our identity and values. In essence, these most basic motivations are the same as our values—the motivation is to achieve, embody, exhibit or otherwise express those values. If one of our values is integrity, for example, the related base motivation is to act with integrity, which can be done in any circumstances, from our profession to our personal relationships to sport—even in our private dealings with ourselves through being honest and realistic. In other words, the fundamental motivations we have are nearly always universal, or at least broadly applicable.

What this means is that with a little consideration, we should be able to connect true motivation to whatever we're engaged in. To be clear, this is not to persuade ourselves to do what doesn't truly fulfill us and then try to rationalize it retroactively—the purpose is to bolster our commitment to what we determine we genuinely need to do, some of which will be, due the basic nature of life, not on our list of preferred activities. Returning to the school analogy, while formal education may not be one of our values, maybe hard work is—and because we need to engage in some amount of structured schooling for many reasons beyond our personal desires, we can apply our motivation to be willing and able to work hard to the process, thereby completely changing our perspective and mindset to one that allows us to legitimately commit to schooling.

This more importantly applies to the many subtasks demanded by the process of working toward our true goals—when all of these little pieces of the much larger puzzle can be connected directly to the underlying motivation driving the whole, becoming and remaining committed to performing them is far easier. Athletic training involves an enormous volume of boring, unglamorous and difficult work that is often not obviously related to the athlete's sport or goals, and this is the kind of training that coaches struggle to enforce. Athletes who change their perspective on these subtasks from seeing them as superfluous and unrelated to essential and directly contributive are the ones who succeed.

Psychological research has convincingly demonstrated people's proclivity to be persuaded by reasons—not even necessarily specific, meaningful or rational ones. This was most famously shown in Ellen Langer's 1977 Harvard "Copy Machine" study[1], in which participants attempted to cut in line at a copy machine. In the attempts in which a reason was supplied, people were over 30% more likely to agree—even though one of the two reasons was "I have to make copies"... something not only completely senseless and without urgency, but identical to the reason the person in front of them was presently using the machine. Even more fascinating, when the reason given was that the participant was in a rush, this only resulted in 1% greater success than simply needing to make copies—that is, the logical reason was essentially no more effective than the illogical one.

With this tendency embedded somewhere deep in our brains, having *any* reason for what we're doing will reinforce commitment to it—we can magnify that effect if our reason is actually in alignment with what truly drives us at the most basic level of our constitution. If our goal is to walk a mile, we instantly recognize that each forward step we take is bringing us measurably closer, even if the end isn't yet visible and we know each of those steps is only about 1/2000 of the entire distance. If instead of seeing all of the mundane, menial little tasks required to achieve a grand objective over a protracted period of time as inconsequential, meaningless hassles, we recognize them as small but progressive steps in the larger process, we're better able to commit to performing them with the consistency and genuine investment required for the greatest success.

COMMUNITY

We're naturally influenced by the natures of those we spend time with, from attitude to habits to manner of speaking to perspective on the world. The more time we spend with given people, the greater that potential influence—this is made obvious by how we tend to think and behave similarly to our families. Jim Rohn famously said, "You're the average of the five people you spend most of your time with." Of course to actually be accurate, that would require you spend identical amounts of time and engaged in the same type of activity with each person. It also implies that we have absolutely no identity of our own and are completely shaped by outside influences. But the fundamental idea he was trying to communicate is sound—we need to choose whom we spend our time with wisely, because it has the potential to influence who we are, and we need to be vigilant about our exposure and response to external influences generally.

Average athletes want to always be the best in the gym or on the field today, while the most motivated and dedicated athletes want to train with athletes better than they are. These athletes understand that training along-side superior counterparts will provide the kind of influence that will drive their own progress, from feeling inspiration, to fueling their natural compet-itiveness, to learning better methods and mental habits. These athletes don't want to just be the best on one field right now—they want to eventually be the best in the world.

Unfortunately, few of us can entirely control the company we keep. Our professions typically dictate whom we're around for many if not most of our waking hours, and often these are far from the inspiring, positive models we'd prefer. Rohn's idea could be seen to imply that we're largely helpless with regard to self-determination—that we're simply amorphous blobs wait-ing for others to mold us into distinctive shapes. But if we determine our own character and reinforce that identity through our choices, we're per-fectly capable of defending against the contrary influences of anyone around us, regardless of the time we're forced to spend with them. If we maintain the level of self-awareness we already know is necessary, being surrounded by influences out of line with our character has relatively little impact be-yond some minor mental fatigue accrued through vigilance. For the tough, whom we choose to spend our time with is about intentionally fortifying our identities and accelerating our personal development, not avoiding contrary influences against which we're helpless—we're seeking the positive to build, not avoiding the negative to prevent deterioration.

Our willing acceptance of complete responsibility for ourselves includes the preservation of our character in spite of any outside influences other than those we've chosen to expose ourselves to for reinforcement or positive impact. Further, rather than being passively battered by others' influence, we have the choice to *be* the overwhelming influence ourselves. Attitude, mind-set, behavior and mood in any community are only democratic among the submissive of the group. *Someone* has to establish these things for everyone else to accept—they don't spontaneously materialize. We can complain about who we're forced to spend our time with because of their negative influence, or we can recognize our own agency and become the model by which others are influenced. This not only diminishes the negative influence, but fortifies support for our character and goals—and in the process, we're helping others escape their own self-defeating mindsets.

DISCIPLINE

Discipline is typically understood to be the basic expression of commitment—the self-enforcement of behavior that's neither the most natural nor the easiest at the moment as a means to achieve another end. It's the result of a more global and long-term view of our lives that allows us to consider how what we do now will affect outcomes in the distant future, and the consequent choices we make to stay on our determined course.

Grabbing a breakfast sandwich, four tacos and some fries at the drive-through demands infinitely less effort than planning, preparing, cooking and cleaning in order to make a legitimate meal. Neither one will have immediately measurable effects on our health or body composition, but one offers instant gratification, and the other offers the present hassle of energy and time investment. In other words, not only is there no immediate feedback from the behavior to positively guide our decisions regarding health and body composition, there's immediate feedback to *discourage* the better choice to achieve our goals. Discipline, guided by a clear understanding of our goals and motivations, is what keeps us diligently cooking our own food regularly and continually progressing toward our goal.

Aristotle said, "Through discipline comes freedom." If we read this literally with the accepted definitions of the words, it's completely nonsensical. Discipline is in fact contrary to freedom—it's the enforcement, whether by self or another, of behavior we'd prefer not to do. That said, Aristotle didn't speak English, and we're not going to be presumptuous enough to believe he didn't know what he was saying. Translations of complex ideas are notoriously difficult and of dubious accuracy—scholars spend careers arguing over them in the absence of a living source with whom to verify their conclusions.

Moreover, unlike what some modern interpretations of this interpretation imply, he didn't say discipline was equivalent or analogous to freedom—he said that the first leads to the second.

Aristotle very likely was describing not the idea of self-discipline in the most granular sense of restricting ourselves from acting freely on a task-level basis, but the broader notion of a disciplined lifestyle characterized by routine and simplicity—a lifestyle that by that nature opens the door to more available time, energy and mental capacity for introspection, reflection, learning, creativity and meaningful experiences—not a lifetime sitting alone hunched with furrowed brow on the edge of a hard, tightly-made bed in a cramped, poorly-lit, bare-walled room defiantly and miserably denying ourselves any possible pleasure.

Discipline is occasionally prescribed as a substitute for motivation as the latter inexorably fades—when we no longer want to do something, we employ discipline to force ourselves to. But this is a misrepresentation of both concepts. Motivation is the ultimate, underlying reason we do something. Discipline can't exist in the true absence of motivation—what's compelling us to be disciplined if we have no motivation? Unless the very act of being disciplined itself is the goal, discipline without motivation to drive it is impossible.

What discipline is a substitute for is enthusiasm. We're enthusiastic early on in our pursuits because we're adjacent to the original inspiration, which is still resonating within us and clearly illuminating the related motivation that drives us to act. As we gain distance from that inspiration, that energy fades and we tend to lose sight of the motivation. In consequence, our enthusiasm for whatever behavior that inspiration set in motion begins to diminish—the novelty wears off and the original blast of energy dissipates. This is the point at which discipline becomes critical—but it has to remain coupled to motivation, which means we need to continually revisit and re-evaluate that intrinsic drive to remind ourselves *why* we're willing to do what we're doing despite the difficulty and the denial of distractions or more immediate enjoyment.

Discipline is the active enforcement of behavior, speech and thought contrary to our natural urges—as such, it demands a significant investment of mental and physical energy. Consequently, there's a very real ceiling governing the implementation of discipline in our daily lives. We simply don't possess adequate resources to make that many conscious decisions and resist that much temptation while also engaging in meaningful, productive activity.

If we know and understand the reasons for our discipline, and they're the underlying motivations that feed our identity and values—we see that it's our own choice and it's benefitting us—our willpower increases and the self-discipline is less demanding on our limited mental resources, extending that willpower's reach.[2] Even so, it remains a limited resource, and we can't expend it carelessly as if it's infinite. This is where habit and routine play their critical roles.

HABIT & ROUTINE

A disciplined lifestyle doesn't take as much willpower as we might want to believe—whether because that belief supports our pride in our presently disciplined lifestyle, or because it gives us an excuse to not make the effort to establish one. Research has found that around 40-50% of our behaviors in a given day are a product of habit, not conscious decisions[3,4]—that is, they require no discipline or willpower to achieve. This may strike a small blow to our egos, but it also means we have a powerful tool to accomplish what we intend if we know how to use it.

A habit is a behavior that's so well ingrained in our brains that we perform it without conscious thought or decision. When it comes to what we consider bad habits, this is a frustrating feature of the human animal, but the system exists because it's imperative for our optimal functioning. The less conscious activity we're forced to engage in, the more energy the body is conserving, and the more of that energy we have available for critical work that demands conscious thought and decision-making, such as managing new and novel experiences, especially ones involving risk. In short, habits reserve more of our limited resources for what's most important.

Routine is essentially the grouping of habits, or the repetition of a sequence of habits, in a given period of time. For example, our days invariably involve multiple routines—the sequence of actions we perform when we first wake and the sequence as we prepare to go to sleep are the most common and obvious examples. We don't consciously work through a series of decisions about what to do each morning and evening when it comes to habits like brushing our teeth, making coffee, and getting dressed, although there are minor decisions scattered throughout these larger routines and habits, such as exactly which clothes to don. If all of these actions required our full attention and consideration, we'd be the least productive creatures on the planet, paralyzed by crushing floods of data from the environment and overwhelmed by evaluating all of the possible options in response. Instead, while we brush our teeth, our minds are free to be contemplating anything from our day's task list to the meaning of life.

If we want to argue that a "disciplined" lifestyle allows us to think and do more—and consequently leads to freedom—we have to concede that the discipline we're describing is in fact not the continual and unrelenting act of applying willpower that eats up our limited energy and cognitive capacity, but the engagement in established habits and routines that allows us to perform the desired behaviors with very little resource investment. Discipline is a demanding activity requiring energy and focus, of which we have a finite amount in any given period of time, meaning its use must be judicious to ensure we're able to enforce the behavior we need to without running dry and encountering a lack of willpower when it's needed most.[5]

Of course, true discipline is in fact required to establish and nurture these habits in the first place, or to break existing undesirable habits—it's very rarely the result of simply deciding once to do something new.

ESTABLISHING NEW HABITS

Before we can begin figuring out the methods of establishing new habits and getting the work done, we have a critical task—determining what those habits need to be. Sometimes this is easy—for example, if we don't exercise at all, starting to exercise regularly is just about the most obvious good habit for us to establish. But other habits and routines that would benefit us individually may not be as immediately and easily identifiable.

In a sense, what we need to do is simple—establish the habits and routines that support the identity we want to embody. The goal is to establish over time the routine of *being* who we are—to make the words, mindset and behaviors of our identity natural rather than consciously chosen each time as they will need to be during the earlier stages of any change. In other words, we're transitioning from *acting* like who we want to be (forcing ourselves to behave differently), to *being* who we are (living naturally in accordance with our identity).

Bruce Lee said, "Learn it until you forget it." This is a concise description of habit formation, but it also describes the development of a skill to such proficiency that it becomes second nature. Many of the habits we need to establish in support of our identity demand some level of skill—most importantly, the habits related to the way we think, like processing and interpreting information, evaluating ourselves, and making decisions. These require not just the creation of habit, but the development of skills through practice over time. We need to be aware that these kinds of changes require more time and effort, but we can be confident that as that time passes and the effort is consistently invested, the effectiveness will continually grow.

In his book *The Power of Habit*, Charles Duhigg breaks the process of intentional habit formation down as simply as possible: "First, find a simple and obvious cue. Second, clearly define the rewards."[6] In other words, once we determine what exactly the habit needs to be, we need to find a clear, unavoidable way to remind ourselves to do it (the cue), and keep in mind why it's worth doing (the reward). James Clear describes the process as making it obvious, making it attractive, making it easy, and making it satisfying.[7] His book, *Atomic Habits*, provides extensive systems for intentionally developing habits effectively.

As we move through the process of determining what habits to pursue, in addition to seeking the behaviors that reinforce our identity, we need to prioritize what Charles Duhigg calls "keystone habits." Keystone habits are those that influence other indirectly related behavior positively and consequently can have a more global effect on us than what the specific change in behavior would otherwise suggest. The mechanism isn't entirely clear, but considerable research has shown that the effects of habits like exercising and bed-making spread far beyond themselves and drive other positive changes in our lives.[8] The accumulation of "small wins" appears give us the attitude that we're capable of success[9]—and an attitude, unlike a specific behavior, is universally applicable, just as finding we have the ability to control ourselves and our circumstances during an adverse experience creates a corresponding mindset that we're then able to impose onto subsequent unrelated experiences.

Exercise and physical activity of all kinds of course have measurable and obvious physiological and psychological effects that can rationally explain its influence on the rest of our life—we have more energy, sleep better, feel more capable, become more confident in our appearance, and experience a frequently repeated sense of accomplishment. It's not particularly mysterious why, then, exercise positively impacts our lives beyond physical adaptation.

The reasons for the effectiveness of other habits may not be as clear immediately, but look for structural changes—habits that alter the structure of our day and behavior in ways that create space for, encouragement of, or otherwise allow more of the habits we want to establish. For example, a consistent wake and sleep schedule allows us to plan and implement new habits like reading and meditation and breathing; meditation and breathing allow us to function at a higher level of performance to achieve more in a given period of time; leaving our phones in another room and closing our email program allows us more uninterrupted focused work time so we can get more done in less time; getting more done in less time makes use feel more accomplished, and leaves us with more energy and time to pursue what inspires us and provides meaning to our lives. These are simple changes with enormous effect.

BREAKING BAD HABITS

Habits appear to be permanently embedded in the structure of our brains. Rather than remove an unwanted habit, we have to either create a replacement, or alter the existing habit to replace the routine associated with an existing cue and reward pairing.[10] That is, we change only the part of the pattern that creates the problem rather than eliminating the entire pattern. Again, for more extensively detailed information on habit building and modification, see the books *The Power of Habit* and *Atomic Habits*.

The next best solution to avoiding the behavior is to reduce or eliminate our exposure to the cue that initiates it, or to eliminate access to the routine—if we can't manage to change the pattern itself, it still may be possible for us to change our environment or surrounding routines in a way that prevents that pattern from ever being set in motion.

The most common example of this is removing the kind of food we're trying to avoid eating from our own home—if we can't manage to break the habit of stuffing Little Debbies down our pie hole every night, we can avoid the actual behavior by simply kicking that plaid-shirted brat out of the house so we don't have exposure to the cue (the presence of tempting pastries), or access to the routine (eating them). While it may feel like less of an accomplishment, the outcome is effectively the same—we're no longer eating garbage every day. Further, in the absence of that pattern, we now have the potential to establish a new habit in its place more easily, and the greater the time spent without engaging in the former habit, the less a resumption of access will compel the old behavior.

TRAINING, HIDING & DELAYING

While there are protocols like the ones Duhigg and Clear discuss in great detail to help us establish or modify habits more quickly and effectively, ultimately it comes down to doing the work. Much like a garden, the initial preparation and planting requires the biggest investment of time and effort, and the demand will diminish over time as plants take root and become established. But just like any plant in a garden, no behavior is truly self-sustaining indefinitely—it requires monitoring and tending. Epictetus wrote, "Every habit and faculty is preserved and increased by correspondent actions—as the habit of walking, by walking; of running, by running." We have to repeatedly *do* in order to reinforce—that is, ultimately, what both creates and preserves a habit. It's also what continues improving the performance of skilled habits into the realm of unconscious competence.

We need to be sure that our effort to find complex methods of habit formation or modification isn't simply an elaborate attempt to procrastinate. At some point, we have to quit searching for tricks and just do it—put our heads down and plow. We can start immediately with the simplest, most accessible behaviors and use them to train our willpower and skill at cultivating habits, as well as accumulate the confidence and momentum generated by the series of small wins. Simultaneously, we can learn more effective methods for habit formation and modification to then apply to the more difficult behaviors on our list. In this way, we're avoiding procrastination, strengthening our willpower, increasing confidence in our ability to make substantial changes, and becoming more effective with our approach to the problem.

Habitualizing and ritualizing desirable behavior is overwhelming beneficial, but there's a potential for creating problems if we take the process too far. The underlying purpose of habit is to eliminate the need for conscious thought and effort—to make the behavior easy. In addition to establishing habits to minimize our workload, we also modify our routines and environments to reduce or eliminate temptation—to clear out the cues that initiate bad habits or create obstacles to the execution of our good habits. Standing in the pantry at night staring at a box of Little Debbies and refusing to eat one (or six) requires willpower—effort and energy. Standing in that same pantry and not eating any Little Debbies because they're no longer there requires no effort at all, no matter how strong the impulse remains.

Willpower can be improved through training much like an athletic trait—as we accumulate practice, our ability to be disciplined increases.[11] The inverse is true as well, unfortunately—the less we use our willpower, the weaker it becomes. The goal is to establish habits and routines and create environments that help us become who we want to be and accomplish our ultimate objectives without hobbling ourselves through excessive comfort and security in the process. If we eliminate all temptation from our daily life through the immaculate sterilization of our environment, our discipline actually weakens—and the moment we're again exposed to an environment we can't completely control, we won't have the willpower to resist cues that prompt undesired behavior. Hiding from temptation isn't becoming more disciplined—ultimately, it's deceiving us into crippling our resolve.

We can avoid this problem without subjecting ourselves to the constant strain of an environment flooded with temptation and the resulting exhaustion of our willpower. By using simple conscious behaviors throughout our day to actively defy urges contrary to our identity and goals, we can train and strengthen our willpower while keeping the habits, routines and environments we've established strictly beneficial.

This can be just about anything that requires we recognize an unwanted behavior that we've started—or better, are about to start—and make a conscious determination to stop, whether by simply abstaining or substituting a desirable behavior. When we pick up our phone to urgently discover what critical things have come to pass on social media in the three minutes since we last checked, we can recognize the habit and not only put the phone down, but place it somewhere out of sight and reach. If we're about to complain when something takes an unexpected left turn, instead we can swallow that rising complaint and ask ourselves what we can do to resolve the problem, and what new opportunities are now available. When feeling crushed as we complete a demanding piece of physical training, we can refuse to lie or sit down, and instead stay on our feet and walk, practicing our rhythmic breathing and focusing on what we've just accomplished rather than on how much our legs want to collapse.

Defying urges to complain or otherwise express suffering—like refusing to sit or lie down when exhausted from training, or tell anyone within earshot how hard it was—is a simple and effective way to steal the power from suffering and infuse it into ourselves. It's a fundamental way to recognize and exercise our power over our circumstances, our behavior and our mindset. This kind of self-possession is a cumulative quality—every instance we employ it fortifies the ability and makes the next experience easier.

To be clear, this is not an implicit recommendation to never communicate suffering or difficulty—there are times that this is appropriate in order to receive needed help from those around us. What we're denying is the compulsion to express it without constructive purpose—to avoid surrendering to an unnecessary and unhelpful behavior that weakens our resolve. Marcus Aurelius wrote, "If it's endurable, then endure it." We need to learn that far more of what we experience is endurable, and to distinguish between an unhealthy compulsion to complain or draw attention to ourselves for validation from a legitimate need for help and support.

We can apply this exercise to procrastination as well. When we look at our day's task list and realize we're about to skip over a line that's likely been skipped over previously, we can resolve to instead begin that task immediately before even having a chance to insert whatever rationalization we already have prepared. Rather than focusing on the presumable odiousness of the task, or whatever collection of reasons we've aggregated to avoid its initiation, we can focus on the benefits of getting it out of the way and off our list forever, remind ourselves that any task is as miserable as we decide to make it, and recall that every time we act in defiance of our urges to avoid, we fortify our resolve. If it's an extensive project impossible to complete in the time available, break it into a series of practical segments that can be accomplished in multiple shorter periods of time.

Consider these simple exercises to be just like any physical exercise—an adequate dose in the appropriate volume and frequency develops the desired ability, while too much intensity too frequently simply exhausts us and sets us back while we're forced to recover. We can perform a few of them regularly each day to stay sharp—to continually strengthen our willpower while also stockpiling the resources for the more significant demands that are sure to come.

HARD WORK

With the natural evolution of societal living and the ever-increasing specialization of professions, we've collectively become progressively further removed from the most basic tasks of survival. The structure of modern society allows the overwhelming majority of us to become entirely focused on extreme specifics—the creation of computer programs, the authoring of books, the assembly of individual automobile components, or even the playing or coaching of a sport. Our basic needs, such as food, water, shelter and the numerous trappings of convenient living we've developed as a species, are provided by other specialists—people whose professions concern harnessing and providing electricity, processing food, treating and distributing residential water supplies, or building homes.

This specialization ultimately has allowed our separation from survival related demands. Pre-industrial societies generally, contrary to the typical imagined scenario, actually spent relatively little time daily working and had considerable freedom for socializing and more intellectual and recreational activities. It's not that we've reduced the amount of work more recently (we've actually increased it, although we're back below the crushing peak of the early industrial revolution era's sixteen-hour days and working children to death in factories stage, with some unethical exceptions), but that we've altered the *kind* of work we participate in regularly. This development is hard to reasonably criticize in totality—it's provided far too much benefit to us individually and collectively—but it's also created an extensive inventory of obvious and sometimes severe unintended consequences.

One of these consequences, which our convenience and security afford us the luxury of ignoring or even failing to recognize, is the absence of truly hard work that the majority of us are required to engage in at all, let alone with any regularity. This absence has utterly skewed our perspective on what constitutes difficulty, inspiring balking at the most minor of inconveniences and demands, and imbues too many of us with a sense of entitlement and condition of fragility. We're more willing to spend countless hours trying to determine ways to avoid hard work than to simply put our heads down and get it done. We can literally purchase anything we need by clicking a few buttons and waiting for it to be delivered to our doors while consuming entertainment from thousands of possible sources from the same comfortable location. The very concept of working for what we have has become an obscure one, and the connection between what we do day to day and what it affords us is often so indirect and convoluted that we find it hard to appreciate.

In a 1906 speech to the American Philosophical Association, psychologist William James said, "The human individual thus lives usually far within his limits; he possesses powers of various sorts which he habitually fails to use. He energizes below his *maximum*, and he behaves below his *optimum*... We are making use of only a small part of our possible mental and physical resources." Over a hundred years later, this has become more accurate than I suspect James could have ever imagined. We spend more of our time and energy actively pursuing methods to reduce effort than engaging in activities that demand true effort, and actively seek meaningless distractions for our minds in place of intellectual stimulus.

This elimination of regular hard work from our daily lives may provide us with incredible opportunities, but it simultaneously robs us of others. There's an inherent power of difficult tasks that can't be replicated with the tedious and mundane activities we've so thoroughly replaced them with. It may be "hard" to get through a long day of data entry on a computer, or to serve rude, whiny customers in a restaurant, but that kind of difficulty is far removed from the sort of work we experience when a task naturally combines both physical and mental challenges.

Work that inextricably connects physical and mental demands creates a unique phenomenon in which the entire being is engaged synergistically and immersed into the experience in a truly interconnected fashion. Arguably this is the apogee of human experience—completely engaging every element of ourselves into an enthralling and fluid symphony of our entire existing complement of abilities, while also demanding the development of new ones in search of solutions to novel problems.

To be fair, this absolute level of activity is uncommon and perhaps can exist only in the most extreme situations, such as survival, in which our lives depend on our concerted physical effort and skill, rational decision-making, imagination and ingenuity, strategic planning, and emotional control. But we can access lower levels of the experience voluntarily through our chosen activities and derive many of the benefits of the kind of hard work our collective innovation has eliminated from our lives.

This is a way to experience a more direct flow of effort to results than we can usually attain. So much of what we do is investing time and effort into tasks contributing to results realized only in the distant future—it becomes difficult at times to remain committed to these kinds of activities. Hard work gives us a chance to see the product of our efforts materialize and to cement the connection in our minds, to gain a deeper understanding and appreciation of what we're able to accomplish and what it takes, and to then be capable of applying that knowledge and confidence to the rest of our lives. It develops elements of our character that are unreachable in any other way, yet influence everything else we do.

Hard work is a self-contained system of effort and results that offers its own intrinsic value along with that of its products. It forces us to commit ourselves to a purpose, to exercise determination, and to utilize existing and develop new capabilities. The form this work takes can vary—it's less an issue of content than structure. It might mean building things, repairing problems in the home or vehicle, creative manual labor in the context of landscaping or property maintenance, or even sport training. Our societal composition generally allows each of us to choose how we express our abilities and engage in hard work rather than nature dictating what's necessary.

What matters is that we immerse ourselves, mentally and physically, to work toward a clear purpose and to complete a meaningful task—that we challenge the abilities of our minds and bodies and remain committed to the purpose until it's achieved.

FAILURE

A critical element of commitment is the willingness and ability to continue pushing ahead through failure—or at least perceived failure. Failing productively has become a hackneyed idea in business and social media, and failure is often touted with an air of wisdom by celebrities of dubious achievement as an unmatched tool for personal growth. John C. Maxwell wrote, "Fail early, fail often, but always fail forward." This kind of thinking has captivated people for some reason (while often admittedly misunderstood or misapplied)—arguably because it's a way for them to instantly and effortlessly revise their depressing personal histories and create a sense of accomplishment when none exists.

In glorifying failure, or embracing the idea that failing ultimately produces success, too many have completely missed the point, misinterpreted essential ideas, or applied the concept inappropriately. In order for failure to have any potential to be meaningful and productive, it has to be the result of the right type of efforts and attempts. Any of us can right now think of hundreds of ways to fail by the end of the day without the slightest potential to gain any wisdom other than that we just spent an entire day making stupid decisions and shouldn't repeat the exercise. I can walk out of my office fifty yards to the edge of a cliff and try to fly down to the river a hundred feet below. I'd be completely confident in two things—first, that I would fail completely, and second, that the experience would provide me absolutely nothing of value.

Failure itself doesn't magically create wisdom or growth or success—the encompassing process does. That process is what determines whether or not any involved failures are actually valuable, and the process includes not just the actions we take, but also the reasons we take them, and the way we evaluate the outcomes. Most importantly, it includes the way we view failure and the actions we take subsequently in response. It's a complex system with multiple inputs and influences—not a simple switch.

When suggesting failure ultimately results in success, failure proponents typically make the enormous mistake of focusing on a single experience rather than the encompassing process of which that incident is a small part. That is, one might point to the great success of a given famous individual and share a story of how he or she failed over and over before finally succeeding, implying—or even explicitly claiming—that those failures are somehow the reason for the success.

But it's misleading to describe that history as a series of failures producing success. In fact, those many failures were all pieces of a single ongoing process—steps along the way from start to finish. A simple analogy would be hiking cross-country through the wilderness to a planned endpoint. We may spend some time hiking in a direction that leads us to an impassible obstruction like a cliff or unfordable river, forcing us to backtrack and determine another course. If we look at this section of the hike in isolation, it could be fairly described as a failure—we failed to go the right way and didn't reach the endpoint. But if, after some recalculation and rerouting, we reach our chosen endpoint, we've succeeded. That means that what we initially viewed as a failure wasn't actually a failure—it was only a single piece of a process (reaching the endpoint) that was completed successfully.

Thomas Edison, when asked how it felt to fail a thousand times before succeeding in creating a functional light bulb responded, "I didn't fail a thousand times; the light bulb was an invention with a thousand steps." In other words, the reporter who asked the question was incorrectly assessing pieces of a single task as distinct tasks themselves, and in consequence, because individually they didn't result in a functioning bulb, deeming them failures. That reporter's logic is the same used typically by failure proponents to paint failure as beneficial. That same logic applied to a one-mile run would call every single stride along the way until the final one a failure because it doesn't reach the length of a mile—likely anyone can see the absurdity of that perspective with such a simple example.

This idea also disregards the stories of success not involving failure—are those successes less successful because they were accomplished more directly? We might argue that the experience of not reaching success directly is replete with important lessons not accessible otherwise, but if we're looking strictly at the purpose of the endeavor, success is measured only by the final result—and failures along the way certainly don't guarantee lessons.

In short, we can't allow ourselves to become inappropriately enamored with the idea of failure being a tool of success through the misinterpretation of events. We need to distinguish between the natural process of attempting a given task or goal, which includes missteps and even backward steps along the way to completion, and genuine failure, which, by definition, means never completing or achieving the intended task or goal.

We can and should develop a productive mindset with regard to failure and how it can be best utilized in support of our objectives rather than allowing it to be discouraging, but that doesn't mean we seek it out or find it particularly valuable relative to other methods. It simply means that we possess the understanding that failure is a temporary step and a brief moment in a greater process, and have the confidence in our character, capability, capacity and commitment to continue pursuing the goal despite any setbacks for as long as it remains meaningful to us.

It's equally critical that we never put ourselves in a fearful position of failure avoidance or risk aversion being primary arbiters of our decisions. That is, we don't avoid failure by not taking risks when appropriate—we avoid it through better preparation and decisions. Success demands a balance between actively avoiding failure through the best possible decisions and planning with what's available to us at the moment, and the willingness to fail temporarily that allows us to take bold action with its attendant risk.

We're willing to fail as a result of extending ourselves to reach great objectives, not to accept perfectly avoidable failure as a result of halfhearted attempts or haphazard choices. We can accept the risk of potential failure that accompanies overreaching because we're committed to both the goal and the process—failure isn't a dead end, but a change of course. Knowing failure is a possibility in any worthwhile endeavor, we resign ourselves to operate under its shadow, prepare as well as circumstances allow, and remain ready to exploit it to our advantage if and when it occurs.

When we look at failure with this attitude, it's arguably better described as testing. That is, we're bringing our ideas to the field and discovering how they perform, and using that feedback as we advance through the process to continually refine our plan to ensure its ultimate success. This attitude instantly transforms any setbacks in the process into constructive data rather than discouraging failures.

PLANNING & PREPARATION

Planning is imperative to any significant pursuit. We don't successfully climb mountains or launch businesses on a whim without any preparation. The process of planning, however, needs to be undertaken with the understanding that the perfect plan doesn't exist because the world defies perfect prediction. There are far too many moving parts in any situation for us to reliably prepare for all possible contingencies—we need to assess and determine our course as well as possible with the given availability of information and inherent time constraints.

It's easy to become paralyzed with over-planning—to continually re-evaluate, revise, second-guess and hedge. Ultimately we have to remember that doing without planning always produces better results than planning without doing—a plan is meaningless and worthless without execution. General George Patton said, "A good plan violently executed now is better than a perfect plan executed next week." Within the context of war strategy and its intrinsic criticalness of timing, this underscores the importance of *acting*. The enemy isn't defeated with a plan, but with action.

However, the typically overlooked word in this quote is "good"—Patton wasn't suggesting cavalierly taking action in the absence of planning, but in taking decisive, committed action in accordance with a *good* plan rather than delaying action in the hopes of a *perfect* plan. This not only emphasizes how imperative timing is to most of what we do, but underscores the impossibility of perfect planning in circumstances comprised of unpredictable elements and the consequent pointlessness of attempting it. Another military aphorism, originating with Prussian commander Helmuth von Moltke, is that no plan survives first contact with the enemy—the ultimate collection of unpredictable elements. Or, as Mike Tyson more succinctly and satisfyingly put it, "Everyone has a plan until they get punched in the mouth."

To continue with the theme, we can consider this approach to planning and preparation as focusing primarily on strategy over tactics. That is, before beginning, we create the overarching plan with a clear end point and purpose, methods of measuring success, and useful markers along the way to guide our decisions and adjust our course as needed. We only finalize the details of how exactly we execute the tasks necessary to fulfill that strategy as we progress and are able to gather more information and feedback to establish optimal tactics at each stage. This provides us the map from start to finish necessary to stay on course overall, but liberates us to move fluidly through the periphery of that path as needed based on the circumstances of the moment created by unpredictable elements.

We can establish contingency plans for the predictable risks and create a toolbox of universal or at least commonly useful tactics to implement or modify as the occasions arise to allow us to adjust more quickly and effectively to preserve momentum, while avoiding getting interminably bogged down in endless details that address issues we're not sure will even exist. This approach allows us to move forward "violently" with a "good plan" without the delay and mental paralysis inherent to attempts to create the perfect plan before even beginning.

WHOLE PROCESS PERSPECTIVE

The most critical element to withstanding failure is preserving a whole process perspective—to never lose sight of the long term and the ultimate goal because of an exclusive focus on present circumstances. A narrow focus causes us to fixate on setbacks and obstacles and allows us to become discouraged and frustrated; being capable of pulling back to see the entire process at any given time allows us to not only better gauge our progress, but to find solutions to the current problems. With too tight a focus, our thinking and options become restricted and tend to be more negative in nature—we view the process in terms of individual problems rather than as a continuous positive motion, however tortuous, toward our purpose.

We need to maintain a stubborn confidence in our ability to prevail, not just with trust in our capability and capacity, but with our understanding that setbacks are temporary at some scale—not necessarily brief, but never indefinite if we can endure. The severity of our setbacks or missteps is influenced to a great degree by our attitude about them—we need to never exacerbate objective difficulty with our subjective evaluations. Getting angry that one plus one doesn't equal three doesn't make the missing one appear any more quickly or easily—a rational mindset and a refusal to feel defeated keep us mentally fit to find or create what we need. Our whole process perspective ensures our evaluation of success takes all progress into account to balance any failures experienced in specific subtasks. It allows us to recognize those failures as wrong turns, not dead ends.

Like smart test-taking strategy, we may be able to temporarily move past a certain failed aspect of the process we're struggling to resolve and accomplish other adjacent or parallel tasks in the meantime. This allows us to maintain momentum rather than getting bogged down and frustrated by a single step of an extensive process, and it can also free our minds to better discover solutions by removing the pressure and extreme focus, much like we often spontaneously remember a word or name we've been searching our minds for once we stop actively trying.

Ultimately no endeavor survives interference and setbacks without commitment. Commitment to the objective is what continues pushing the process forward through resistance, around obstacles, and over objections. Our most meaningful pursuits are never without their trials—arguably a great deal of their meaning and value is derived from the very struggles we're forced to endure for their achievement. The willingness to commit to the fight endows us with the power to overcome and accomplish.

VIOLENCE

Violence is a subject charged with enormous potential for discomfort, uncertainty and revulsion, but it's one we all need to confront. Many of us will make it to our deathbeds without a single violent encounter—for that, we can appreciate our good fortune. But none of us can reliably predict such an outcome. Many soldiers never see combat, while pacifists are mugged on the street. Many police officers never fire their weapons in the course of duty, while people who've never touched a firearm are killed by them. Like adversity generally, we can make assumptions of probability based on our profession, lifestyle and locale, and we can prepare suitably. But also like adversity, when it comes and of what it's comprised are unknown until the moment we encounter it.

Ultimately the decision of whether or not we're willing to commit violence must be entirely individual. In no way does being tough prescribe one decision over others—what it does require is knowing exactly what we're willing to do in any given situation, and having the commitment to stand by that decision in what may be the most trying and traumatic experiences imaginable. This decision can't be left for the moment our action is demanded. Such moments are nearly guaranteed to be incredibly brief and chaotic—they don't afford us the luxury of stepping aside and contemplating the meaning and potential consequences of every possible response and the value of what we're protecting or sacrificing. The emotional, psychological, ethical, practical and legal implications need to be understood and accepted before we ever find ourselves in a position requiring such a decision.

Varg Freeborn frames this consideration as concisely as possible in his book *Violence of Mind*: "What are you willing to kill or die for?"[12] Of course, a violent encounter can involve a level of violence anywhere on the spectrum short of killing and dying—we need to consider what our self-imposed limits and provocations are within that spectrum. In other words, what is worth executing a given level of violence to us? What are we willing to sacrifice to achieve our pre-determined end? What are we willing to sacrifice as a result of our chosen boundaries?

It's important to keep in mind that being willing to commit an ultimate level of violence doesn't mean we don't retain the ability to behave on a gradient as the circumstances demand and allow. Being willing to kill doesn't mean being willing to kill for anything—the protection of property, for example, shouldn't have the same boundaries as the protection of a child. If the value to us of something we own exceeds or even approaches the value of a life, we're in need of extensive professional mental help, not lessons and reflection on the execution of violence.

Being violent isn't tough—what's tough is being willing to be violent if necessary for a meaningful end; or, being willing to sacrifice our lives if we truly believe the act of killing is never justified. Being tough is the commitment to our values—the resolve to do whatever is necessary to defend them.

The overwhelming priority with regard to violent encounters is their avoidance—violence should always remain the last resort, to be employed only when all other options are exhausted or determined impossible. Avoidance includes a number of behaviors and decisions, from not unnecessarily exposing ourselves to risk to not being responsible for provocation or escalation—we have no need to commit violence if an encounter never rises to that level of intensity, or we prevent an encounter from even occurring at all. This is largely dependent on our awareness and the ability to assess our environment and circumstances in order to respond suitably.

We also need to always consider the possibility of removing ourselves from a situation that appears to be escalating toward violence or has the potential. Many situations will preclude this option, but in others, we have the choice to escape—and that choice might only exist very early on in an encounter and the window may close abruptly if we fail to take advantage of it. However, in other situations, the option may persist or present itself later in the encounter—it should always be considered along with its potential consequences relative to remaining engaged.

Our final non-violent option is defusing—attempting to de-escalate an encounter before it begins an inexorable trajectory to violence. This can assume a number of forms, from reasoning to the way we're speaking to simply changing our posture or our position relative to an adversary to one less inherently threatening. Such actions need to be taken with appropriate precaution. De-escalation doesn't mean creating vulnerability—we can make these attempts without sacrificing our awareness and readiness.

If these options fail, we're left with a violent encounter, whether we want it or not, and whether or not we think the circumstances warrant it. Freeborn describes the cascading priority of objectives of any encounter succinctly: avoid; escape; win the fight.[13] When being committed to avoiding violence fails, we're left to commit to engaging in violence according to the limits we've determined for ourselves in order to prevail.

No matter how much we've contemplated what we're willing to do and for what, and how clearly defined our own limits are, they have no bearing on our adversary's system of operation. Any encounter is likely to involve asymmetric boundaries—that is, what our adversary is willing to do will not match what we are. If we're never the source of instigation or escalation, we will likely be at a disadvantage in terms of boundaries. Our opponent has already demonstrated, by initiating a violent encounter in circumstances in which we wouldn't resort to violence unprovoked, a greater willingness to employ violence, which suggests their willingness to escalate most likely also extends beyond our own for any given situation.

A petty disagreement in a bar, a traffic dispute, or a simple argument between spouses can escalate to murder—all it takes is one person being willing to kill and unable to control their impulses. Freeborn writes, "Once you open that door to violence, anything from aggressive to homicidal can come out; you don't get to choose which one, and there's no putting it back in once it comes out."[14] In other words, once we're engaged in a violent encounter, the level of violence will be dictated by the more violent participant regardless of how that relates to our own boundaries—our only choices at that point, if escape is not possible, are either to match that level of violence and fight to win, or to accept the consequences of refusing to meet the demand... up to and including harm to or death of ourselves or our loved ones.

Committing to winning this kind of encounter means having no doubt about what we're willing to do and why. If the lives and safety of our family are in jeopardy, are we willing to kill or potentially die trying to protect them? What if the life in jeopardy is that of a perfect stranger? Or a casual acquaintance? We need to know before finding ourselves in such a position what we are and aren't willing to do, because these kinds of situations will demand decisive action that can't be undone.

It's important to be very clear about the consequences associated with all violence—the emotional and psychological impact of being violent and potentially crippling or killing another human being, the legal ramifications of our choices, and other repercussions that may affect our families or friends as a result of our decisions. This requires being familiar with pertinent laws regarding violence—knowing what exactly the local laws allow us to do in order to protect ourselves or others. What we deem in the moment to be warranted may not be viewed that way legally, and our efforts may result in imprisonment or financial ruin. These consequences have to be considered if our objective is protecting others, such as families that would suffer as a result of them.

Critically, we need to prepare for this specific type of adversity like for any other. It goes far beyond carrying a concealed weapon, watching MMA regularly, and fancying ourselves little Rambos. It needs to be approached soberly and earnestly with the gravity of the issue always at the forefront of our minds—this isn't training for recreation or sport, but for life and death. We need to invest the time and effort into training with legitimate instructors and relying on credible resources—and never overestimate our abilities and become too comfortable.

This is not morbid fantasizing—it's rational calculation and preparation in the face of a reality in which human on human violence is always a looming possibility.

FOCAL POINTS

- Commitment is what allows the other elements of toughness to actually be put to use—without commitment and the resulting action, they're nothing but ideas.

- Motivation is what compels our decisions and action. It won't always be consistently accompanied by enthusiasm long term.

- In order to truly determine our identities and the course of our lives, we need to understand our motivations and their sources.

- Discipline is not a substitute for motivation—it can only stand in for enthusiasm.

- Much of what we do every day is the product of habit rather than discipline or conscious choice.

- Proper habits and routine preserve cognitive resources to invest in higher order thinking to allow meaningful experiences and achieve goals beyond the basic tasks of daily life.

- Hard work offers important lessons and experiences we can't replicate otherwise and should be voluntarily sought out.

- Failure is inevitable in the course of meaningful pursuits. It should be avoided as well as proper planning and preparation allow, but never feared and avoided through aversion to reasonable risk.

- Failure needs to be viewed with a whole picture perspective to be seen as a temporary setback in an overall process rather than a distinct event and final result.

- We need to determine our willingness to engage in violence and establish clear boundaries, and understand and accept the consequences of our actions or inaction.

ACTION

Commitment is action. Reading this book and contemplating the ideas is a start—but without acting on them, it's also a short trip to a dead end.

MOTIVATION

When contemplating your identity and values, you've already learned your underlying motivations, at least in broad terms. Expand on this with some direct consideration and write your thoughts down in your evaluation journal. Consider questions like:

- Why are you reading this book? What compelled you to pick it up? What's missing in your life? What falls short of meeting your ideas of who you are? What do you want to gain?
- What are the true fundamental reasons for your choices? What is it that you can always rely on to be there when you need to be reminded of why you're working hard and enduring struggle?
- Make a habit of pausing and noticing what you're doing day to day, and try to connect the behavior with its motivation. This is an exercise in both evaluating the wisdom of your various decisions, and continuing to gain a more extensive and nuanced understanding of who you truly are.

HABIT IDENTIFICATION & UPDATING

Reflect on your typical day and identify what behaviors are habitual rather than the result of conscious decisions in the moment based on present circumstances. For each identified habit, ask yourself if that behavior reflects your true identity: If you were exactly who you wanted to be, would you still engage in that same behavior in that same way? If so, move on; if not, ask how that habit can be modified or replaced to support your identity. Add these necessary changes to the goals section of your evaluation journal (more on that below).

MEDITATION & BREATHING

Add the practice of meditation or at the very least breath work to your daily routine. Use the protocols described previously in the book, or get a bit more advanced and use the protocol from *Stress Less, Accomplish More* by Emily Fletcher. In any case, meditation and breath work can be combined with your journaling exercises to derive as much benefit as possible from both—begin each journaling session with your meditation or breathing protocol for maximal effectiveness.

Of course, as discussed previously, controlled breathing and even simple meditation protocols can be employed at any time as needed in response to the circumstances. Put the tools in your possession to good use.

HARD WORK

If regular hard work isn't already a part of your life, make it one now. Even if your profession requires it, you may consider adding more or new non-work-related activity strictly for the sake of your personal gratification and growth. This activity will be closely tied to your pursuit of greater capability, as any work you undertake in this vein should inherently force the improvement of existing skills and the development of new ones. As much as possible, make this activity useful as well—find ways to address existing needs and solve existing problems rather than exclusively inventing new ones. What needs to be done to the house, property or vehicle that you may be able to handle yourself with a bit of research and focused effort? What can be done to help family, friends or neighbors? Can you volunteer with a charitable organization like Habitat for Humanity, or establish an apprenticeship with a craftsman? Get creative and be ambitious—you don't have to become an instant jack-of-all-trades, but that status is an admirable goal.

JOURNALING

Among a wide array of personal growth advice, keeping a daily journal may be the most consistent recommendation. It's a simple, nearly zero-cost and minimal time investment tool with considerable power. The exact protocol is up to you based on what your experience determines to be most effective, but the following is a solid template:

Morning Journal This was covered in detail in the Character chapter of the book. If you do only one journaling exercise, this is the one to choose. This is your chance to reflect on how well you're meeting your standards, define and fortify your identity, and begin each day with a refreshed, open mind.

Evaluation Journal This is the second journal introduced in the Character chapter. In this journal, you can do all of your longer term evaluation, reflection and planning. You've already done the identity and values exercises from the Character chapter, and you should have at least scheduled your first regular check-in if not already done at least one. You've also read about (and should have started if not finished) the exercises for this journal in the Capability and Capacity chapters.

The evaluation journal can be used as more of a reference volume—this is more "permanent" information you can refer back to as needed and update along the way. Rather than daily considerations, this is global information and contemplation that guides your daily activity, and the framework against which that activity can be evaluated.

Shortly you'll read about the final addition to this journal: goal setting and evaluation.

Training Journal You've of course already started your new physical training program, so you've of course also started your training journal to track your activity and evaluate your progress. Don't underestimate the importance of this more utilitarian tool.

GOAL SETTING & TASK PLANNING

In your evaluation journal—or a goal-specific journal if you prefer—create your initial goals and plans. Based on what you've learned so far, what do you need to do, and what do you want to accomplish? Be sure to make your goals clear and measureable—they need to be objectively defined or creating steps to achieve them and accurately evaluating progress will be impossible. A goal like *get better* is meaningless even if it expresses a fundamental purpose—it provides no point of aim and no guidance for determining a successful process. Instead of a vague goal like *get better at running*, create a hard target—*I'm going to improve my 2-mile trail run to under 15 minutes.* That's as straightforward and measureable as it gets. Notice as well the offensive mindset in the language—*I'm going to* not *I want to.* Set yourself up immediately for success with confidence and assertiveness.

Step 1: Write down all of your current goals, no matter how ambitious or seemingly impossible they may be. This is not the time to determine whether or not they're reasonable or possible, but a chance for you to see what it is that you truly want to achieve. Get them out of your head and onto paper before you start doubting yourself. Remember, no one else needs to see this, so don't hold back.

Step 2: Next consider how each goal aligns with your identity and values—if there's discordance, you need to determine which needs adjustment. Is the goal not truly what you want or need (i.e. are you thinking of it because it seems like what someone in your position is supposed to do?), or does the existence of this goal make you realize you need to adjust the definition of your identity and values?

Step 3: Organize this list by prioritizing based on need over desire. Which of these goals supports the demands of your profession, lifestyle and locality, and which support activities or abilities you simply want to perform or acquire because they interest you? You'll likely find that some accomplish both, and those should be emphasized whenever possible. Determine which of these goals you're going to begin pursuing now, and which will be set aside for a later date.

Step 4: Once you've determined which primary goal or goals are on the agenda now, create a series of intermediate building goals for each that will lead to their achievement. What are the shorter steps and benchmarks along the way that will allow you to plan a process of reaching the primary goal? These intermediate goals give you simpler, closer targets that allow better and easier focus, lay out a clear path leading to the true end point to keep you on track over a protracted course, and allow effective evaluation and measurement of your progress.

If we use *build a house* as an example of a primary goal, that's an overwhelming task and its completion is distant—it's tough to plan for it, tough to determine a timeline, and even tougher to stay focused and know whether you're on track for success at any given point along the way. To resolve this natural problem with being ambitious, we can create intermediate goals that lead to the final product—establish the build site and secure permits; ensure utilities access; create architectural plans; excavate and pour foundation; framing; roofing and siding; electrical and plumbing; interior surfaces and trim; etc. Each of these intermediate goals is a much simpler target to aim for and can be planned and executed confidently, and the execution of each intermediate goal demonstrates our progress toward the primary goal, no matter how distant it may still be.

Step 5: Create a clear plan for each intermediate goal. This is the level at which you establish actionable steps. If your primary goal is *I'm going to attain a black belt in Brazilian Jiu Jitsu*, the intermediate goals are really obvious: attain a white belt, blue belt, purple belt, brown belt…

Now for each of these steps, you can create tasks that will lead to their accomplishment. To get that white belt, the task is simple: find an instructor and establish a training schedule. To progress to the next intermediate goal— the blue belt—you're likely going to need to take some additional steps. You may need to increase the frequency of your training, spend time outside the gym practicing and studying, attend a clinic with a visiting instructor, etc. In this way, you're able to relatively easily create clearly defined tasks that ultimately wind up being the steps to achieving the primary goal.

You don't need to create the task lists for every intermediate goal up front—only the next one. In fact, it's better not to get too far ahead in planning at this level of detail. Circumstances change, and you're going to learn more about the process along the way that you can apply to planning the subsequent tasks. Think of this like an outline for a book—create the title (primary goal), then establish a series of chapters (intermediate goals), and then write each chapter in order (create and execute the tasks).

At this level, it's now also possible to establish timelines. To achieve a black belt, you may be looking at ten or more years—that's far too long a time period to use as a guideline. Too much can happen during that time to force changes in course and adjustments to the intermediate plans, and it's impossible to know how long each step will take at the outset. By breaking it down to small tasks, it's far easier to comprehend the time scale and more reasonable (and possible) to assign timelines.

Step one in the belt example—find an instructor and begin training— can be easily assigned a timeline (and it should be a short one). The next step of blue belt will be harder to determine, but as you gain experience, you'll be able to get a better sense of it. Always recognize when certain goals require flexible timelines—adjusting timelines in these cases is necessary, and refusing to do so is guaranteeing failure for no good reason. Other goals can have fixed timelines—a certain performance accomplished at a competition scheduled for a specific date is an obvious example—adjusted only in response to truly disastrous incidents that leave no choice (e.g. an injury that forces you to postpone competing until a later date).

Step 6: Finally, track your progress and adjust your course as needed. It's a good idea to set a regular check-in schedule to maintain accountability as well as to ensure you're on the best track to achieve the next goal. Once weekly, spend some time during your evaluation journal routine considering and noting your progress toward your goals—are you completing your planned tasks as needed and on time? What isn't working and needs to be adjusted to get you back on track or moving more efficiently? What has worked well, and can you apply that to other aspects? Where are you in the total process, and how much have you accomplished so far? Be sure to always look at this from the perspective of how far you've come rather than how far you have left to go. Finally, consider how your pursuit of and dedication to these goals has affected you—how has it changed your mindset, your confidence, your sense of identity, your enthusiasm, etc. Week to week you may not notice dramatic change, but on a larger scale, it will be impossible to miss.

VIOLENCE PREPARATION

- Spend some time examining your values and your beliefs regarding violence—in at least broad terms, what are you willing to do for what reasons? Over time, flesh these out to greater specificity.
- Read the book *Violence of Mind* by Varg Freeborn—this is the best resource for truly understanding violence, self-defense, and the related considerations.
- Find a legitimate self-defense instructor and work with them to develop at least a minimal level of competence—it's not a bad idea to return periodically for tune-ups and more skill work. Your investment in this kind of training needs to match your determinations on your boundaries—you need to be capable of supporting your willingness to engage with the necessary skills.

CHAPTER 6
FINAL THOUGHTS

If this book has given you the impression that to be truly tough is to be permanently and inescapably dour and deprived, if becoming tough seems completely out of reach to you, or you're confused about how to start or overwhelmed by the prospect, I've failed completely in communicating the ideas as intended. Being tough isn't a distant endpoint, and is less about what we do than how we do it—and why.

I can't motivate you. I can't create desire for you. I don't believe in external motivation as an effective driver of anything significantly meaningful. As a coach, I can provide incentives and consequences in many forms in many cases, but that's not genuine motivation. I can maybe even inspire an athlete to a great performance with a rousing speech that appeals to that moment's mood. I can possibly inspire through example. But that's not creating the *desire* within an individual—it's simply pushing and prodding and coercing, and the moment those efforts are removed, so is the drive.

Motivation must be intrinsic to be effective on any scale other than brief. You either want something, or you don't. Motivational self-help material often points to the fact that extremely successful people are such because of the intensity of their desire for something, then follow with the advice to somehow possess more intense desire... but desire is natural and spontaneous. You can't fabricate it. It's not something you create—it's there or it isn't, and when it's there, you can't miss it.

I can give you practical tools to be successful. I can lay out a plan in gory and unendurably boring detail. But it's your ongoing decision about how to use those things—to determine your own path to meaning and purpose and apply these tools to the process. That's not something I'm capable of helping you with—we all need do it on our own.

It may seem a daunting prospect, but step back and reframe the picture. Standing in the foothills and gazing up at the distant snowy peak you intend to summit can be overwhelming and discouraging, or it can be inspiring and galvanizing. This is truly your first decision in this pursuit: will you allow the enormity of the challenge to dissuade you or compel you? You choose to view every step toward that summit as either a reminder of how far you still have to go, or a measure of how far you've come.

We're repeatedly told that we can't change the world, we can only change ourselves. But this logic fails to consider the fact that each of us is an integral part of the world—changing ourselves is unavoidably and undeniably changing it. Our individual changes alone may be fractional to a nearly imperceptibly small scale, but they're repeatedly magnified by our influence of those around us. Such influence can be exponential in its reach as it spreads through the various networks into which each of us is directly and indirectly tied. Every positive step we take in our own lives is pushing the world, however infinitesimally at the moment, in the right direction.

In his book *Flow*, psychologist Mihaly Csikszentmihalyi describes the way in which life, by nature absent of universal meaning, can be given meaning and purpose by each of us:

> If a person sets out to achieve a difficult enough goal, from which all other goals logically follow, and if he or she invests all energy in developing skills to reach that goal, then actions and feelings will be in harmony, and the separate parts of life will fit together—and each activity will "make sense" in the present, as

well as in view of the past and of the future. In such a way, it is possible to give meaning to one's entire life.[1]

I believe we should strive for perfection. Any goal short of it is arbitrary in some way and therefore makes little sense, and invariably becomes a limiting self-fulfilling prophecy—by definition, it *is* a limitation. But how we define perfection here is critical. Perfection is a state of being, an active condition, not a single finite point in time or space. It's not an endpoint that we someday reach to achieve completion—it's a continuous process of forward motion.

Perfection of course is unattainable in the strictest sense, but therein lies the benefit—in seeking perfection, the task is never truly finished, and we have a defined but infinite pursuit to organize and motivate our choices and behavior, measure and evaluate our success, and deliver accomplishment and gratification. We need definite, objective goals along the way that serve as landmarks, steps and points of measurement, and which provide us a continual series of achievements to fulfill our broad and varying needs, remind us of our fundamental motivations, and frequently stoke our enthusiasm.

It's only the ultimate goal or goals that need to remain forever incomplete—and not because we've failed to complete them, but because by our intent and their very nature they are incompletable. This requires more subjective ideas, but subjective doesn't necessarily mean vague or impossible to understand. These ultimate goals need to be tied more to the notions of character and values—the elements of our lives that define us and dictate our sense of fulfillment—rather than the more objective metrics that describe the myriad intermediate goals we check off throughout our lives as part of an all-encompassing process.

We might initially look at the seeking of perfection, regardless of how we define it, pessimistically as a way to ensure failure—if we choose to pursue something that can never be completely achieved, failure is the only possible outcome, and we should expect to be perpetually demoralized and disappointed. But consider your experiences more closely—have you been more energized, enthusiastic and enthralled by actually accomplishing a goal, or by the process of pursuing it? Even if the feelings of each were identical, one is a finite point in time, and the other is an enduring experience.

We all have two fundamental choices in life—what our purpose is, and whether or not to pursue it. Discover that purpose, and begin your unrelenting pursuit.

UNIVERSAL BASICS OF CAPABILITY

The following are abilities everyone should work on developing irrespective of profession, locale and lifestyle. These are capabilities and knowledge that will serve as a foundation for survival and self-protection, and as a result, the survival and protection of our loved ones and those for whom we're responsible. With luck, most of these will never be needed, but the goal in any circumstances is to know and be capable of more than we need—especially when those circumstances have severe consequences for inability and failure.

SURVIVAL SKILLS

Learn and practice the minimum skills for survival. The best method to learn is through live courses with qualified instructors and related experience, but supplement this with reputable books and online information as needed. It's a good idea to keep a reliable resource on hand as well that can be referred to as needed, such as the pocket-sized but thorough *SAS Survival Handbook* or *Bushcraft 101*. Likewise, it's important to build and maintain survival kits or go-bags of various levels both for the home and car. Recommended contents for these can be found in reputable books and websites.

The most important basics include:

- Locating and treating drinking water
- Locating or building adequate shelter
- Starting and maintaining fire
- Signaling and communication methods
- Map and compass use and basic land navigation without them
- Basic food procurement and preparation methods
- Common knots and their uses

FIRST AID

Basic emergency medical treatment can save lives (including your own) and doesn't require a great deal of knowledge. Live courses are best for learning these skills, but supplement with books and online resources from reputable authors and organizations.

- ABC (airway, breathing, circulation) protocols
- CPR (adult, child and infant)
- Choking protocols (adult, child and infant)
- Basic wound care and tourniquet use
- Heat/cold exposure and dehydration recognition/treatment

HOME SAFETY

Learn the basic functions of the home and utilities, not just for emergencies, but for everyday independence and safety.

- How to turn off gas supply to the house
- How to turn off house and individual fixture water supply
- How to turn off or reset individual breakers in electrical panel, or to shut power off to the house
- How to use heating systems and potential non-utility back-ups like fireplaces or wood burning stoves
- How to use a fire extinguisher or otherwise put out fires in the home and kitchen

CAR SKILLS

Most of us drive regularly; some of us frequently and in high volume or long distances. Unless we live in relative isolation and truly depend on the function of our cars, most of us don't need to become expert auto mechanics, but in all cases knowing at least the basics can prove invaluable.

- How to change a flat tire
- How to fill a radiator when low and overheating
- How to jump start a car
- How to drive a manual transmission
- How to drive in snow/ice and how to get unstuck in snow or mud
- How to use paper maps for navigation

TOOL USE

Familiarity and comfort with common tools provides us with immense and broad abilities. Having even the most rudimentary understanding of mechanical systems—the literal nuts and bolts—and construction gives us the ability to make repairs and build various contraptions, whether in emergencies or for simple convenience. Much of this ability can be gained through self-directed experience, but courses exist, and plenty of books and online resources provide quality information and instruction, such as *thisoldhouse.com*.

Learn first to use all the common hand tools—hammers, screwdrivers, all types of wrenches (crescent, box/open-end, Allen), all types of pliers, all types of hand saws. Then move on to the most common power tools—drills and drivers, saws (miter, circular, saber, jig, table, chain), long handled tools (sledgehammer, ax/pick, shovels), air compressor and common fittings, sanders and grinders. Keep at least a basic toolbox with hand tools, and spend time using them whenever opportunities arise.

SELF-DEFENSE

We don't necessarily need to train as professional fighters for the sake of self-defense. Any good self-defense instruction includes information and methods for awareness and avoiding potential danger in addition to the methods of actually physically defending against attack. This is a critical skill that demands quality live instruction and training—do your homework on the background of potential instructors and organizations and choose wisely. This is not about appearance, but substance. *Violence of Mind* by Varg Freeborn is required reading.

PHYSICAL ABILITY

Physical fitness and capability were discussed in detail previously, but one skill that deserves inclusion here is the ability to swim. There's no need to swim at a world-class skill level—this is an issue of safety and survival. None of us should be at risk of death simply by finding ourselves in a body of water. Swimming courses and private lessons are generally easy to find.

FIREARMS

You don't need to be a gun enthusiast, a world-class marksman, or own any guns yourself; you can even hate guns. But being familiar with (and not intimidated by) firearms and their basic operation and safe handling is a valuable skill, and in no way will force you to change your opinion on gun ownership, law or anything else. This, like survival and self-defense, should be learned in-person from a qualified instructor. Learn to safely handle and operate (including resolving basic malfunctions), load and unload, and fire both pistols and rifles with reasonable accuracy and confidence. You may get to the end of your life never touching a firearm again—or your basic ability may some day save your life or the life of a loved one.

TRAINING TEMPLATES

FOUNDATIONAL MOVEMENTS

Following are some of the most generally valuable exercises that meet the criteria for each foundational movement type. Note that this is an abbreviated list—many more exercises for each category exist, as well as many variations of each listed, and can be found at becomingtough.com/exercises.

SQUAT
- Back squat
- Front squat
- Split squat
- Step-up

DEADLIFT
- Deadlift
- Snatch/clean pull
- Deficit deadlift
- Stiff-legged deadlift
- Straight-legged deadlift

PRESS

- Press
- Bench Press
- Push-up
- Dip

PULL

- Pull-up
- Chin-up
- Pull-down
- Bent Row

RUN/WALK

- Distance running
- Interval running
- Distance walking
- Walk/run intervals

JUMP

- Vertical jump
- Box jump
- Broad jump/double-leg bounding
- Single-leg jumps/bounding

CARRY

- Farmer carry
- Shoulder carry
- Overhead carry
- Stress carry

DRAG/PUSH
- Forward sled drag
- Backward sled drag
- Sled push

CLIMB
- Rope climb
- Wall climb

HEART & LUNGS
- Run/walk
- Bicycling
- Rowing
- Swimming
- Cross-country skiing

ACCESSORY
- Sit-up variations
- Back extension variations
- Plank variations
- Trunk rotation variations
- Anti-rotation variations
- Grip training

TRAINING TEMPLATES

The first template below is appropriate for experienced athletes, the second is more suitable for individuals at an intermediate training level, and the last is for those with no training experience at all, who have been sedentary for a significant period of time, or who otherwise need to begin extremely conservatively. These templates can be used to get started quickly, but should be considered just that—starting points. Eventually a training program suited more precisely for your needs and abilities should be developed.

In all cases, alternative exercises of the same movement type can be plugged into place as needed to suit your needs or available equipment and space. Note that these are templates, not complete training programs—the details of weight, reps, sets and times will need to be determined individually.

The final template provided requires no training equipment at all—this is the *No Excuses* template, and its purpose is exactly what the title suggests. If you're sedentary and have little or no experience with training or exercise, it's going to be very easy to formulate seemingly reasonable excuses to avoid getting started. This template removes some of the biggest barriers to entry—now you're down to excuses you can't as easily accept. Get started now. It's only as intimidating as you decide it is.

More information, help and complete training programs can be found at https://becomingtough.com/training.

ADVANCED TEMPLATE

This training template is suitable for experienced athletes who have significant training histories and access to a wide variety of training equipment.

MONDAY

- Rope Climbs
- Pull-ups
- Dumbbell rows

Circuit:
- Sled drag
- Farmer carry
- Sandbag Zercher carry
- Overhead sandbag throw

Accessory:
- Weighted sit-up
- Side star plank
- Sledgehammer rotation

TUESDAY

- Snatch
- Snatch pull
- Back squat
- Run sprint intervals

Accessory:
- Dead bug
- Windmill

WEDNESDAY

Rest, recovery cardio, or skill work

THURSDAY

- Push Press
- Press
- Push-ups
- Long run

Accessory:
- Hanging leg raise
- Anti-rotation landmine
- Wrist roller

SATURDAY

- Clean & Jerk
- Deadlift

Circuit:
- Air bike
- Sandbag shoulder
- Burpee

Accessory:
- Single-leg RDL
- Russian twist
- L-sit
- Back extension

INTRODUCTORY TEMPLATE

This training template is suitable for those with reasonable experience lifting weights and using a variety of common exercises.

MONDAY

- Back squat
- Bent row

Circuit:
- Farmer carry
- 200 m run
- Sled drag

Accessory:
- Sit-up
- Russian twist

WEDNESDAY

- Overhead squat
- Press
- Long run/bike

Accessory:
- Plank
- Side Plank

FRIDAY
- Deadlift

Circuit:
- 1 min bike/run
- Walking lunge
- Push-up

Accessory:
- Dead bug
- Superman hold

NO EXCUSES TEMPLATE

This training template is suitable for those with little or no experience with training, or who have been sedentary for a long time and need to ease back into exercising. It requires no equipment (but basic equipment like dumbbells can be used if on hand) and little skill.

MONDAY

- 1-Arm row – 3 x 10-15

Circuit – 3 times without resting:
- Farmer carry x 50 m
- Sit-up/crunch x 10-30
- Squat x 10

WEDNESDAY

- Walk/jog – 20-30 minutes

Circuit – 3 times without resting:
- Push-up x 10
- Plank x 10-30 sec
- Step-up x 10/leg

FRIDAY

- Deadlift – 3 x 10

Circuit – 3 times without resting:
- Jog/run x 1 min
- Squat-thrust x 10
- 1-arm row x 10-15

LOADING

If you have no equipment like dumbbells, use household items for weights.

- 1-arm row: Loaded plastic bag, backpack, large detergent bottle
- Farmer carry: Loaded plastic bags, backpacks, suitcases
- Deadlift: Use the same items you used for farmer carries—hold one in each hand and lift/return to the floor at the sides of your feet, or hold one item with both hands directly in front of you.

SCALING

Movements can be scaled down to be made accessible at any level.

- Squat: Squat as deep as you can safely. Hold onto a table or similar as needed to assist yourself.
- Push-up: Make easier by starting on the knees instead of the toes, or by leaning against a wall or table to bring your body more upright.
- Step-up: Use a single stair riser or curb if needed.
- Plank: Plank from the knees and on the hands with straight arms to make easier, or lean at an angle against a wall or table.

NOTES

CHAPTER 2 **CHARACTER**

1   Laurence Gonzales, *Deep Survival* (New York: Norton, 2017), 31, 33.
2   Marcus Aurelius, *Meditations* (Edinburgh: Black & White Classics, 2014), 11.18.5b.
3   Malcolm Gladwell, *Talking to Strangers* (London: Allen Lane, 2019), 73.
4   Kathy Mitchell, "How Writing Improves Your Brain and Helps You Heal," *Book Meditation Retreats*, January 18, 2018, https://www.bookmeditationre-treats.com/news/writing-brain-health.
5   Amanda L. Chan, "6 Unexpected Ways Writing Can Transform Your Health," *Huffpost*, November 12, 2013, https://www.huffpost.com/entry/writ-ing-health-benefits-journal_n_4242456.
6   Nancy Olson, "Three Ways That Handwriting with a Pen Positively Affects Your Brain," *Forbes*, May 15, 2016, https://www.forbes.com/sites/nancyol-son/2016/05/15/three-ways-that-writing-with-a-pen-positively-affects-your-brain/.
7   Stanford University. "Stanford Study Finds Walking Improves Creativity." Stanford News, April 24, 2014. https://news.stanford.edu/2014/04/24/walk-ing-vs-sitting-042414/.
8   Emily Fletcher, *Stress Less, Accomplish More* (New York: HarperCollins, 2019), 133.

CHAPTER 3 **CAPABILITY**

1   Laurence Gonzales, *Deep Survival* (New York: Norton, 2017), 180

2   Martin Broadwell, "Teaching for Learning," *The Gospel Guardian*, February 20, 1969, http://www.wordsfitlyspoken.org/gospel_guardian/v20/v20n41p1-3a.html (accessed April 14, 2020).

3   Sarah Gingell. "How Your Mental Health Reaps the Benefits of Exercise," *Psychology Today*, Sussex Publishers, March 22, 2018. https://www.psychologytoday.com/us/blog/what-works-and-why/201803/how-your-mental-health-reaps-the-benefits-exercise.

4   "Individual Variation and the Genetics of Sleep," *Healthy Sleep*, December 12, 2007, http://healthysleep.med.harvard.edu/healthy/science/variations/individual-variation-genetics.

5   "How Much Sleep Do We Really Need?" *National Sleep Foundation*, Accessed May 12, 2020, https://www.sleepfoundation.org/articles/how-much-sleep-do-we-really-need.

6   "Sleep and Disease Risk." *Healthy Sleep*, Accessed May 12, 2020, http://healthysleep.med.harvard.edu/healthy/matters/consequences/sleep-and-disease-risk.

7   "Sleep, Performance, and Public Safety," *Healthy Sleep*, Accessed May 12, 2020, http://healthysleep.med.harvard.edu/healthy/matters/consequences/sleep-performance-and-public-safety.

8   Mah, C.D., K.E. Mah, E.J. Kezirian, and W.C. Dement (2011). The effects of sleep extension on the athletic performance of collegiate basketball players. Sleep. 34: 943-950. https://dx.doi.org/10.5665%2FSLEEP.1132.

9   "Sleep and Athletes." *Gatorade Sports Science Institute*, Accessed May 12, 2020, https://www.gssiweb.org/sports-science-exchange/article/sse-167-sleep-and-athletes.

10 John Axelson and Vladyslav Vyazovskiy, "Banking Sleep and Biological Sleep Need," *Sleep* 38, no. 12 (2015), 1843-1845. Accessed May 13, 2020. https://dx.doi.org/10.5665%2Fsleep.5222.

11 Alex Hutchinson, "Banking Sleep Ahead of Time Can Stave off Exhaustion, Study Shows," *The Globe and Mail*, February 23, 2017. https://www.theglobeandmail.com/life/health-and-fitness/fitness/banking-sleep-ahead-of-time-can-stave-off-exhaustion-study-shows-health/article34120978/.

1   Martin Seligman, *Learned Optimism* (New York: Random House, 2006), 44-48.

2   Angela Duckworth, *Grit* (New York: Scribner, 2016), 190.

3   Ben Sherwood, *The Survivors Club* (New York: Hatchet Book Group, 2009), 42.

4   Lt. Col. Dave Grossman, *On Combat* (Warrior Science, 2008), 373.

5   Ben Sherwood, *The Survivors Club* (New York: Hatchet Book Group, 2009), 37.

6   Mihaly Csikszentmihalyi, *Flow* (New York: Harper Perennial, 2008), 23.

7   Martin Seligman, *Learned Optimism* (New York: Random House, 2006), 14.

8   Utpal M Dholakia, "4 Reasons Why an Optimistic Outlook Is Good for Your Health," *Psychology Today*, July 31, 2016. https://www.psychologytoday.com/us/blog/the-science-behind-behavior/201607/4-reasons-why-optimistic-outlook-is-good-your-health.

9   Martin Seligman, *Learned Optimism* (New York: Random House, 2006), 174.

10 Dr. Al Siebert, *The Survivor Personality* (New York: Perigree, 2010), 199.

11 Martin Seligman, *Learned Optimism* (New York: Random House, 2006), 16.

12 Dr. Al Siebert, *The Survivor Personality* (New York: Perigree, 2010), 131-132.

13 Alex Osborn, *Your Creative Power* (Lanham: Hamilton Books, 2009), 19.

14 Steven Callahan, *Adrift* (New York: Mariner Books, 2002), 154-155.

15 Martin Seligman, *Learned Optimism* (New York: Random House, 2006), 111-115.

16 Martin Seligman, *Learned Optimism* (New York: Random House, 2006), 15.

17 Émile Coué, *Self Mastery Through Conscious Autosuggestion* (Salt Lake City: Project Gutenberg, 2008), iBook.

18 Dan Ariely, *Predictably Irrational* (New York: Harper Perennial, 2009), 204-214.

19 Mihaly Csikszentmihalyi, *Flow* (New York: Harper Perennial, 2008), 119.

20 Emily Fletcher, *Stress Less, Accomplish More* (New York: William Morrow, 2019), 27-28.

21 Matthew Thorpe, "12 Science-Based Benefits of Meditation," *Healthline*, July 5, 2017. https://www.healthline.com/nutrition/12-benefits-of-meditation#section7.

22 Jeremy Adam Smith, et al., "10 Things We Know About the Science of Meditation," *Mindful*, November 12, 2018, https://www.mindful.org/10-things-we-know-about-the-science-of-meditation/.

23 Madhuleena Roy Chowdhury, "5 Health Benefits of Daily Meditation According to Science," *Positive Psychology*, May 18, 2020. https://positivepsychology.com/benefits-of-meditation/.

24 Mihaly Csikszentmihalyi, *Flow* (New York: Harper Perennial, 2008), 10.

25 Varg Freeborn, *Violence of Mind* (Violence of Mind, 2018), 44.

26 Varg Freeborn, *Violence of Mind* (Violence of Mind, 2018), 46.

27 Craig Caudill, *Extreme Wilderness Survival* (Salem: Page Street Publishing Co., 2017), 22-23.

28 Dr. Al Siebert, *The Survivor Personality* (New York: Perigree, 2010).

29 Robert M. Sapolsky, *Why Zebras Don't Get Ulcers* (New York: Holt Paperbacks, 2004), 22,27,32.

30 Bruce Siddle. Quoted in Lt. Col. Dave Grossman and Loren Christensen, *On Combat* (Warrior Science, 2008), 136.

31 Angela Duckworth, *Grit* (New York: Scribner, 2016), 188-89.

32 Scott Weingart, Podcast 164 – The Day I Didn't Use Ultrasound by Mike Mallin, *EMCrit Blog*, December 26, 2015, https://emcrit.org/emcrit/day-i-didnt-use-ultrasound/.

33 Susanne Vogel and Lars Schwabe. Learning and memory under stress: implications for the classroom. *npj Science Learn* 1, 16011 (2016). https://doi.org/10.1038/npjscilearn.2016.11

34 Lt. Col. Dave Grossman and Loren Christensen, *On Combat* (Warrior Science, 2008), 39.

35 Mike Lauria, "Stress Inoculation Training," *EMCrit RACC*, December 31, 2015, https://emcrit.org/emcrit/on-stress-inoculation-training/.

36 "What Is Exposure Therapy?" American Psychological Association. American Psychological Association. Accessed April 16, 2020. https://www.apa.org/ptsd-guideline/patients-and-families/exposure-therapy.

37 Christophe André, "Proper Breathing Brings Better Health," *Scientific American*, January 15, 2019, https://www.scientificamerican.com/article/proper-breathing-brings-better-health/.

38 Mark Divine, *The Way of The Seal* (White Plains: Readers Digest, 2013), 138.

39 Daniel Goleman, "A Feel Good Theory: Smile Affects Mood," *The New York Times*, July 18, 1989, https://www.nytimes.com/1989/07/18/science/a-feel-good-theory-a-smile-affects-mood.html.

40 Noel E. Brick, Megan J. McElhinny, and Richard S. Metcalfe, "The effects of facial expression and relaxation on movement economy, physiological, and perceptual responses during running," *Psychology of Sport and Exercise* 34, January (2018), 20-28, https://www.sciencedirect.com/science/article/pii/S1469029217303461.

41 R. I. M. Dunbar, et al., "Social laughter is correlated with an elevated pain threshold," *Proceedings of the Royal Society B Biological Sciences*, 2012 Mar 22; 279(1731): 1161–1167.

42 Ranganathan, Vinoth K., et al., "From mental power to muscle power—gaining strength by using the mind," *Neuropsychologia*, 2004; 42(7): 944-56.

CHAPTER 5 **COMMITMENT**

1   Langer, E., Blank, A., & Chanowitz, B. (1978), "The Mindlessness of Ostensibly Thoughtful Action: The Role of 'Placebic' Information in Interpersonal Interaction," *Journal of Personality and Social Psychology*, *36*(6), 635–642.

2   Charles Duhigg, *The Power of Habit* (New York: Random House, 2014), 150-151.

3   Charles Duhigg, *The Power of Habit* (New York: Random House, 2014), xvi.

4   James Clear, *Atomic Habits* (London: Random House Business Books, 2018), 160.

5   Charles Duhigg, *The Power of Habit* (New York: Random House, 2014), 137.

6   Charles Duhigg, *The Power of Habit* (New York: Random House, 2014), 36.

7   James Clear, *Atomic Habits* (London: Random House Business Books, 2018), 54.

8   Charles Duhigg, *The Power of Habit* (New York: Random House, 2014), 100, 108-109.

9   Charles Duhigg, *The Power of Habit* (New York: Random House, 2014), 112.

10 Charles Duhigg, *The Power of Habit* (New York: Random House, 2014), 20, 62, 92.

11 Charles Duhigg, *The Power of Habit* (New York: Random House, 2014), 139.

12 Varg Freeborn, *Violence of Mind* (Violence of Mind, 2018), 11.

13 Varg Freeborn, *Violence of Mind* (Violence of Mind, 2018), 6-9.

14 Varg Freeborn, *Violence of Mind* (Violence of Mind, 2018), 15.

CHAPTER 6 **FINAL THOUGHTS**

1   Mihaly Csikszentmihalyi, *Flow* (New York: Harper Perennial, 2008), 214-215

BIBLIOGRAPHY

American Psychological Association. "What Is Exposure Therapy?" Accessed April 16, 2020. https://www.apa.org/ptsd-guideline/patients-and-families/exposure-therapy.

André, Christophe. "Proper Breathing Brings Better Health." *Scientific American*, January 15, 2019. https://www.scientificamerican.com/article/proper-breathing-brings-better-health/.

Ariely, Dan. *Predictably Irrational.* New York: Harper Perennial, 2009.

Aurelius, Marcus. *Meditations.* Edinburgh: Black & White Classics, 2014.

Axelson, John, and Vladyslav Vyazovskiy. "Banking Sleep and Biological Sleep Need." *Sleep* 38, no. 12 (2015), 1843-1845. Accessed May 13, 2020. https://dx.doi.org/10.5665%2Fsleep.5222.

Brick, Noel E., Megan J. McElhinny and Richard S. Metcalfe. "The effects of facial expression and relaxation on movement economy, physiological, and perceptual responses during running." *Psychology of Sport and Exercise* 34, January (2018). 20-28. https://doi.org/10.1016/j.psychsport.2017.09.009.

Broadwell, Martin. "Teaching for Learning." *The Gospel Guardian*, February 20, 1969. http://www.wordsfitlyspoken.org/gospel_guardian/v20/v20n41p1-3a.html.

Callahan, Steven. *Adrift.* New York: Mariner Books, 2002.

Caudill, Craig. *Extreme Wilderness Survival.* Salem: Page Street Publishing Co., 2017.

Chan, Amanda L. "6 Unexpected Ways Writing Can Transform Your Health." *Huffpost*, November 12, 2013. https://www.huffpost.com/entry/writing-health-benefits-journal_n_4242456.

Chowdhury, Madhuleena Roy. "5 Health Benefits of Daily Meditation According to Science." *Positive Psychology*, May 18, 2020. https://positivepsychology.com/benefits-of-meditation/.

Coué, Émile. *Self Mastery Through Conscious Autosuggestion.* Salt Lake City: Project Gutenberg, 2008. iBook.

Csikszentmihalyi, Mihaly. *Flow.* New York: Harper Perennial, 2008.

Dholakia, Utpal M. "4 Reasons Why an Optimistic Outlook Is Good for Your Health." *Psychology Today*, July 31, 2016. https://www.psychologytoday.com/us/blog/the-science-behind-behavior/201607/4-reasons-why-optimistic-outlook-is-good-your-health.

Duckworth, Angela. *Grit.* New York: Scribner, 2016.

Divine, Mark. *The Way of The Seal.* White Plains: Readers Digest, 2013.

Dunbar, R.I.M, Rebecca Baron, Anna Frangou, Eiluned Pearce, Edwin J. C. van Leeuwen, Julie Stow, Giselle Partridge, Ian MacDonald, Vincent Barra, and Mark van Vugt. "Social laughter is correlated with an elevated pain threshold." *Proceedings of the Royal Society B Biological Sciences*, 2012 Mar 22; 279(1731): 1161–1167. https://doi.org/10.1098/rspb.2011.1373.

Fletcher, Emily. *Stress Less, Accomplish More.* New York: Harper Collins, 2019.

Freeborn, Varg. *Violence of Mind.* Violence of Mind, 2018.

Gatorade Sports Science Institute. "Sleep and Athletes." Accessed May 12, 2020. https://www.gssiweb.org/sports-science-exchange/article/sse-167-sleep-and-athletes.

Gingell, Sarah. "How Your Mental Health Reaps the Benefits of Exercise." *Psychology Today*, March 22, 2018. https://www.psychologytoday.com/us/blog/what-works-and-why/201803/how-your-mental-health-reaps-the-benefits-exercise.

Gladwell, Malcolm. *Talking to Strangers.* London: Allen Lane, 2019.

Goleman, Daniel. "A Feel Good Theory: Smile Affects Mood." *The New York Times*, July 18, 1989. https://www.nytimes.com/1989/07/18/science/a-feel-good-theory-a-smile-affects-mood.html.

Gonzales, Laurence. *Deep Survival.* New York: Norton, 2017.

Grossman, Lt. Col. Dave and Loren Christensen. *On Combat.* Warrior Science, 2008.

Healthy Sleep. "Individual Variation and the Genetics of Sleep." December 12, 2007. http://healthysleep.med.harvard.edu/healthy/science/variations/individual-variation-genetics.

Healthy Sleep. "Sleep and Disease Risk." Accessed May 12, 2020. http://healthysleep.med.harvard.edu/healthy/matters/consequences/sleep-and-disease-risk.

Healthy Sleep. "Sleep, Performance, and Public Safety." Accessed May 12, 2020. http://healthysleep.med.harvard.edu/healthy/matters/consequences/sleep-performance-and-public-safety.

Hutchinson, Alex. "Banking Sleep Ahead of Time Can Stave off Exhaustion, Study Shows." *The Globe and Mail*, February 23, 2017. https://www.theglobe-andmail.com/life/health-and-fitness/fitness/banking-sleep-ahead-of-time-can-stave-off-exhaustion-study-shows-health/article34120978/.

Lauria, Mike. "Stress Inoculation Training." *EMCrit RACC*, December 31, 2015. https://emcrit.org/emcrit/on-stress-inoculation-training/.

Mah, C.D., K.E. Mah, E.J. Kezirian, and W.C. Dement (2011). The effects of sleep extension on the athletic performance of collegiate basketball players. *Sleep* 34: 943-950. https://dx.doi.org/10.5665%2FSLEEP.1132.

Mitchell, Kathy. "How Writing Improves Your Brain and Helps You Heal." *Book Meditation Retreats*, January 18, 2018. https://www.bookmeditationretreats.com/news/writing-brain-health.

National Sleep Foundation. "How Much Sleep Do We Really Need?" Accessed May 12, 2020. https://www.sleepfoundation.org/articles/how-much-sleep-do-we-really-need.

Olson, Nancy. "Three Ways That Handwriting with a Pen Positively Affects Your Brain." *Forbes*, May 15, 2016. https://www.forbes.com/sites/nancyol-son/2016/05/15/three-ways-that-writing-with-a-pen-positively-affects-your-brain/.

Osborn, Alex. *Your Creative Power*. Lanham: Hamilton Books, 2009.

Ranganathan, Vinoth K., Vlodek Siemionow, Jing Z.Liu, Vinod Sahgal, and Guang H. Yue. "From mental power to muscle power—gaining strength by using the mind." *Neuropsychologia* 2004; 42(7): 944-56. https://doi.org/10.1016/j.neuropsychologia.2003.11.018.

Sapolsky, Robert M. *Why Zebras Don't Get Ulcers*. New York: Holt Paperbacks, 2004.

Seligman, Martin. *Learned Optimism*. New York: Random House, 2006.

Sherwood, Ben. *The Survivors Club*. New York: Hatchet Book Group, 2009.

Siebert, Dr. Al. *The Survivor Personality*. New York: Perigree, 2010.

Smith, Jeremy Adam, Hugh Delehanty, Barry Boyce, Sharon Begley, Grace Bullock, Willem Kuyken, Jeremy Hunter, Oren Jay Sofer, and Kira M. Newman. "10 Things We Know About the Science of Meditation." *Mindful*, November 12, 2018. https://www.mindful.org/10-things-we-know-about-the-science-of-meditation/.

Stanford University. "Stanford Study Finds Walking Improves Creativity." *Stanford News*, April 24, 2014. https://news.stanford.edu/2014/04/24/walking-vs-sitting-042414/.

Thorpe, Matthew. "12 Science-Based Benefits of Meditation." *Healthline*, July 5, 2017. https://www.healthline.com/nutrition/12-benefits-of-meditation#section7.

Vogel, S., Schwabe, L. Learning and memory under stress: implications for the classroom. *npj Science Learn* 1, 16011 (2016). https://doi.org/10.1038/npjscilearn.2016.11

Weingart, Scott. "Podcast 164 – The Day I Didn't Use Ultrasound by Mike Mallin." *EMCrit Blog*, December 26, 2015. https://emcrit.org/emcrit/day-i-didnt-use-ultrasound/.

Greg Everett's background spans an unusual array of professional and personal experiences, from working on an ambulance, to authoring a dozen books, to coaching the sport of weight-lifting at the world championship level. He's competed in sports ranging from weightlift-ing to bicycle trials to tactical shooting, trained and participated in many more from Brazilian jiu jitsu to boxing to rock climbing, and has been backpacking through the Sierra Nevada and Cascades for almost thirty years. His book, Olympic Weightlifting, is the world's best sell-ing on the subject, his instructional content across multiple media is used by athletes and coaches around the world, and he wrote, shot, directed, produced and edited the first docu-mentary film on the sport of weightlifting in the US, American Weightlifting.

CPSIA information can be obtained
at www.ICGtesting.com
Printed in the USA
LVHW110318080221
678680LV00042B/857/J